POPULAR CULTURE
AND MASS COMMUNICATION IN
TWENTIETH-CENTURY FRANCE

POPULAR CULTURE
AND MASS COMMUNICATION IN
TWENTIETH-CENTURY FRANCE

Edited by

Rosemary Chapman

and

Nicholas Hewitt

The Edwin Mellen Press
Lewiston/Queenston/Lampeter

Library of Congress Cataloging-in-Publication Data

Popular culture and mass communication in twentieth-century France /
    edited by Rosemary Chapman and Nicholas Hewitt.
        p.   cm.
    Includes bibliographical references and index.
    ISBN 0-7734-9499-5
    1. Mass media--France. 2. France--Popular culture--History--20th
century. I. Chapman, Rosemary, 1951-   . II. Hewitt, Nicholas.
P92.F8P66   1992
302.23' 0944' 0904--dc20
                                                                    92-8511
                                                                      CIP

A CIP catalog record for this book is available
from The British Library.

The Edwin Mellen Press
P.O. Box 450
Lewiston, NY 14092
USA

The Edwin Mellen Press
Box 67
Queenston, Ontario
CANADA L0S 1L0

The Edwin Mellen Press, Ltd.
Lampeter, Dyfed, Wales
UNITED KINGDOM SA48 7DY

Printed in the United States of America

"La culture d'un pays est sa manière de vivre, l'ensemble des activités qui s'y développent et des intérêts qui s'y expriment"

<u>*Pierre Sorlin*</u>

TABLE OF CONTENTS

LIST OF ILLUSTRATIONS

FOREWORD

This volume is based upon the proceedings of the annual conference of the Association for the Study of Modern and Contemporary France, held at the University of Nottingham on 13-15 September 1991, on the theme of FRANCE: CULTURE AND SOCIAL IDENTITY.

The Editors would like to express their grateful thanks to the Committee of the Association for their assistance in the organisation of the programme and to the University of Nottingham for so generously funding the preparation of the final manuscript. Their thanks are also due to Ms Alison Connor, who undertook the translation of the chapter by M. Thierry Groensteen, and to Mrs V. Roddis for working so efficiently and so patiently on the typescript.

Rosemary Chapman
Nicholas Hewitt

January, 1992

PREFACE

In his analysis, in the first chapter, of the French Ministry of Culture's own survey of the nation's cultural activity, *Les Pratiques culturelles des Français 1973-1989*, Brian Rigby discerns a noticeable shift in emphasis on the part of the Government statisticians regarding the definition of cultural activity itself. He notes that "the 'centre of gravity' of cultural practice has now moved quite decisively away from the traditional idea of culture based on books, live theatre and visits to art galleries". Whilst there is some paradox in the fact that a Ministry which has such a distinguished and enviable record in the promotion of this very area of high cultural activity should chart with apparent equanimity a movement away from this activity to an essentially audio-visual culture, the survey does show how necessary it may be to broaden the definition of culture to include activities hitherto neglected by cultural historians.

It is the purpose of this present volume to rectify in some measure this neglect, by indicating areas of popular or mass culture which may prove significant in their own right and may constitute fruitful areas for further research, and by providing essential demonstrations of the breadth of modern French cultural experience. The French population reflected in this volume is not made up of bookish theatre-goers and connoisseurs, but of people deeply engaged with the mass-media, receptive yet vulnerable to techniques of modern advertising, often belonging to ethnic minorities, and devoting themselves to weekly rituals such as the *tiercé*. Their experience of sculpture is as likely to be gained from contemplation of the local war-memorial as from visits to the municipal art gallery and their reading-matter is as likely to consist of volumes of *bande dessinée* as it is of the latest literary prizes.

Clearly, this is not historically a new phenomenon. Rosemary Chapman, in Chapter 2, recalls the debate on the definition of culture conducted by the Proletarian Writers, particularly Poulaille, in their journalistic activity, and Tony

Chafer, in Chapter 10, raises the question of "whose culture?" through the history of education policy in French West Africa.

It is, however, probably advertising which constitutes one of the most privileged areas of contemporary cultural activity, both in its influence and its complexity. Geoffrey Hare, in Chapter 3, demonstrates the increasing control of advertising over French radio in the last ten years, and Michael Palmer, in Chapter 6, provides an important historical survey of the rise of the great advertising agencies from their origins in the Nineteenth-Century press. The detrimental effect of contemporary advertising in reinforcing gender stereotypes is argued strongly by Renate Gunther, in Chapter 5, a point taken up by Maggie Allison in Chapter 4 with respect to media coverage. In Chapter 7, however, Pierre Sorlin sketches a picture of modern advertising which is signally different from its own stereotype: instead of a rapacious industry crudely insulting the viewer's intellect, he depicts a group of intellectually-trained professionals playing to an audience who is every bit their intellectual equal and who derives aesthetic pleasure from the decoding of the product. In this light, the divide between high and low culture becomes considerably blurred.

The world of class and consumerism is explored to considerable effect in Etienne Chatiliez's film of 1988 *La Vie est un long fleuve tranquille*. Where Bill Marshall, in Chapter 9, provides a Bakhtinian reading of the film in terms of carnival and reversal of class, Jill Forbes, in Chapter 8, uses the film to discuss the role of the family in modern French cinema and the way in which that role reflects structures of ownership and management within the industry itself. Similarly, in his analysis of "Ethnic Minorities and the Mass Media in France" in Chapter 11, Alec Hargreaves takes up Renate Gunther's discussion of advertising and gender with respect to television depiction of the North African community.

Contemporary culture is composed of a broad range of activities and artefacts often ignored in the cultural histories. In Chapter 12, Philip Dine discusses the importance of the *tiercé* since 1945, whilst in Chapter 13 Thierry Groensteen explores the still doubtful legitimacy of the *bande dessinée*. In Chapter 14, William Kidd argues that the war-memorials erected after the 1914-1918 and the 1939-1945 Wars are often important examples of popular art in their own right and significant indicators of French attitudes in the periods following both conflicts. Finally, in Chapter 15, Rodney Ball takes up Pierre Sorlin's conclusion to his analysis of advertising, that all advertising is, ultimately, a reflection of the current state of the language, and explores precisely how that language is evolving and how written French, once the preserve of rigorous "correctness", is now caught between the intrusion of the popular spoken language and the inflationary effects of jargon.

This convincing picture of a language which is no longer sure of its formality and its privileged high-cultural status may stand as an image of French cultural activity as a whole, as recognised by the French Government's own statistics. The variety of cultural practices explored in this volume, however, indicate that the erosion of the line between high and popular culture opens the way to research which is both richer and more complex.

Nicholas Hewitt

1. *LES PRATIQUES CULTURELLES DES FRANÇAIS 1973-1989:* A STUDY OF CHANGING TRENDS IN THE PRESENTATION AND ANALYSIS OF GOVERNMENT STATISTICS ON CULTURE

BRIAN RIGBY

In 1990 the Département des Etudes et de la Prospective du Ministère de la Culture et de la Communication published the results of its most recent survey on the cultural practices of the French people.[1] This survey brought the Ministry's statistics up to 1989. The two previous surveys had been done in 1973 and 1981.[2] In order to achieve continuity with the previous surveys, and also to permit useful comparisons to be made, the 1988/1989 *enquête* asked largely the same kind of questions of its sample of 5000 French people over the age of 15:

"Qui va au théâtre, au concert, au cinéma, dans les bibliothèques? Qui lit quoi? Combien de Français jouent d'un instrument de musique? Quels rapports constate-t-on entre la culture classique et les pratiques liées au développement des médias? Quelles inégalités territoriales? Quelles inégalites sociales?"[3]

On reading the new edition, one can see, however, that there were

---

[1] Département des Etudes et de la Prospective. Ministère de la Culture et de la Communication, *Les Pratiques culturelles des Français 1973-1989*, Paris, Editions La Découverte et La Documentation Française, 1990. The volume is divided into two main parts: 1) "Les pratiques culturelles et leur évolution" by Oliver Donnat, pp.17-141; 2) "Les pratiques culturelles dans l'espace des loisirs" by Denis Cogneau, pp. 143-282.

[2] Ministère de la Culture, Service des études et recherches, *Pratiques culturelles des Français en 1974*, Paris, La Documentation Française, 1978, 2 vols; Ministère de la Culture, Service des études et recherches, *Pratiques culturelles des Français. Description socio-démographique. Evolution 1973-1981*. Paris, Dalloz, 1982.

[3] *Les Pratiques culturelles des Français 1973-1989*, p.5.

clearly some misgivings on the part of those conducting the new exercise, since by 1988/1989 there had obviously developed a recognition - even in Ministry of Culture circles - that such were the enormous changes that had taken place since 1973 in the social and cultural sphere, that to repeat the same exercise might be to apply rather blunt and outdated methods and criteria for the analysis of cultural practices in modern France. In the "Avant-propos" the authors also freely admit that a quantitative survey of the *Pratiques culturelles des Français* type is a very imprecise and inadequate means of understanding the detail of French cultural practices. As is pointed out, this survey cannot deal with practices that concern less than 2% of French people. Therefore, more than a million and a half individuals need to engage in a certain cultural practice before the *enquête* includes them in the statistics. At times the authors throw their hands up in despair at the inability of this kind of survey to deal with the diverse and different cultural practices in modern France, as for example here in the case of music:

> "Quels sont les points communs en effet entre les jeunes banlieusards qui créent un groupe rock, les musiciens des fanfares et harmonies qui demeurent très présentes, notamment en milieu rural, et les membres d'une chorale parisienne?"[4]

In the "Avant-propos" it is immediately stressed that the most significant and large-scale cultural developments in the preceding decade had been the increase in the amount of time people had come to devote to watching television and listening to music at home. But the authors are also quick to point out that, although what they call this "culture d'appartement" is constantly on the increase, it would be wrong to deduce from this that France as a society had turned in upon itself. In all sections of French society the statistics show that people are going out more in the evenings than they did in 1973, although

---

[4] Ibid, p.5.

this development is, in fact, predominantly a characteristic of very specific groups. What the authors also point out is that, if the French are going out more in the evening, it is for general sociable and convivial purposes, rather than to engage in traditional and classic cultural practices, such as going to the theatre or to a concert. Even after thirty years of deliberate governmental intervention in the cause of diffusing high culture, and even though there has been an enormous increase in the number of people in society with educational qualifications (upon which, of course, high cultural practice has been considered to depend), there has been no corresponding increase in the percentage of people engaging in high cultural practices, which still belong distinctively to a relatively small group of professional and highly educated people.

What *has* changed, however, is that there has been a striking increase in people's involvement with modern forms of audio-visual culture. This leads the authors of the "Avant-propos" to conclude that the "centre of gravity" of cultural practice has now moved quite decisively away from the traditional idea of culture based on books, live theatre and visits to art galleries. This relatively new, and of course rather belated, recognition in Ministry of Culture circles does promise to have enormous significance for the way in which cultural practice is conceived of by the State, and possibly - although not necessarily - for the way in which cultural practice is funded and organised in the future. Be that as it may, what does seem likely, however, is that one of the first "casualties" of this new awareness may well be the kind of survey of cultural practices which I am considering here, and which have been such a characteristic feature of the work of the Ministry of Culture. Over the years the Ministry has, of course, become a veritable powerhouse for the gathering, production and analysis of statistics across the whole cultural field in France, and it has created a bank of data relating to culture which I doubt can be matched by any other country in the world.[5]

No doubt the collection and analysis of statistics will continue with equal and indeed increased assiduity, since the Ministry of Culture and Communication is obviously here to stay. What is less clear is what kind of statistics they will be, and what they will be used for, when the French State continues to lose its overriding ambition to increase the rates of participation of French people in high cultural practices, which, despite some modifications, has after all been the principal driving-force and justification of the Ministry of Culture since its inception in 1959.[6] Up till now, and the 1990 edition of *Les Pratiques culturelles des Français* carries on the tradition, the analysis of cultural statistics has underlined the fact that high cultural practice is determined by the educational level, the socio-professional situation, the cultural heritage and the social origins of the practitioners. However valid the approach, and however important the findings, one has to admit that the exercise has by now become a rather mechanical, stale and depressing business, since it simply ends up repeatedly reaffirming what was already revealed and displayed by Pierre Bourdieu back in the 1960s.[7]

If the Ministry of Culture's work of over thirty years is to be judged by its success in increasing participation rates in high cultural practices, as traditionally defined, then it has, of course, failed, as its own statistics so painstakingly show. It is, therefore, difficult to believe that the Ministry will just carry on in the future gathering and analysing statistics in such a way that it will be seen as perpetuating this record of failure. So I suspect that the 1990 edition of *Les Pratiques culturelles des Français* may well be the last which

---

[5] To gain some idea of the extent of this activity, see the bibliography in R. Wangermée and B. Gournay, *La Politique culturelle de la France*, Paris, La Documentation Française, 1988.

[6] See: E. Ritaine, *Les Stratèges de la culture*, Paris, Presses de la Fondation Nationale des Sciences Politiques, 1983.

[7] See, in particular: P. Bourdieu and A. Darbel, *L'Amour de l'art: les Musées d'art européens et leur public*, Paris, Minuit, 1966.

organises its questionnaires in such a way that the statistics continue to point up the gap in high cultural practice between the majority of the French people and those relatively few people (defined by the high educational qualifications, their socio-professional situation and their social and cultural background) who remain the constant audience for traditional high culture.

The 1990 *enquête* now concedes that governmental action in the cultural sphere can in no way compete with, let alone outweigh, the overwhelmingly powerful influence in people's daily lives of the modern mass media. In other words, there now seems to be an acceptance that a ceiling has been reached in terms of participation rates in high culture, and there is a recognition that, effectively, no progress will be made if the Ministry continues to worry about the statistical take-up of high culture by underprivileged groups.

However, if the 1990 *enquête* shows that it is fully aware of the weaknesses in its approach to the description and analysis of modern cultural practices, it did none the less saddle itself with this approach for the 1988/1989 survey and Olivier Donnat's text on the evolution of cultural practices is perforce dedicated to highlighting the continuing inequalities in the cultural sphere, despite all the undoubted efforts of the Ministry of Culture in increasing "l'offre culturelle" and in pursuing an active policy of democratisation and decentralisation. However, while highlighting continuing inequalities, the author now tries not to construct too pessimistic an interpretation on the basis of the statistics.

If one excludes "la culture d'appartement" (that is, the home-based culture of the mass media), then the statistics show that only 10-15% of the French population engage in traditional and highly regarded cultural practices. Such a central traditional cultural practice as reading is shown to be definitely on the decline and the average number of books read by individuals per year has gone down very noticeably between 1973 and 1989. This decrease is described as "une des évolutions majeures qu'a connues le champ culturel ces quinze dernières années".[8] In total, some 25% of French people had not read one book in the previous year, and when this is broken down further into socio-professional and even geographical categories, the figures are even more striking: 50% of *agriculteurs* had not read a book, and 33% of *ouvriers* had not, as opposed to only 3% of *cadres* and "professions intellectuelles supérieures", and only 6% of Parisians. However, in order not to be too pessimistic, or to appear to subscribe to cultural attitudes that might seem too traditional or elitist, the author hastens to add that the fact of reading a book is not in itself evidence of high cultural practice, since only 6% of readers, in any case, prefer to read "littérature classique" and only 1% prefer to read poetry. Therefore, despite these statistics, which in the past would have been considered as very depressing by a Ministry of Culture concerned to diffuse high cultural practices, the author refuses to adopt a miserabilist stance and does all he can to put an optimistic gloss on the figures, even when it concerns the 13% of French people who do not possess one single book. According to the author, "l'absence de livres au foyer n'est pas forcément synonyme d'un dénuement culturel total".[9] What is very interesting about this is that here we find an authoritative text coming from the Ministry of Culture and Communication taking issue with the whole idea of "dénuement culturel", as this had been traditionally defined. One is, therefore, impelled to wonder to what degree the Ministry is now ready to forget that its "mission" was to reduce cultural inequality and to provide access to culture to those traditionally seen as deprived of it.

In order to analyse the evolution of cultural practices since 1973, the author selects six highly regarded, traditional practices so as to see what patterns have emerged between 1973 and 1989: "les sorties au théâtre, au concert de musique classique, à un spectacle de danse; les visites d'expositions,

---

[8] *Les Pratiques culturelles des Français 1973-1989*, p.80.

[9] Ibid, p.100.

de monuments historiques et de musées". He explains this choice by emphasising that these six practices "constituent pour l'essentiel le 'noyau dur' de la culture classique, celle que les acteurs de la vie culturelle des années soixante se proposaient de démocratiser en s'attaquant aux obstacles matériels (inégalitiés spatiales de l'offre, prix des places ...) qui entravaient l'accès au plus grand nombre".[10] Before giving the figures, he notes that "en 1988 le bilan peut paraître sévère". Indeed, the new set of statistics still show that 76% of French people have never been to a "spectacle de danse" in their life; 71% have never been to a classical concert; 50% have never been to a play; 51% have never been to an art exhibition. Only in the case of visits to historic monuments and museums do the figures drop to around 25%. There has, therefore, been no change in 15 years in the rate of high cultural practice, and no change in the social composition of the publics for high culture, as traditionally defined. If anything, the figures show a decline. Moreover, what is clearly revealed is that what people, in fact, prefer to do when they go out is go for a meal, go to watch a film or go to the fair.

With this awareness in mind, the 1990 edition of *Les Pratiques culturelles des Français* seems to me to initiate a new departure in its increased readiness to consider cultural practice as falling firmly within the context of general patterns of leisure and sociability. However, as already indicated, what the new statistics still show beyond any doubt is that the groups which constitute the traditional publics for high culture are *also* the groups which quite simply go out more and engage in a whole range of culture and leisure activities well beyond those traditionally regarded as the key high cultural practices. These groups (along with Parisians, young people and *célibataires*) have a life style which makes of them a new privileged elite who can avail themselves of all that the modern city can offer them in terms of leisure and cultural possibilities. Access to high culture has now been exchanged for an idea of access to the outside

---

[10] Ibid, p.105.

world (and to city night life in particular), a world in which high culture plays a significant part, but none the less only a part within a much broader notion of what it means to live a modern and open life. The cultured/uncultured opposition in cultural discourse is now replaced by that of open versus closed, sociable versus solitary, mobile and flexible versus static and fixed.

The first dimension of this open life style, according to the author, is its *culturedness* - it is dubbed "le rapport cultivé et aisé à l'extérieur"). This life style is presented as the modern way of living, as "un art de vivre dans le monde du loisir aujourd'hui".[11] "La réclusion chez soi" - especially if one is a worker who stays in to watch "La Roue de la Fortune" - is presented as the "repoussoir" to this modern life style and serves as a contemporary form of "barbaric" behaviour in the sense that Bourdieu gives this term.[12] Not only do such people spend their time closeted in their domestic space, but they also engage in the lowest form of cultural practice (in the eyes of cultured people) - namely, watching game shows on television.

The second dimension of the modern leisure style is its *youthfulness*. As a group, adolescents have a high rate of going out, and, as is well known, openness to the outside world decreases as people grow older and take on professional and domestic responsibilities.

The third dimension of the modern leisure life style is its *maleness*. Women and girls are said to be less "modern" in their "rapport à l'extérieur", and less open to modern cultural practices:

"La division des rôles familiaux héritée du XIXe siècle, qui donne à l'homme l'extérieur et à la femme la garde de l'intimité perdure

---

[11] Ibid, p.153.

[12] See, in particular, P. Bourdieu, *La Distinction, critique sociale du jugement*, Paris, Minuit, 1979. See also the chapter "Popular culture as barbaric culture: the sociology of Pierre Bourdieu" in B. Rigby, *Popular Culture in Modern France. A Study of Cultural Discourse*, London, Routledge, 1991, pp.96-130.

à tel point qu'une analyse factorielle des pratiques de loisir sur les 15-24 ans montre qu'une jeune femme n'est pas aussi facilement une femme jeune, sur le plan de l'extraversion et de la conquête du présent qu'un jeune homme est un homme jeune. Ainsi les filles lisent moins souvent des bandes dessinées ou de la science-fiction, écoutent moins souvent du rock, sortent moins que les garçons."[13]

Rather than focussing upon access to high culture, and highlighting the social, economic and educational inequalities which put up obstacles to high cultural practice, the authors of *Les Pratiques culturelles des Français* now choose to focus upon the "rigidités" - be they temporal, spatial, economic or "symbolic" - which adversely affect, not now "le niveau culturel" of French people, but rather "le niveau de sociabilité et le niveau de sorties à l'extérieur", even though these "rigidités" are exactly of the same kind as those that have all along been detected as the factors that have hindered cultural practice, as traditionally defined:

"Le capital culturel, somme de capital scolaire acquis et de l'héritage culturel transmis par les parents, constitue le principal passeport pour l'extérieur de chez soi, à la fois garantie de compétence verbale et scolaire, pour certains capital de relations sociales et héritage culturel incorporé, pour beaucoup condition d'un train de vie. La détention d'un fort capital culturel donne accès à un 'grand cumul' de sorties diversifiées, la 'culture de sorties'.

Par l'intermédiaire du capital culturel, il y a cumul et concentration des contacts et des relations sociales, ainsi que des sorties à l'extérieur."[14]

In his analysis of the statistics for "sorties", the author refutes the

---

[13] *Les Pratiques culturelles des Français 1973-1989*, p.162.

[14] Ibid, p.168.

prevalent notion of "la sociabilité populaire" and points out that in all groups of society "le niveau de sociabilité" always has a positive correlation with the level of educational qualifications. The higher the qualifications a person has, the more likely that person is to have a regular pattern of going out in order to engage in a *variety* of leisure and cultural practices. Even among young people there is a definite correlation between their rate of going out and the level of their educational qualifications:

> "Les effets de diplôme sont surtout sensibles à partir du bac; en effet, les détenteurs d'un CAP ou d'un BEPC ne semblent pas disposer d'une facilité de sortie très supérieure aux sans-diplôme. Le capital culturel scolaire des sorties noctambules fréquentes, c'est au moins le bac."[15]

The category of person who can most avail *himself* of a wide range of evening leisure and cultural facilities is, therefore, a youngish (about 25), highly educated, single and independent male living in Paris. It also helps, believe it or not, if he is very left-wing and an atheist. Not surprisingly, the category of person who is least likely to avail *herself* of a wide range of evening leisure and cultural activities is a woman aged 65 or over, living alone in a rural commune, without educational qualifications and who is a right-wing Catholic to boot.

Although the analysis of the statistics in *Les Pratiques culturelles des Français* claims to be scientific and objective, there is no doubt in my mind that it is, in fact, underpinned and directed by the idea that a regular pattern of going out several times a week in the evening to engage in a wide variety of leisure and cultural practices is the superior way of living a modern, open, mobile, flexible and fulfilled existence. The author actually says as much: "la 'culture de sorties' ... s'impose comme le bien rare des loisirs. C'est le *nec plus ultra* du rapport à l'extérieur ...". It is opposed at the other end of the scale to

---

[15] Ibid, p.169.

a life characterised by claustration in the home and by a very reduced range of leisure and cultural options, that is to say the life lived largely by old people, *agriculteurs*, *ouvriers* and women (categories of people who, on average, go out less than once a month). These groups stay at home and devote the largest part of their leisure time to watching TV. Such people are said to be suffering from "un handicap social majeur", which prevents them from enjoying a rate of going out in the evening comparable to that of certain privileged groups, and especially "les diplômés des études supérieures longues qui sont aussi devenus cadres supérieurs et qui savent rester autant 'modernes' que les adolescents."[16] Such people clearly add the trump card of eternal youth to their social, economic and educational advantages, in their ability to continue to renew themselves culturally and remain open to new cultural forms and practices.

The author, therefore, gives a rather rhapsodic view of trendy, successful, educated professionals living the good life which, presumably, is now to stand as the ideal which all French citizens should try and aspire to, even if, as the survey itself insistently demonstrates, educational, social, economic, gender and age factors will largely prevent them from doing so:

> "Le capital culturel gouverne l'accès à la modernité. Plus on détient de capital culturel, plus on peut et on sait rester jeune... Le capital culturel donne une autre tournure aux étapes de la vie et préserve ainsi d'une réclusion chez soi accélérée et assure une autre disponibilité d'esprit pour affronter les inventions de la modernité et les menaces de 'ringardisation'."[17]

So, in its eagerness to be up-to-date, and in its willingness to recognise the equal validity of all forms of leisure and cultural practice, the Ministry of Culture and Communication is obviously displaying its own flexibility and

---

[16] Ibid, p.268.

[17] Ibid, p.285.

openness to cultural developments in a modern technological society. Central to this case for openness and modernity is the Ministry's strategy of stigmatising "staying at home" as a handicapped condition. It strikes me, however, as deeply inconsistent and ambiguous that, at the very moment that the Ministry finally comes to acknowledge the overwhelming significance of television in modern culture and in people's lives, it also manages to end up giving such a miserabilist view of what the practice of television viewing means for the majority of people. In using the television-viewing habits of less privileged and less educated people as the contemporary form of the degree zero of leisure and cultural practice, it yet again perpetuates the long-standing hostility to the mass media within French State cultural policy. Now, however, television viewing is not being opposed to going to the Théâtre National Populaire, but rather to the general practice of going out regularly and enjoying a full life away from the home.

It has to be said, however, that the survey itself offers contradictory evidence on its attitude to television. As the volume proceeds, the miserabilist portrayal of a working class which spends nearly all its leisure time watching bad television becomes the principal foil to the presentation of leisure and cultural life styles which are turned to the outside world. In the earliest parts of the volume a more optimistic version was presented on the basis of the statistics. The volume begins, in fact, not only by insisting on the centrality of television in modern culture, but also by stressing the similarity of television-viewing habits across all sections of the population. So, although it is pointed out that it is still possible to show how different groups of people use television in different ways, according to their educational, social, economic and professional situations, the overall thrust of the analysis at this point in the volume is to stress that the gap between different practices is nothing like as wide in television viewing as it is in other forms of cultural practice. It is, for instance, indicated that, although highly educated people do not watch game

12

shows, uneducated working-class people *do* watch programmes that are considered to be cultured and which appeal to educated audiences (*Apostrophes, Océaniques* ...). What is more, in the conclusion to the section dealing with television viewing, it is made quite clear that, taken overall, television is by far the principal leisure and cultural resource of *all* French people:

> "On ne doit pas faire oublier que la télévision est aujourd'hui omniprésente, que son usage est massif et généralisé, que cette pratique est celle qui occupe le plus de temps dans les loisirs des Français, et que ceux-ci ont finalement à son égard des comportements assez peu différenciés. Le fait de souligner la propension plus faible des cadres supérieurs ou des Parisiens à regarder la télévision chaque jour ne doit pas faire oublier que les uns comme les autres sont néanmoins à plus de 50% chaque jour devant leur petit écran."[18]

If the authors of *Les Pratiques culturelles des Français 1973-1989* had themselves taken to heart their own injunction not to forget the overwhelming similarity in the way nearly all categories of French people watch television, perhaps they would not yet again have pursued into a newly defined field of leisure and culture the same preoccupations with patterns of distinction and difference, and, in so doing, once more helped to consign the working class to the same old position of cultural barbarism, and continued to perpetuate a negative idea of the cultural role of television in modern French society.

---

[18] Ibid, p.55.

2. _ **PROLETARIAN CULTURE AND JOURNALISM**

ROSEMARY CHAPMAN

This chapter examines the contribution of journalism to the development of proletarian culture in the inter-war years in France. It focusses specifically on the activities of the proletarian writers grouped informally around Henry Poulaille to demonstrate the difficulties of writers who insist on their working-class identity and yet assert their independence from all political parties, notably from the Communist Party. Three different types of journalistic activity undertaken by Poulaille and his group are studied, illustrating the problems of any attempt to create an alternative, class-based culture in isolation from, or in opposition to, the main trends of contemporary political life.

The relationship between proletarian culture and journalism immediately presents a paradox: a current of proletarian culture which exists in French cultural life, but which is attacked rather than welcomed and promoted by the Left, (and in particular by the Communist Party), and which is marginalized during the Popular Front period rather than flourishing. In order to explore this paradox I shall need to give a brief account of the context of this non-aligned proletarian culture. Firstly, why did the Communist Party not support the emerging working-class writers? Secondly, why was it unlikely that the group of writers around Poulaille should become part of mainstream cultural life on the Left?

The fact that it is a group of non-communist writers who are the most active in developing proletarian culture in the 1930s is partly a result of the shifting priorities of the communists in this period. Despite pressure from Moscow in 1927 when all Western communist parties were urged to develop a revolutionary proletarian literature in their own countries, French communists gave a low priority to cultural activity, concentrating their efforts on political activity. Even so, Henri Barbusse did set up *Monde*, the weekly journal in 1928, and one of its three objectives stated in the first issue was as follows:

> "Travailler à dégager, et peut-être même à susciter en quelque mesure les premiers efforts, déjà sensibles, quoique encore dispersés et tâtonnants, d'un grand art de masses aux perspectives collectives et panhumaines".[1]

Yet even this statement suggests a hesitation between the notions of "dégager" and "susciter", that is between encouraging what already exists and creating a new, revolutionary proletarian art. In the pages of *Monde* in the late 1920s there is criticism of the ideological flabbiness of writers such as Dabit, Doff and Poulaille, but no real sign of a positive alternative. In the view of Moscow, *Monde* was more a platform for Barbusse's internationalism and published too wide a range of non-communist authors. The French communists were severely attacked at the 1930 Kharkov conference, for their sluggish response to the policy of proletarian culture. For a short period in 1931 and 1932 articles in *L'Humanité* called for contributions from its working-class readership to constitute the core of proletarian cultural activity. Léon Moussinac worked from late 1931 to set up the Association des Ecrivains et Artistes Révolutionnaires, the French section of the International Union of Revolutionary Writers. It had Vaillant-Couturier as general secretary and Francis Jourdain as chairman and one of its aims was to create proletarian literature in France. But within weeks of the official launch of the AEAR in Spring 1932 the whole political and cultural debate then shifted in accordance with the USSR's changes in policy.[2] The Soviet Union now called on Western

---

[1] *Monde*, No. 1, June 9th 1928, p.1.

[2] The Soviet Association of Proletarian Writers (RAPP) was dissolved by the Central Committee of the Soviet Communist Party on April 23rd 1932. For further details on the significance of this, see J.-P.A. Bernard, *Le Parti communiste français et la question littéraire 1921-1939*, Grenoble, Presses Universitaires de Grenoble, 1972.

communist parties to see as their dual aim the fight against fascism and the defence of the USSR. This, it was felt, could best be achieved by encouraging a broad front of support, including sympathetic writers and intellectuals. The policy of proletarian culture was abandoned as being too divisive and likely to exclude the much more prestigious support of eminent figures such as Malraux and Gide. The new literary style to be encouraged was socialist realism. These changes in Moscow meant shifting priorities for the French Communist Party. This in turn meant that it was left to the non-communist proletarian writers to pursue their aims in their own way and using the channels open to them.

The second point is why the proletarian writers did not take their place in the mainstream of cultural life on the Left in the mid 1930s. In terms of his eminence and his contacts in the literary world Poulaille was well placed to stimulate proletarian writing. In the inter-war years he wrote semi-autobiographical novels, numerous studies of proletarian literature, in journals and in his 1930 study *Nouvel âge littéraire*. His writings reached an international audience. He became the unofficial leader of the Groupe d'Ecrivains prolétariens de langue française, founded in 1932. Employed from 1923 by the publisher Grasset in the press office, Poulaille was able to advise new writers about prospective publishers and editors. He became the natural focus of activity for new, usually isolated, working-class writers. But Poulaille's political views did not suit the broad coalition of communists, socialists and radicals that was emerging in the mid 1930s, starting with the Joint Programme of Action of July 27th 1934 between Socialists and Communists. Poulaille himself was an anarchist, with a lifelong hatred of party politics and a particular distrust of the French Communist Party both for their apparent acceptance of Stalinism and for their willingness to compromise with reformism in the period of the Front Populaire. It was his refusal of any alliance with the Communist Party or any of its front organisations which above all other factors was to determine the place of proletarian culture between the wars.

16

Nevertheless, despite the political isolation I have just outlined, proletarian writers did establish a presence in the journalism of the inter-war years in a variety of ways. There are three distinctive types of journalistic activity to consider.

Firstly - the journals set up by Poulaille himself. Three of these - *Nouvel Age*, 1931, *Prolétariat*, 1933-4, and *A Contre-courant*, 1935-6 deserve particular attention.[3] Each of these ran to 12 issues before collapsing, in each case for financial reasons and not for lack of contributions. The editorial boards were composed of writers from working-class or from "paysan" origins. The editorial board of *Nouvel Age* included writers such as Giono, whose first novel had been published by Grasset thanks to Poulaille, Giono's friend Henri Jacques, and the author of *Hôtel du Nord*, Eugène Dabit, all of whom were briefly attracted by Poulaille's enterprise, but quickly moved off to pursue their literary careers.

The major advantage of this form of journal was the amount of editorial freedom the team enjoyed. In the case of *Nouvel Age* the journal was a further step in the collaboration between Georges Valois and Poulaille. Valois financed the year's publication without involving himself in editorial matters and was glad for his other publishing activities to benefit from the considerable interest which *Nouvel Age* aroused both in France and abroad. In many ways *Nouvel Age* was the ideal platform for proletarian culture. Poulaille published

---

[3] Poulaille created or co-created the following reviews:
Le Journal sans nom (with Marius Bouquinet, Henri Maslin and Marcel Morin. 1 issue, November 10th 1925.
Nouvel Age. 12 issues, January-December 1931. Editorial board: Poulaille, Dabit, Gachon, Giono, Jacques, Peisson, Rémy.
Bulletin des écrivains prolétariens. "Organe du groupe des écrivains prolétariens de langue française". 4 issues, March-June 1932.
Prolétariat. 12 issues, July 1933-July 1934. Editorial board: Poulaille, Gachon, Gerbe, Massé, Peisson, Rémy.
A Contre-courant. 12 issues. July 1935-October 1936. Editorial board: Poulaille, Gachon, Massé, Peisson, Romagne.
L'Equipe des Arts et des Lettres. 3 issues, May-July 1939. Literary director: Poulaille. Artistic director: Joseph Lacasse.

many new proletarian writers, translations of Soviet, American, Norwegian, Dutch writers. The journal adopted no single political line but was in no way apolitical. In 1932 Poulaille wrote:

> "Nous avions, puisque tous se réclamaient de la révolution, pensé que communistes, socialistes, révolutionnaires et libertaires, pouvaient travailler de concert à la recherche de l'expression de classe, seule véritable base de la littérature prolétarienne."[4]

But the independent journal, in full editorial control of the proletarian writers, had its drawbacks. The financial problems proved insurmountable. *Nouvel Age*, much the most ambitious of Poulaille's journals never managed to sell more than 1,000 copies including regular subscribers. The initial printing of 3,000 copies was reduced to 2,000, but there were still heavy losses. The publisher Valois attributed the journal's lack of sales not to its quality, which was excellent, but claimed:

> "nous nous sommes trouvés devant un boycottage en règle de la part des librairies littéraires et de la plupart des organes littéraires bourgeois".[5]

If *Nouvel Age* was considered far too revolutionary for the bourgeois literary establishment, it was not sufficiently orthodox to gain communist support. Indeed, according to Poulaille, he received an ultimatum from the communists informing him that unless he fell into line with Party discipline *Nouvel Age* would be boycotted by communist readers, critics and contributors. The later two journals, *Prolétariat* and *A Contre-courant* faced the same problems of low readership, financial difficulties and attacks from Right and

---

[4] Henry Poulaille, "Sur *Nouvel Age*", *Les Cahiers bleus*, No. 108, 1931, p.18.

[5] Extract from a letter by Valois reproduced in K.-A. Arvidsson, *Henry Poulaille et la littérature prolétarienne française des années 1930*, Paris, Jean Touzot, 1988, p.240.

Left. So the considerable achievement of the proletarian writers in creating a series of platforms for proletarian culture in France can only be seen as a partial success.

The other two forms of journalistic activity depended on establishing a platform for proletarian writing within the existing range of newspapers and journals in France, which presented a different set of opportunities and problems.

A number of journals offered Poulaille's group space to publish proletarian writing and articles about proletarian culture.[6] What is interesting about this "borrowed" space, is that each of the papers or journals must have seen proletarian literature as being somehow in tune with their own very different ideological positions, if only for a brief period.

The proletarian writers were first of all invited to provide material for *Monde*, where Henri Barbusse was still editor and in early 1932 was still maintaining a certain editorial independence from the Communist Party. Early in 1932 Barbusse wrote to Poulaille expressing his hope that Poulaille might contribute to *Monde*, this being just at the time that Poulaille was under strong attack from orthodox communist critics such as Fréville in *L'Humanité*. Then in April Marc Bernard appealed in the pages of *Monde* to working-class readers to send in their work to be considered for publication in the journal. After a few selections of submitted writing the Groupe des Ecrivains prolétariens took over responsibility for the "Pages et documents de la vie populaire" which ran for 9 issues between July and October 1932. New writing

---

[6] Poulaille edited a page, or pages, of proletarian writing in:

Monde. 'Pages et documents de la vie populaire'. Usually 4 pages per issue. Appeared 9 times between July and October 1932.

Esprit. Poulaille edited 5 'Cahiers de littérature prolétarienne' between July 1936 and September 1937.

La Flèche. 'Littérature prolétarienne et documents populaires' appeared once on January 30th 1937, with an introduction by Poulaille.

Le Libertaire. A page entitled 'Ecrits prolétariens' was published 3 times from March to May 1937.

by Malva, Autry, David and Ayguesparse was published, as was an extract from Marx and Engels on Balzac, and articles on a range of topics including proletarian literature, Gorky, Nazism, Spain and the dissolution of the Soviet Association of Proletarian Writers (RAPP). The timing of this collaboration was crucial. *Monde* was itself facing financial difficulties and the proletarian writers helped the journal to survive by agreeing to wait for payment. In the Summer of 1932 Barbusse was becoming deeply involved in antifascist activities, setting up the Amsterdam-Pleyel movement and organising the Congrès mondial contre la guerre impérialiste which took place on August 27th-29th 1932. In the following few months the Communist Party also changed its strategies, as explained earlier, to give a high priority to antifascism and broad front policies. So rather unexpectedly for Barbusse, he was far nearer to mainstream communist thinking by late 1932 than for a number of years previously. From now on *Monde* moved back into the influence of the Communist Party and further collaboration with Poulaille's group was unthinkable as more orthodox communists moved onto the editorial board to implement the ideological line of the Communist Party.

The second journal to offer space to the proletarian writers was *Esprit* which published five quite substantial selections of texts between July 1936 and September 1937. It is certainly surprising that Poulaille's group whose works were consistently criticised on the conservative Right for their near total disregard of religion and spirituality should be welcomed in a Catholic journal, even a progressive one. There are two possible reasons for this, apart from opportunism on Poulaille's part. *Esprit* was willing to take a stance on issues of political principle, arguing like Poulaille for the liberation of Victor Serge in the USSR, at times critical of the Front Populaire, denouncing Stalinism. Secondly, Mounier was anti-capitalist, anti-bourgeois, showed a strong concern about working-class poverty and felt that only a revolution could right the wrongs he saw. According to Senarclens in his study on the *Esprit* movement, the working-class represented for him: "la fraîcheur, la pûreté, les promesses de l'enfance ingénue".[7] If the "peuple" are children, then politics belongs to the realm of wicked adulthood. In his presentation of the first of the "Cahiers de littérature prolétarienne", Mounier writes of the aim of proletarian literature to "retrouver le peuple dans sa pûreté originelle" arguing that: "Le peuple est atteint comme nous tous par les maladies de l'époque, et cependant il est toujours la grande réserve".[8] While Poulaille had no sympathy for Mounier's notions of a spiritual revolution, he firmly believed that political and cultural renewal must come from the working class alone. His own presentation of the first of the "Cahiers de littérature prolétarienne" is headed simply "Des hommes voudraient parler" stressing that proletarian writers are in effect silenced in contemporary society and that by giving the working class a voice one gives them power. Two further weekly journals offered Poulaille space in the course of his collaboration with *Esprit*. These are much less significant except to show the diversity of platforms available to a non-conformist group. In 1937 Bergery's *La Flèche* was distanced from the political establishment on the Right and Left. It claimed to be anti-capitalist and anti-communist, and to be seeking a "third way". The final journal, *Le Libertaire* was ideologically the closest to Poulaille, being "L'organe hebdomadaire de l'Union anarchiste". *Le Libertaire* denounced parliamentarianism and its product the Front Populaire. Poulaille in his opening article expresses his political and literary views far more clearly than in any of the other journals in this section:

> "Et à l'heure où l'on oublie dans les partis politiques la lutte des classes, et où l'on voit se perdre, peu à peu dans les organisations ouvrières le sens de classe, sur les prétextes d'une mystique de front populaire - d'affront populaire souvent - il est nécessaire de

---

[7] P. de Senarclens, *Le mouvement 'Esprit' 1932-41*, Lausanne, L'Age de l'Homme, 1974, p.126.

[8] *Esprit*, No. 42, March 1936, p.928.

faire le point pour ce qui est des choses de l'esprit".[9]

What these four journals represented for Poulaille's group was firstly, publishing space without the financial responsibility of their own journals and secondly, the chance of reaching a wider and a different readership - although even the influential *Esprit* had fewer than 4,000 readers. The dangers were that any such collaboration was likely to be shortlived as proletarian literature was not the primary concern of those journals and that even though Poulaille might have editorial freedom within his pages, proletarian writers were bound to be associated, in the minds of the readers with the views of the journal concerned, which makes a long-term collaboration with a journal like *La Flèche* or even *Esprit* undesirable.

The third form of journalistic activity to consider is literary editorship. Poulaille was literary editor of *Le Peuple*, the CGT daily paper from 1924 until war broke out in 1939. Given his horror of all political associations this might seem strange. But Poulaille had always believed in the role of the syndicalist movement as the natural form of organisation of the working class. He supported the principle of the 1906 Amiens Charter, quoted in one of his novels, which stipulated that the syndicats should have no formal link with any political party. After the Congrès de Tours the CGT had divided from the CGTU which was sympathetic to communism. It was not until 1935 that the two organisations agreed moves towards reunification, in keeping with the widespread mood of "rassemblement". This was finally ratified at a special congress in March 1936. For most of this period, then, the CGT offered Poulaille a way of reaching the heart of the workers' movement, without compromising his political principles.

In terms of editorial freedom *Le Peuple* and its editor until 1936, Francis Million, allowed Poulaille the independence he needed, although some of the

_____

[9] *Le Libertaire*, March 18th 1937, p.5.

other journalists on the paper did not share Poulaille's and Million's view of the importance of culture to the working-class reader. Million's support is clear - as in his New Year message to the readership in 1934, where he refers to recent improvements in the paper and states that his aim is to make *Le Peuple* "le meilleur instrument d'influence, de combat et d'éducation mis entièrement à la disposition du mouvement ouvrier".[10] This coincides with Poulaille's own statement in *Nouvel âge littéraire* concerning the function of the literary historian, the creative writer and the journalist: "Il y a une éducation complète des masses à entreprendre et journaux et revues devraient s'y employer".[11]

In the course of fifteen years the literary columns underwent some changes in format but the space devoted to literature and culture remained fairly constant. In addition to the "page littéraire" (usually weekly) there were regular shorter items (book reviews or extracts from new works, for example), and in the course of a year *Le Peuple* would serialize on average twelve full-length novels, two novels running concurrently. Up to half of these were novels by writers from the rural or urban working-class, such as Emile Guillaumin, Tristan Rémy, Louis Guilloux, Marguerite Audoux, one or two per year would be by foreign writers such as Dos Passos, Sinclair Lewis, Tolstoy, Gorky or Hamsun, and the rest by French writers such as Zola and Chamson.

The "page littéraire" fulfilled a number of functions:-

1)   The discussion of proletarian culture and its acquisition particularly in the series "L'écrivain et l'ouvrier" published from 1926-7 and which expounded Poulaille's views on a culture by the working class and for the working class.

2)   Evidence of the existence of an authentic proletarian voice in

---

[10] *Le Peuple*, January 1st 1934, p.1.

[11] *Nouvel âge littéraire*, Paris, 1930, p.37.

literature by the publication and promotion of proletarian writers.

3) Access not only to French but also to foreign literature in articles, extracts and serialisations.

4) Access for the working-class reader to a culture more broadly based than proletarian literature. (This became an increasingly important aspect of *Le Peuple* from 1933 onwards when the paper was modernised in terms of its layout, the number of photographs and other illustrations, and the grouping of articles under more specialised regular rubrics. Examples of the range of material included are series on European painting, on great composers, on science, on working-class history, on popular traditions).

The relative importance of these four functions does shift in the period examined. The use of the pages as a forum for cultural debate declines. In the mid 30s onwards there are still many proletarian writers published, but the term proletarian is used as the norm, not as a polemical term. The tone does however seem to become a bit more bland, possibly as a result of Million's campaign to increase readership in the mid 1930s when sales rose dramatically for many left of centre papers.

To summarize: the proletarian writers' journalistic activity takes three main forms, each with its drawbacks.

1) Independent journals. The independent journals represent a financial burden and only manage low circulation, not having the support of a network - be it of the literary establishment, major newspapers, well-known figures or of the communist press. So these journals were doomed to be specialized and, paradoxically exclusive - produced by proletarian writers and read by other

proletarian writers, aspiring writers or convinced supporters. No mass readership was possible.

2) Pages in other journals - borrowed space. This is interesting in terms of the light it throws on those journals welcoming the proletarian writers. Often it is a sign of their own non-conformism and their wish to challenge the status quo. Borrowed space depends on the generosity of other groups/individuals and there is some risk of contamination by association if those platforms continue too long. The writings will reach a new readership, but they are likely only to be of peripheral interest to those readers.

3) *Le Peuple* - literary editorship. This is much the most significant of the three in terms of readership (around 16,600 by the end of 1939), and in terms of continuity. A number of proletarian writers are involved both as journalists and as creative writers (gaining precisely the sort of apprenticeship to writing that critics like Guéhenno felt they lacked). The cultural element in *Le Peuple* does achieve the twin aims of education and of developing the readers' awareness of themselves as members of a class which can create and control culture. *Le Peuple* hardly represents a mass readership, but in the context of the inter-war years it was a good audience to target.

To conclude: journalism in the inter-war period does help to widen working-class access to the cultural process. This access is both active and passive. Members of the proletariat are active as producers, presenters and critics. The readers, the consumers, are offered a range of cultural experience which their elementary schooling will not have offered them. This culture is not only that which is enjoyed by the educated bourgeoisie, but also a culture which has come from their own class. The process might well have been more far-reaching were it not for the fact that proletarian culture remained doubly marginalised in the inter-war period - firstly through the domination of the publishing world by an educated bourgeoisie and secondly through the proletarian writers' opposition to the policies of the Communist Party and their refusal of any political alignment.

3. THE LAW OF THE JINGLE, OR A DECADE OF CHANGE IN FRENCH RADIO

GEOFFREY E. HARE

The construction and perception of social identity is a complex matter. One aspect of social identity is that which is implicit in the notional audience that the broadcasting media construct for their own institutional purposes. The thrust of this chapter is to examine how the notional audience constructed by French radio institutions has changed significantly over the last decade, and to conclude by asking what social identity this medium projects onto its listeners, still over three-quarters of the population.[1]

The Traditional Pattern of Radio Broadcasting

Describing French radio in 1980 was straightforward: in competition for the national audience there were four or five "generalist" radios, each with a similar diet of programmes. Four commercial radios called "périphériques", since they transmitted from outside France, had the lion's share of listeners on long wave. They were RTL (Luxembourg) and Europe 1 (near Saarbrücken, Germany), especially dominant in the north and east, and Radio Monte-Carlo (RMC) in the south, dwarfing their little sister Sud-Radio (Andorra) in the south-west. Radio-France's equivalent public service radio station, France-Inter, with no brand advertising, tried to cultivate an image of difference, but basically devoted its day's programmes to what was seen as a homogeneous national audience, albeit with different needs at different times of the day: for example, 6 am to 8.45 am: news, current affairs and press reviews; followed by

---

[1] In addition to the items listed in the bibliography, this chapter is based upon interviews conducted in 1990 with the following: Jean-Noël Jeanneney, Director-General of Radio France from 1982 to 1986; Robert Latxague, Rédacteur en chef, Radio-France Isère and Andrew Menderstam, Chair of RFM.

middle-of-the-road music and game-shows for a mainly house-wife audience up to the 1 pm news; more music and talk in the afternoon; news and current affairs from 7 pm to 8 pm; then music aimed at the younger end of the market until close down.

The only other radio stations of note were Radio-France's two low audience, high culture stations: France-Culture and France-Musique. The first programmed music and drama, and a lot of high level discussion of a wide range of subjects from philosophy and the arts to science and international affairs. The second concentrated on classical music and discussion of same. Local radio was limited to a few minutes of "décrochage" per day by the 15 regional stations of Radio-France. There was little real choice of programme therefore, and a limited choice of programme supplier: state control of broadcasting was not really challenged by the existence of the "périphériques", since the latter were indirectly controlled through state-dominated holding companies like the SOFIRAD and Havas.

Radio was available all through the day for listening to or accompanying various activities as background. There were 25-30 million radio sets in 1980 for a population of over 50 million. The portable transistor radio on the kitchen table had replaced the earlier big valve radio in its fixed position in the sitting room. Listening tended however still to be a home-based and often a communal activity, at least at breakfast and at other meal times.

There were signs however of a sea-change waiting to happen, which was to increase competition, massively open up radio broadcasting to the private sector and displace the centre of gravity of radio output to the FM wave band (offering in principle higher sound quality) - 6 out of every 10 listeners are now tuned to FM -, multiply the supply of programmes a hundred-fold, fragment the audience into small targeted segments, and turn radio listening into a solitary activity on personal stereos or the car radio where everyone has their own receiver and is able to listen to their chosen station.

This was to happen simultaneously with the growth of external competition for audiences from an increasing supply of television programmes. There are now six national terrestrial or off-air broadcasting channels (as opposed to three in 1980), over a hundred city cable networks, a French DBS satellite (not to mention other European ones received in France) and a number of local TV channels. Television is available 24 hours a day on some channels. Breakfast TV in particular offers competition at a traditionally high audience time for radio. Changes in the political, economic and technological domains have come together to effect this sea-change. The body of this chapter will review the key forces at work in these domains as they have developed, making the 1980s an unprecedented decade of change as regards radio broadcasting in France.

Political Change and the FM Band

In 1980, the signs of change were first of all only in the Socialist Party's manifesto, which promised to take the broadcasting media out of the hands of government. There was a possibility that within a year François Mitterrand would replace Valéry Giscard d'Estaing as President of the Republic and be able to install a left-wing government in power and set in train various media reforms in the direction of greater broadcasting freedom.

More important than political change (which, it could be argued, was being pushed by social change), was the existence, since about 1973, of a growing number of illegal pirate radio stations (perhaps 50 or so by 1978) broadcasting with relatively cheap equipment on the FM wave band in an attempt to break the state monopoly. The state authorities in turn jammed and raided them whenever possible. Many were run by broadcasting fanatics, or music lovers, who simply wanted to exercise their freedom of expression over the air-waves. Others set up pirate stations for political reasons, such as the Socialist Party's Radio Riposte in 1979, which in addition to being jammed by the state broadcasting authorities was the object of legal proceedings naming Mitterrand and other socialist leaders. Others still wished to break the state monopoly in order to set up commercial radio stations as a vector of paid advertising.

Public service radio had foreseen the inevitability of evolution in radio broadcasting in response to a new demand: they not only put France-Musique and France-Culture on FM, but more especially created new local and thematic (or focussed) radio stations aimed at segments of a hitherto national audience. In 1980 Radio-France's Director General Jacqueline Baudrier set up on an experimental basis three local radios and two thematic radios, as an attempt to get new state controlled public service radios established on the ground. The local radios were intended as trials for different sizes of geographical areas of coverage: Radio Melun-FM (broadcasting at town level), Radio Mayenne (at the level of the *département*), and Fréquence-Nord (broadcasting from Lille at the regional level). The thematic radios targeted two age groups: the young up to the age of 25 or so with Radio 7, and the retired ("le troisième âge") with Radio Bleue. The aim was, over time, to extend the number of local public service radios to several dozen, and to extend Radio 7 broadcasts nationwide. This was not to be sufficient to cope with social demand.

The election of Mitterrand as President in May 1981 and the declaration, on 14th May 1981 by the Socialist Party communication spokesman (and later Minister) Georges Fillioud, that the new government would break the state monopoly on broadcasting lit the blue touch paper for an explosion of (still illegal) "radios libres". Suddenly, it seemed, everybody with a spare attic room was setting up a transmitter and playing records for their "quartier", including, from June 1981, Jean-Paul Baudecroux, in a 10th floor flat, Porte des Lilas. His station, NRJ, was to become financially and in terms of size of audience the most successful of local private or commercial radios. The anarchy created by dozens of stations on limited air-waves cried out for regulation, and within

6 months, following the Holleaux Commission's report, a new law was promulgated (on 9th November 1981) aimed specifically at regularizing the situation of the "radios libres".

In the spirit of the Socialist Party's mistrust of the "grandes puissances d'argent" (which had also inspired the legislators at the Liberation to ban all independent commercial radio) the new law was to ban all advertising income from the authorized radios. The new "radios locales privées" had to operate as non-profit-making associations, could not set up networks of transmitters, and could not be run by town councils. They also had to broadcast on specific frequencies with strict limits of transmission strength (up to 50 watts) and area (within a 30 km radius).

A long period of judicial limbo ensued during which time anarchy continued to reign. The licensing authority (first the Commission Holleaux, and then from mid-1982 the HACA or Haute Autorité de la Communication audiovisuelle) took an inordinately long time to draw up its list of authorised stations. In Paris there were 155 applications for the limited number of frequencies on the FM band and it was not until April 1983 that the first licences were granted - only 22 in the city of Paris. Some stations cynically ignored the agreed transmission strength or allocated frequency. Others sinned through lack of technical expertise. The financial problems of these stations (despite the distribution of grants of £10,000 from a special fund - le fonds de soutien à l'expression radiophonique - fed by a tax on TV advertising income) led many to resort to more or less open advertising or sponsorship. Patrick Meyer's RFM, in particular, supported by Coluche, set out deliberately to break the commercial advertising ban and was jammed in Paris for 423 days in 1981-82. Pressure and confusion built up, until President Mitterrand appeared to contradict his Minister and give the go-ahead for commercial advertising (27th March 1984), the day after Fillioud had reaffirmed his continuing hostility to it. The law of 1st August 1984 authorised independent radios to operate as private companies and take advertising income. The Socialists' acceptance of private enterprise in broadcasting was widened, when, following the Bredin report (mid-1985), they created two new commercial TV stations, and set in train the withdrawal of the state from the "périphériques", Europe 1 being sold off to the publishing group Hachette (March 1986). The Chirac Government completed this process by asking the Sofirad to sell its shares in RMC.

The growth of a loyal FM audience was fairly rapid - as shown by the strength of feeling and the numbers of young NRJ supporters in a massive demonstration in Paris on 8th December 1984, after the HACA had tried to ban NRJ and other radios for persistent violation of transmission strength and for setting up networks. Government was unable to pluck up enough courage to send in the police and seize their transmission equipment, thus further exacerbating the lack of respect for the legal framework and the broadcasting authorities, and encouraging the law of the jungle on the FM band. The estimated audience of local private radios (RLP) was 4.3 million in 1984, by 1988 36% of the listening public, and still growing.

The "périphériques" had to react to the economic blow of their audience being nibbled away, especially that of the high-spending section of 15-25 year olds and even 25-34 year olds, with its consequent effect on advertising income. Realising that the majority of listeners would henceforward be on FM, the périphériques, hitherto limited to long-wave stations, successfully negotiated the attribution of frequencies for themselves on FM when the official broadcasting band was extended to include 104-108 MHz in January 1986. They effectively began broadcasting on FM from 7th March 1986. By this time then it was clear that the centre of gravity of radio broadcasting had swung to the FM band.

New Technology and National Networks

The technological possibilities of the FM band had been opened up by political decision, and forced on traditional broadcasters by economic necessity.

Another significant technological step forward was the launch, mainly for business and defence communications, of the satellites Telecom 1 in 1984 and Telecom 1C in 1988. These low power telecommunications satellites, not to be confused with the high power Direct Broadcast Satellite TDF1, came to be used by the RLP for the setting up of networks - radios transmitting the same programme in different towns. The central programming station distributes the programme via the satellite to its affiliated stations or transmitters which relay the entire programme (or part of it) locally on FM. Originally networks were banned, but gradually local stations were either bought up or given the franchise to broadcast programmes produced by the station to which the locally owned station was affiliated. They were legalised in the 1986 audivisual law reform. NRJ, the biggest network was believed to control 108 stations at the last count, ensuring it about 10% of the national audience. Among six or seven major networks which are trying to establish themselves is RFM, part owned since 1989 by the British group Crown Communication (owners of LBC and Independent Radio News).

The future of broadcasting then from 1986 onwards (commercial pressures pointing the way) was in the form of national FM band networks. The importance of networks with formatted programming has also been recognised by the "périphériques", but rather late and they have lost ground on the competition. Simply putting their traditional programme on the FM band was not enough. RMC has lost a third of its listeners since 1986. Realizing it is the only way to keep the younger end of the market in their basket of audiences to sell to advertisers, they have all tried to set up a network of "music-and-news" stations to deliver targeted programmes to that segment of the market, quite separate from their generalist programmes, which are no longer listened to by the 15-24 year olds. Europe 1 is setting up a form of network of independently owned local stations subscribing to programmes supplied by its subsidiary Europe 2 (since 1987). Additionally, they are offering advertisers a basket of audiences, under the name Puissance 3, made up of the complementary audiences of Europe 1, Europe 2 (25-45 year olds) and the Skyrock network (15-35 year olds). RTL, having failed to buy Radio Nostalgie, bought up Aventure FM to create a network called Maxximum (aimed at 15-30 year olds), which has since merged with Métropolys (June 1991), with the CLT (owners of RTL) keeping a 30% stake. RMC, in their turn, in early 1989, bought the Nostalgie network, whose turn-over proceeded to triple in 1990.

This trend was tending to isolate the independent networks such as NRJ, which reacted by taking control of a second smaller network Chérie FM (25-45 year olds) and absorbing the network Pacific FM (November 1989), in an attempt to offer advertisers complementary audiences. The upshot of all this is that now the "périphériques" are competing on the same ground as the new networks, and the independent local radios and smaller networks are falling prey to both in this battle for audiences.

Regulation and Licensing

The complexities of relationship between local stations, programme suppliers or franchise holders, and advertisers pose problems in relation to concentration of ownership and variety of programme, problems which the regulators began to address only in 1990.

The last ten years have not been an easy period for regulators. The authority of broadcasting's regulatory bodies has suffered first of all through lack of longevity: they have come and gone with changes of government: the HACA (dating from 1982) was replaced by decision of the Chirac government in 1986 by the CNCL, which in turn, in January 1989, was transformed by the Rocard government into the CSA. Their authority, particularly in the case of the HACA, has also been diminished through lack of power to enforce their own decisions and lack of support from the Elysée or from government. The CSA is only just beginning to establish the necessary order in the law of the

34

jungle that is French radio. In his speech inaugurating the regional regulatory body in Dijon (7th December 1989), the President of the CSA, Jacques Boutet, recognised the perverse effects of the "cacophony" which has developed along with the massive increase in number of stations (some 1800 of all kinds at the time). Examples of this anarchy include one station deliberately or innocently jamming another, pirating of frequencies, illegal buying up of stations and frequencies, "confusion des genres", disregard for the law, and a plethora of bankruptcies. His objective is to turn this "paysage qui tient encore parfois de la forét vierge" into a French garden - planned and ordered.[2]

It is too late to go back on the existence of networks even if the regulators wanted to. However the CSA, while allowing for commercial networks in its new regulatory framework, is attempting to protect other forms of broadcasting organisation, which otherwise might be eaten up by the "poids lourds" of national commercial radio. Unlike the HACA, the CSA has full control over allocation of frequencies, and greater powers of sanction.

Licences for radio stations throughout France are being reallocated region by region by CTRs (Comités techniques radiophoniques) appointed by the CSA. There are 12 such regions and CTRs in metropolitan France, with 4 more for the overseas *départements*. The CSA has defined 5 categories of radio which may henceforward apply for broadcasting licences. The five categories are:

A. *Non-commercial stations*. Eligible for help from the Fonds de soutien, they must receive less than 20% of income from commercial (brand-name) advertising or sponsorship and be genuinely "radios de proximité".

B. *Local or regional independent commercial stations*. Covering an area with a population of less than 6 million potential listeners, their programming must be preponderantly of local/regional interest.

C. *Local or regional commercial stations affiliated to or franchised by a*

---

[2] *La Lettre du CSA*, 4 January 1990, p.9.

35

network. Local again means an area of under 6 million inhabitants. Programmes must include significant time devoted to local programmes (at least 20%), but they may subscribe to another programme supplier (usually a network), whose programmes must not be financed by local advertising revenue. Contracts with the supplier cannot bind the local station for more than 3 months. Changes of franchise or network are subject to the agreement of the CSA.

D. *National commercial "thematic" stations.* They are essentially music-and-news networks, with no local "décrochages" either in programming or publicity, so income is from national advertising only, leaving local income solely to finance local programmes, in categories A-C.

E. *National commercial "generalist" stations.* They are essentially the "périphériques", offering a lot of news and information, culturally orientated programmes, as well as game shows and a variety of musical output. Again, no local "décrochages" will be allowed, financing being from exclusively national advertising.

A given application must be clearly for one category only and in awarding licences the CSA will attempt to achieve a balance and a complementary variety of types of radio in a coherent pattern, which is intended to last.

The deconcentration of decision-making is not complete - the CTR recommends, the Paris-based CSA decides, - allowing the CSA to oversee the national picture, as President Boutet has stated. In particular the CSA wishes to safeguard authentic non-commercial radio, guaranteeing the "vocation associative" of such stations, and to safeguard local radio. As regards existing networks, which will have to apply for licences in each locality, they are not all guaranteed to remain. One of Boutet's fellow CSA commissioners, Roland Faure, chiefly responsible for radio matters in the CSA, declared in November 1989 that he felt there were too many national commercial networks for the available advertising income. It remains to be seen whether the CSA will attempt to accelerate the process of market forces by eliminating 2 or 3 of them in the licensing process. There are already limits on concentration of ownership. A national network serving over 30 million potential listeners cannot control a second network serving more than 15 million potential inhabitants. The owners of RTL have chosen a minority holding in a national "music-and-news" network (Métropolys) in preference to wholly controlling a smaller one (Hit FM).

Public Service Radio Adapting to Competition

Public service radio meanwhile has not been sitting idly by, watching its audience figures drop in this climate of increased competition. Of course, long-term planning at Radio-France has not been helped by frequent changes of Director General. Mme Baudrier gave way to Michèle Cotta in 1981, who on her elevation to the presidency of the HACA, handed over the reins to Jean-Noël Jeanneney in 1982. The Chirac government replaced him in 1986 with Roland Faure, who, on his appointment to the CSA was in turn replaced by Jean Maheu in February 1989. Despite these changes, Radio-France has pursued a relatively coherent strategy, but not without set-backs.

Jeanneney carried through two important policies: going as much as possible for FM frequencies and a networking strategy with the opening of a large number of local stations (standing at 42 in all by 1991 and covering 50% of France). Radio-France claimed very early to have the biggest network of stations in the country, all of which feed each other rather than feeding on each other's audiences (as some employees felt) in a policy of broadcasting cannibalism. The most successful format as regards size of local station seems to be that of the *département*, with particular success in terms of listeners in the rural *départements*. The city stations are less successful (Nice, Lyon, Marseille, and Toulouse have been turned largely into FIPs, "radios musicales d'accompagnement".

Under Faure, the other line of diversification begun by Mme Baudrier, the opening of thematic stations, was taken further with the opening of the increasingly successful 24 hours rolling news station, France-Info, which from its 2.5% of total audience in September 1988 had gone up to 4.5% in March 1989, and is at 7.7% in June 1991. However France-Info was created at the expense of Radio 7, whose demise looked inevitable after doing less and less well in competition with the RLP. Budgetary cuts by the Chirac government also helped force this change. The other thematic station, Radio Bleue, on the other hand, has significantly increased its daily output (to 12 hours per day in 1990), as have France Musique and France Culture.

Another innovation, begun under Jeanneney and realised under Maheu (November 1989), has been the creation of two upmarket cultural programmes (mainly compiled from France Musique and France Culture) broadcast to a European-wide audience in digital stereo sound on the TDF1 satellite: Victor (as in Hugo) the cultural and information programme, and Hector (as in Berlioz) the serious music programme.

Changes of top personnel at Radio-France have nonetheless not helped counter competition in one crucial area: the audience for its national flagship station France-Inter. After a drop in audience at the time of the 1981 and 1982 changes Jeanneney's new head of Programmes, Jean Garetto redesigned the schedules with success, so that, from 13.5% of total radio audience in 1983, Inter had gone up to 17.3% by the end of 1986, which, for the first time in many years, put them ahead of Europe 1 in audience figures. Subsequently, frequent changes of management and direction have seen a constant fall in audience to 10.9% at the beginning of 1990, a figure partly (but not wholly) compensated for by the continuing rise of France-Info. Radio listening as a whole went up during the Gulf War by 3%, especially the figures of France-Info (9.7%), but fell back again in the second quarter of the year. However

38

Radio-France, if it totals up its audiences for its national stations and local stations can still claim to be "le premier réseau de France" with 23.5% of the radio audience in June 1991, ahead of RTL on 18.8%.

Public service broadcasting in the early 1990s enjoys a friendlier government (and hence less austere funding) than under the Chirac regime (1986-1988), when it lost control of Radio-France Internationale. It has established a national network of local stations (some of which it will come under renewed pressure to close) and successful thematic stations, and has not neglected new channels of communication such as digital sound via satellite and innovations like RDS (Radio Data System). However, the audience figures of France-Inter continue to be worrying, as does the 1990 operating deficit. Radio-France will not be well placed to ask for increases in licence fee revenue if they start to lose listeners again. The loss of their popular Sunday morning show *L'Oreille en coin* is symptomatic of internal dissension - the whole team went to Europe 1 in 1990 after disputes between its producer Jean Garetto and the new Head of Programming, Pierre Bouteiller.

The Growing Impact of Market Forces

After ten years of rapid change the dominant impression is that the decade has seen the triumph of market forces.

The laws of the market have encouraged a fragmentation of the audience through the triumph of formatting. By formatting is meant niche marketing or targeting a particular segment of the total listening public for easier sale to advertisers, and thereto offering a very specific type of programme. The formats dominating the networks are variations on "music-and-news", with NRJ, FUN and Skyrock aiming at the 15-25 year olds, RFM and Europe 2 at the 25-45 year olds, and Nostalgie mainly the over 40s. Formatting has also been adopted by public service radio, with noticeable success in the case of France-Info, the only French station with a news-only format, and also with Radio Bleue, music and news, now for the over 50s, which has its commercial competitor in Paris in the form of Radio Montmartre. Compared to the American market where 23 different programme formats have been identified (each with sub-divisions), the French market has still some way to go in terms of audience fragmentation. Radio formatting designed to sell an audience clearly illustrates the primary importance of marketing in French radio.

Market forces have also favoured concentration of ownership, whether in the form of wholly owned networks, or affiliated stations, or franchising or programmes, or advertising networks. The present position is that, of the 1800 or so radio stations in France about 300 are non-commercial or community radios, some 500 are independent commercial stations, and about 1000 attached to commercial networks. The present government, in its new regulatory framework, has recognised the dangers of the earlier, more liberal, deregulated (or rather non-regulated) approach, and the CSA is providing some protection to local commercial independent radios ("radios de proximité) and non-commercial "radios associatives". However, the range of community radio in the provinces, where the networks dominate, in no way mirrors that in Paris (Radio Notre-Dame, Radio Protestante, Radio Shalom, Radio Beur, Radio Orient, Fréquence Gaie, etc.). In Paris or elsewhere only a few radio operators resemble the pioneers whose joint efforts broke the state monopoly ten years ago.

A further way in which market forces have had an impact is that the "périphériques" whose dominance over the commercial radio scene was threatened by their slowness to react to technological and social change, have found ways of using their financial resources to buy back their leading role in French radio. Whether, like RMC or RTL, by majority or minority ownership of FM networks, or, like Europe 1, by acting as programme supplier (arguably a more fragile position), they are still in a relatively strong position within

French radio broadcasting. The only newcomers to challenge them are Baudecroux's NRJ (with 5 million listeners, over 100 stations, a 200 million Franc annual turnover, and 63 million Franc profit in 1988), and to a lesser extent Skyrock and, in a small way, RFM.

Like any other enterprise, once expansion slows on the home market, where the listening audience is now more or less saturated, French commercial radio is looking to expand abroad. Europe 2 is broadcasting in Prague, Europe 1 has a foot in the door in Moscow, FUN is in Poland, Rumania, Czechoslovakia and the USSR. Several French radios are moving into Belgium, and looking at Italy and Germany.

The pattern of French radio broadcasting in the 1990s seems set - the 1980-81 changes have shaken themselves out. Radio listening as a whole has stabilized too at about 76% of the population, after the shock of increased TV competition in the mid 1980s. This figure is broadly comparable to total British audience figures. However the loss of a million radio listeners (2.8%) of total) between 1989 and 1990, particularly in the 15-24 year old bracket, reminded investors that FM radio is not a licence to print money. RMC and Sud-Radio were forced to lose 10% of jobs. Advertising revenue has tightened and may tighten further, and one or two networks may fail (as Kiss FM did in March 1991), and others merge (like Métropolys and Maxximum in 1991). These failures and mergers have led to somewhat increased concentration of ownership - but not necessarily (in the cases mentioned) at the expense of diversity of programmes. However, under the emerging authority of the CSA, a more stable situation seems likely to impose itself unless major technological innovations or political change again disrupt the status quo.

French Radio and Social Identity

How do we relate these changes to social identity? The most useful set of arguments are those around the notion of the construction of an audience

41

by the media.[3] This way of looking at the audience involves the idea that a given media organisation can be said to develop a model of the audience to suit its own needs and that people do not exist as an audience until they have been constructed as such by the media. Now, we have seen that one of the main changes in radio in the last decade has been the growing dominance of the commercial networks. To exist today commercial radios need to sell their audience to advertisers. The radio station promises to deliver a particular type and size of audience to companies who have bought advertising slots at particular times of the day. Thus programming policy (production and scheduling) is predicated on the principle of creating a particular type of audience rather than on the basis of providing listeners with "what they want to hear". In defining this audience, emphasis is not so much on numbers as on "demographics": defining the audience in terms of certain demographic characteristics which identify a particular consumer group. This may be illustrated with reference to one such new radio, the small, but successfully targeted station, RFM.

Within a year of taking over RFM in 1988, Crown Communication decided to change the format to target a segment of the market they identified as being hitherto underexploited in France: the 25-40 year-old "actifs" living in towns of over 100,000 people, more male than female, from the A+B social class categories (to use the British classifications, as they do). They can sell this audience, who may be described as "French Yuppies", to advertisers in the automotive industries (cars, petrol, insurance - 70% of their advertising income is motor car related), to France Telecom and to advertisers of certain other new products.

The programming format they have used to build up this audience

---

[3] See: Manuel Alvarado, Robin Gutch and Tania Wollen, *Learning the Media. An Introduction to Media Teaching*, Basingstoke, Macmillan Education, 1987, pp.257-258, and Michael Gurevitch et al., (eds), *Society, Culture and the Media*, London, Routledge, 1990, p.169.

features more news and information than most music stations: service information on weather and driving conditions, time checks, "l'agenda du business man", and 11 minutes of news per hour at the important morning "drive time", as well as news on the hour through the day ("Le monde en 80 seconds"). An unexpected feature (but one which gives a certain *cachet*) is their relaying of the BBC Overseas Service international news in French every evening at 11 pm (for 3 minutes). Time given to news bulletins is of course still very restricted in comparison to music, which dominates air-time. In terms of choice of music, RFM combines its regularly up-dated play-list of new pop singles with what it calls "classics" (pop records from the 1958-1975 period). RFM's "animateurs" (who include the nationally known Eddy Mitchell and Antoine de Caunes) are individualised much more than say those on NRJ where the music is all important, and RFM's tone is more ironic or caustic than other stations.

They constantly monitor their format in terms of the target audience through market research and "panels". To quote their sales brochure, "RFM maîtrise les attentes du marché et se donne les moyens d'ajuster régulièrement sa grille de programmes et ce, pour satisfaire la cible privilégiée des 24-40 ans, Actifs, Citadins qu'elle a décidé de fidéliser". To facilitate the advertiser's task they quote percentage penetration of given segments of the market and prices per 1000 contacts/listeners of their standard slots. Market research between May and September 1989, on either side of their changed format, showed a clear shift towards the centre of their targeted audience.

Now, the very act of targeting an audience, as illustrated by the case of RFM, is going to play a part in constructing that audience. Who the actual radio listeners are can only be identified *post-hoc*. The radio station must start out with an idea or model of its target audience. This idea (or construct) is then less descriptive than predictive. Successful formatting and promotion means the initial construct will become reality in terms of the listeners actually attracted to the station, and the format will be constantly refined by audience research to steer the composition of the audience towards the desired target. This is what is meant by the notion of media organisations "constructing an audience" for its own purposes, "constructing" in the meaning both of conceptualizing and building up in reality. Since the dominant model in French radio is the commercial one, and since the commercial sector is ever more dominated by a small number of national networks, the audience model with which radio broadcasters are operating is one of a very few variations on consumer models conceived in advertising agencies or by marketing people. Put another way, the dominant (one might even say sole) characteristic of social identity which is being used by the programmers is one which conceives of the audience simply as consumers.

This would seem to involve two dangers: exclusion and stereotyping. Firstly, it tends to exclude from the explicitly addressed audience any groups with lower purchasing power - one cannot imagine a commercial radio targeting the unemployed, for instance, even though they are potentially a large listening group with lots of time on their hands. Secondly, the formatter envisages in the abstract a particular type of listener, and these expectations work to stereotype the nature of the audience as addressed. Formatting privileges a one-dimensional concept of the listener (the listener as consumer) rather than involving a multifacetted definition involving the complexity of what an audience is and what social identify is, complete with all their class, race, gender, age, family, religious, cultural, political and economic facets.

The fact that a particular stereotypical model of an audience is used by formatters does not necessarily mean that the broadcasters address the listeners over the air solely as consumers. But the danger must be there, since the station's audience model is so central to its raison d'être, and to the organisation's implicit ethos or system of values. I am not aware of any recent content studies of French radio to test this hypothesis. Perhaps it is a fruitful

44

area of future research.

However, perhaps we do not have to prove that individual broadcasters address their listeners simply as consumers for us to be worried. The very structure of French commercial radio broadcasting is moving in the direction of grouping its listeners in consumer categories, so that what one listener has in common with the others in his or her radio sub-culture is his or her consumer characteristics.

The effects of media on their audience are not easily established of course. However, one commonly agreed idea, after Blumler and Gurevitch,[4] is that media effects may be seen primarily in terms of the shaping of the categories and frameworks through which audience members perceive socio-political reality. In this light, we would have to say that commercial radio networks in France, by their very institutional structure and working practices, stand for a one-dimensional view of social identify. For commercial radio networks, "society" means "consumer society". Is this the framework radio audiences are also learning to use? Again further research is needed.

The networks are the dominant force in French radio, but they are not the only form of radio, although (as seen above) market forces are having a growing impact on all forms of radio broadcasting. In this context, the importance of the licencing body, the CSA becomes clear, in protecting public service radio, community radio and local radio, as safeguards to variety of approach and to pluralism in constructing parts of the radio audience. The 1989 law gives the regulators this power, and they claim they are exercising it to defend public service radio, to protect generalist stations from the hegemony of the formatters, to protect local independent stations from the national networks, and to protect community radio from everybody else. In this light, three recent events are worthy of comment. In late 1990 the CSA passed over an application for a licence from a Marseilles-based Islamic radio (Radio-Islam-

---

[4] See: Michael Gurevitch et al. (eds), *Society, Culture and the Media*, p.262.

France, RIF). In November 1990 a genuinely local radio, Radio FMR, after 9 years of broadcasting in Rouen, was forced into liquidation through lack of means. In June 1991 the President of the Skyrock network went on hunger strike to protest at the CSA's decision not to award his network a licence for Caen and Le Mans. The first was controversial and regrettable, the second is sad and ought to be avoidable, whereas the third is merely derisory.

4.   FROM *ELLE* TO S/HE

MAGGIE ALLISON

At a time in history when the image is paramount, influencing us in our choice of coffee, deodorant, partner and Prime Minister this chapter will discuss image and its work in transforming or confirming our perceptions.

It will exploit the blip culture aspect of image, taking blips through time and blips through media genres in order finally to examine the interrelation between French and British media treatment of key women figures on either side of the Channel.

What it will not do is look in detail at *ELLE* magazine, nor rehearse here the she/he debate, but rather assume that these represent two somewhat distant points on a continuum of images of women, let us say from the passively embellished clothes horse to a thinking human being, agent of her own destiny. The examples used will illustrate some of the problematics in travelling the continuum referred to. They will be drawn from French fashion magazines of the 1920s and 1940s, culminating in a comparison of French and British journalism in 1991.

The aim is to demonstrate via the progression over time from the fixed image on the printed page to the moving image on our small screens that a convenient parallel showing a shift from *femme figée* to *femme active* is not, however, a serious proposition, given that a number of constants remain when we consider the "work" of the image.

If we are assailed by images we are with every instance assailed by lenses, and in relation to representations of women this lens is commonly regarded as being male dominated.[1] In mainstream media treatment of "serious" women, the legacy of the repeated essences or constants remains, producing clichés *dans les deux sens du terme*, and thwarting real development of new viewpoints. Conceptualisations of *"femme-muse"* and *"femme amuse"* are more likely via a male-on-female lens: *"femme s'amuse"* creates the possibility of a new dynamic, but raises problems for the male to female lens, and *"femme se muse"* certainly does, but also for the female viewpoint since at this juncture there is a need to subvert the usual male-subject-female-object channel and develop a female subject viewpoint. Women here become serious viewers, controllers of image and of meanings, capable of changing the picture.

Berger has said that "men act and women appear".[2] Exemplifying this by referring to the process of joking he says in relation to woman:

> "Every one of her actions [...] is also read as an indication of how she would like to be treated. If a woman makes a good joke this is an example of how she treats the joker in herself and accordingly of how she as a joker-woman would like to be treated by others. Only a man can make a good joke for its own sake."

There is, however, more to this: if humour is a subversion of the norms of discourse, then woman joking, and at the same time subverting the rules for participation in discourse, is moving from an "appearer" to an "actor/player" and via this double subversion becomes the "joker in the pack", stepping outside her allotted frame and thereby fracturing the iconography of woman as non-player. It is my contention that women on the world stage create this disruption for media representation and are made to perform a balancing act, walking the

---

[1] For further discussion of lens and looking see Rosemary Betterton: "Introduction: Feminism, femininity and representation", in *Looking On*, ed. by Rosemary Betterton, London, Pandora, 1987, pp.11-13.

[2] John Berger, *Ways of Seeing*, London, BBC and Penguin, 1977, p.47.

tightrope between joking and appearing. For if man acts he also appears; the act has an actualisation and also an appearance, that of a man of action such that the mere appearance of a man is equatable, iconographically, with action or potential action. A woman of action, therefore, refutes the parallel equation: woman equals inaction. But she certainly is not joking.

A corollary to this is that males who are perceived to be behaving outside their alloted frame of seriousness can be equated with females, and young ones at that, as in a criticism of one male world figure of another (we believe Yeltsin of Gorbatchev) in Spring 1991:

"Ceux qui ont les positions les plus élevées de l'état ne doivent pas se comporter en jeunes filles capricieuses."

The main work of this chapter, then, will be to analyse three different sets of documents and texts, spanning sixty or more years, and examining ways in which mainstream French and British media manipulate such notions of "*caprice*" and "*jeune fille*" in relation to "the serious woman", that is, women in positions of power, perpetuating myths which can only be harmful to other women.

First we shall consider the portrayal of women's heads in fashion publications of the 1920s and the 1940s; this will be followed by an analysis of a fashion profile in the British press of Norma Major, thirdly there will be a comparative assessment of the French and British media treatment of the appointment of Edith Cresson as French Prime Minister.

Let us begin, then, at the top, that is with the head, its accoutrements, and some of its verbal images:

"head; fat head; pin head; big head; keep your head; heads will roll; head over heels; off your head; *tête; en tête; entête; grosse tête; tête dure; tête bien sur les épaules; plus la tête à moi; petite tête; femme de tête; têtu; je ne sais plus où donner de la tête; signe de la tête; tête de passoire; tête de linotte; drôle de tête; à tue-tête; changer de tête; ça va, ta tête?..."*

Illustrations of couturier designed hats of the late 1920s show the head stripped of natural adornment and firmly encased in a close-fitting cloche, a container from which one can imagine nothing of significance emerging. Two striking examples of this are to be found in the Le Monnier hats, modelled by a certain Mlle Mariette de Rovira in a Spring 1928 edition of the fashion magazine *Femina*, the one being described as:

> "Une toque en bandes de crin roulé havane, sur laquelle une petite voilette est posée d'amusante façon [...]."

and its twin as:

> "Une ravissante toque combien printanière et parisienne à la fois [...] Elle est en violettes blanches et violettes noires."

The head is clamped in something resembling a luxuriant fungus, the expression in the eyes is vacant, the lips tightly pursed in each case and, as one looks at the two-page feature with the faces turned inwards, Mlle de Rovira is seen to be contemplating this extraordinary spectacle of herself on the opposite page.

By the early 1940s Le Monnier hats, and those of other designers, were beginning to sprout various extras perched at dangerous angles on the forehead but to prevent woman taking off into flights of fantasy there is also evidence of a shrouding of the face, fixing the head firmly to the shoulders. Alternatively, there is evidence of headgear strongly reminiscent of the raspberry pavlova or the cream cake. Is woman in wearing and "consuming" these hats also labelled as a consumable? Consume and you shall be consumed, in visual if not in literal terms.

If the head has nothing to say the hat must say it all: we are informed in the fashion hints page of the 1946 winter edition of *Signes* that:

"La tête s'empare toujours du signe le plus expressif."[3]

An examination of the cover page of this edition is, therefore, instructive since the female/feline face depicted there has no substance whatsoever, being composed entirely of *gribouilles, sinon griffes*, its vacuous expression and outline created entirely of the nebulous cigarette smoke of presumed sophistication.

The text informs us further:

> "Il n'est pas exact que les chapeaux soient petits. Le chapeau de la paix est moyen. Il trouve son équilibre entre le confetti de l'avant-guerre et le chapeau-coussin des années 43. De plus en plus, il tend à s'appuyer sur la nuque, en la couvrant parfois [...] tendant à incorporer dans une même ligne la robe et le couvre-chef. Ce n'est pas la seule idée du moyen-age que contienne la mode actuelle, tentée par son charme naïf."

From our present day standpoint we can make short work of transferring these epithets and remember that not only was woman being re-feminised and weaned away from her active war-time role, she was even being pushed into the Middle Ages for good measure, the head being refused an independent role from that of the body. Even though here for our purposes the head is being considered in isolation it is to be regarded as a metonymic for the person: if the head is assumed to be devoid of content or independence,

---

[3] John T. Molloy corroborates this in his *The Women's Dress for Success Book*, New York, Warner, 1977, p.80: "If women want the world to take off its hat to them then they would be better if they kept their own hats on. For a man or a woman a hat is a traditional symbol of power, authority and position".

then so can the person, and the head and body can be assumed as one monolithic vacuity in Western fashion codes. When the female head does have an independent life this becomes problematic for the male lens view of the world.

This preoccupation with the fixing of the female head is endorsed in an article entitled: "Le décolleté du visage" by Louis Cheronnet in the May 1945 first edition of *Cahiers de l'Artisane: COUTURE*, in which we are given an analysis of different types of "classic" *décolleté*, with the *"type bâtard"* apparently the most effective:

> "C'est le décolleté "en bateau" ou "corbeille", qui découvre du même coup la poitrine et le haut des épaules et semble retenir la robe comme par miracle."

Such statements are in keeping with the whole article which begins:

> "La femme a passé son temps, à travers les siècles, à nous montrer ou à nous cacher les trésors les plus nobles de son corps. Cheveux, bras et jambes, cou et gorge, épaules et poitrine ont été tour à tour dissimulés ou généreusement offerts à l'admiration masculine. Il est vraisemblable que ce petit jeu de cache-cache vestimentaire n'a pas fini de lui plaire et qu'elle continuera encore longtemps à y employer le meilleur de son imagination. Pour les hommes, le résultat est le même: le secret leur paraît aussi séduisant que la révélation."

The lens in this instance is all too obvious, as are further developments in the text as to the décolleté in the depiction of the Virgin Mary in art. The head, then, behatted, shrouded, drawn to the shoulders and now flanked at its other extremity by a gaping décolleté bordering on the seductive and the maternal, not to say the untouchably pure, no longer has any serious "work" to do. For head read: woman.

This realisation is further corroborated by a discussion of the winter

1949/50 female silhouette in an article of Lucien François entitled: "Il court il court le fourreau".

Anyone who has attempted even to stride out in skirts as pencil slim as those described here will know that "courir" is out of the question and that the encasement of woman *de la tête aux pieds* is well and truly on course: she is now hobbled, if not hobbling from the high heeled shoes required to complete the pencil-slim picture. Indeed there is worse since *la femme-fourreau* depends on the giants of haute couture to define her and this definition is far from certain for:

> "La silhouette, pour l'hiver 1949-50 est modelée par une ligne qui n'ose pas dire son nom. Ce n'est point pourtant que chaque couturier n'ait trouvé à la baptiser, mais aucun n'emploie le mot vrai. "Ligne Looping" dit Marcel Rochas. "Ligne Jaillissante" dit Jacques Fath. "Ligne Ciseaux" dit Christian Dior [...] "Ligne Roulee-Boulee" [...] "Ligne Cerf-Volant" [...] "Ligne Stop and go" [...] "Ligne Cigare" [...] "Ligne Tour Eiffel" [...]"

The list continues, since:

> "Chaque couturier a trouvé un moyen personnel de mouvementer, d'habiller ou d'actualiser le fourreau, tel qu'il était de mise vers 1923, avant que la taille ne glisse presque aux genoux. Car le style de la mode actuelle est bien inspiré par l'autre après-guerre, seulement il se camoufle encore."

Hence woman, yet again, cannot be permitted to step out, this time into the fifties, at least not without having relived the image of the *après-guerre* woman according to high fashion, once she has deduced what that is. We could say that *femme élancée ne saurait s'élancer qu'à ses risques et périls*, for the illustration of the *Ligne Fourreau* takes the viewer's eye up to the head, beyond the small, pruned face and the vacant eyes of the model atop which sits a questionmark of feathers. Action woman's time has not yet come. The apparently phallic symbolism of the *Ligne Fourreau* culminates in interrogation: women are not meant to be in the business of making active statements but rather that of being perpetually "not in the know".

But for those who, forty years on, doff their hats, literally roll up their sleeves, metaphorically, and choose to engage with the world, let us assess their treatment at the hands of the media. In making the transition from *"tête de femme"* to *"femme de tête"* it is useful to look at an intermediate category, that of *"femme de chef"*.

The example to be developed here is that of a profile of Norma Major in the *Sunday Express* of 2 June 1991 and will be drawn on later in discussion of Franco-British media treatment of Edith Cresson.

We have travelled from the *Tante Yvonne* image of the 1960s via *Anémone* and others, past zero Heath consort and through the discreet *Danièle Mitterrand* and the I'm-just-Dennis phase of the 80s, to find ourselves with girl-next-door Norma, preferring the backwaters of Huntingdon to the rough seas of Number 10. But in the long term such self-effacement does not make good media copy, hence the *Sunday Express*'s assessment of the state of the art of Norma Major (NM) six months on.

The half page article with colour photographs entitled: **Major chic** (or should we read this as Major chick?) gives a before and after type description taking us from the November night of Major's accession to the Leadership of the Tory Party to Norma Now, after sixth month of *his* office. **A true blue change of style for Norma**, reads the byline, quite unremarkable in its predictability; it does, however, mean that the page should be read in terms of colour, in addition to other salient features, preferably in the first instance without reference to captions. As Burgin has pointed out:

"We rarely see a photograph *in use* which does not have a

caption or title [...]"[4]

thus skewing our own reading of the image. Reading the article clockwise therefore, from top left to bottom right blue dominates - or almost - since the extreme top left is taken with the dark-suited John Major, and the extreme bottom right with the black shod feet of Norma - or almost - since these feet stand on the plinth of a caption defining her in terms of colour, outlining her and indicating where she should put her feet, namely, in court shoes. Scanning left to right and immediately prior to encountering the full-length new blue image of NM, we cross the feminising and glamourising stream of pink taffeta in two evening shots, showing the same outfit but different accessories for no-nonsense Norma. This blip into the frivolous is, however, firmly encased between the far right, all blue, and the more homely centre shot, not quite full length and rather posed with floral overtones, but with just sufficient carved cleavage to be traditionally feminine, imitating the evening time neckline. Bottom left there is the professional model echo, nameless, but clearly an idealised version of NM, approximately half her age, several kilos lighter and sporting a jacket with a large English rose style floral pattern, but minus feet, and with an accompanying descriptive text headed: **Flower Power**. Finally from the professional woman model's lesson on how to wear clothes and pose in them, the eye travels back upwards, top left, to the shy, unfortunate Norma, supposedly caught off guard on the evening of her spouse's triumph.

It is common knowledge that few protagonists are allowed to engage direct eye contact with the camera and this set of photographs is no exception to the rule: admittedly in the shot top left both figures are addressing a different camera from the one via which we are allowed our point of view, but the subject of the article, NM, is in fact, objectified throughout and not

---

[4] Victor Burgin, "Looking at Photographs" in *Thinking Photography*, ed. by Victor Burgin, London, Macmillan, 1982, 136-71, p.141.

permitted to face camera directly, even in the more formally posed central shot. This is in definite contrast to the direct address to camera of the one professional photographic performer, the model: moreover NM's sideways glance in the centre shot, although leading out of the picture, is less obviously leading out of the frame of the half page spread than is the hand wave of John Major, top left. She is engaged within the frame but he is allowed to engage beyond it.

The overall reading of the visuals, then, is that Norma Major, in spite of the pretended revamp does not have the authority to address us directly as an independent individual, nor to lead us out of the overall frame - indeed, she herself forms the right hand pillar of the ensemble, as befits the right hand woman of the Premier, in response to John Major who frames top left, himself framed by the doorpost of Number 10. If it cannot be denied that the final, far right photograph has NM looking more confident and in control, we must rocognise that this is because she is foregrounded full length, standing on her own two feet, presumably carrying out an individual engagement. This would appear to be an all female gathering. By contrast in the shot top left she is hunched against her partner who is a full head taller. This is a classic example of the theories on function ranking and ritualisation of subordination developed by Goffman.[5]

However, our analysis cannot rest there, for the article claims that:

"Instead of the shapeless conservative blue suit of last year, Mrs Major now sports a slimmer, more fashionable silhouette. In the same colour, which must now be *de rigueur* for her role, she now looks younger in a double breasted suit with a black-buttoned long-line jacket."

Closer inspection reveals that the "before" and "after" suits are one and

---

[5] Erving Goffman, *Gender Advertisements*, New York, Harper and Row, 1976, pp.32-6.

the same but that NM has, in the far right photograph, simply had time to button up before going public. Further perusal reveals that this had, in fact, been printed in reverse, such that NM can now look inwards onto the page, remaining thereby contained in the article and also produce what we now see to be an illusory symmetry of two right profiles followed by two left profiles in the foursome of photographs of which she is the focus. Is this reversal an innocent accident or a deliberate and quite common device to produce contrived coherence on the page? We suspect the latter, but such a reversal produces a number of interesting twists. One: is Norma a closet feminist, since finally her rings now appear on her right rather than her left hand. Two: is she a cross dresser, her double breasted jacket now fastening the male way. Three: has she bribed a friend in the print room, for we are now seeing NM as she would see herself (her preferred image?) in a mirror. If we are confused we should take heart, for the sub-title **Subtler steps to a new image** explains all. This can only be referring to the *Sunday Express*'s own processes rather than any conscious efforts of NM.

Ultimately, however Norma may appear via media intervention to have grown in sophistication and stature, the largest, most confident depiction of her here has her facing across the page in the direction of supposed real authority, that of her Prime Minister husband to whom she is most definitely a consort. But her consort role is not simple, since John Major's authority is still on loan from the previous incumbent at Number 10: NM must fill the female slot at Number 10 and assume some of the legacy of that authority. Her vestments must, therefore, be clones of those of Thatcher to lend authority to the man who was Thatcher's consort-cum-protégé, as Foreign Secretary and Chancellor, and just one of her bevy of a whole cabinet of consorts. Hence, NM is not just John Major's right hand woman but also a substitute for the mother of son-of-Thatcher.

Caroline Evans and Minna Thornton, in their article, "Fashion,

Representation, Femininity"[6] have useful contributions to make here, distinguishing between two things:

1. The avoidance of superfluous detail in women's clothing, providing a more masculine impression of power:

> "Chanel's early work exemplifies the modernist project in design to dispense with superfluous detail and decoration and to espouse the cause of functionalism. Perhaps the functionalist or anti-decorative move in art and design may indicate a cultural rejection of the feminine in favour of an exclusively masculine model of power."

2. The concept of phallicism in dress, drawing on the work of Flügel:[7]

> "He (Flügel) argues that phallicism is a defence against anxiety. It is manifested in elements in themselves innocuous, even meaningless, but which have come to represent masculinity in our culture: dark colours (associated with sobriety), thickness and stiffness (associated with moral "uprightness") and tightness (often symbolizing self-control) - all the characteristics of traditional male tailoring, in fact."

Whereas Thatcher made full use of the latter, particularly dark colours,[8] NM is pictured here in her "ideal uniform" with fluid skirt and embroidered lapels, details sufficient to draw her back from the brink of the "genuinely" authoritative look. But it is still only she who can sport the true (royal) blue for the party cause: such a shade would, paradoxically, detract from John

---

[6] Caroline Evans and Minna Thornton, "Fashion, representation, femininity", *Feminist Review*, 38, 1991, 48-66, p.50.

[7] Quoted from J.C. Flügel, *The Psychology of Clothes*, London, Hogarth Press, 1930, by Evans and Thornton, op. cit., p.53.

[8] A fuller analysis of the use of dark and light blue is made in the Panorama programme *The Marketing of Margaret*, BBC 1, 13 June 1983.

Major's play for authority, were he to wear it at the despatch box. She is able to effect for him the "work" of the Thatcher uniform, as exemplified in the Heath cartoon (*Independent*, 5 March 1991), portraying John Major in a Margaret Thatcher style suit - fastened the male way, of course - complete with pearls and MT initialled handbag with the caption:

"Nice to see John's got his image right at last"

In the light of the above analysis let us turn now to the case of Mme Edith Cresson.

Whereas Norma Major, emerging from comparative obscurity, could be subjected to a total media (re)make, as much in terms of class as in terms of femaleness or authority, Edith Cresson presented a different challenge, already having a "history" with the media due to previous terms of senior office. She also, as Prime Minister, was saddled with the history of images associated with her peer, Margaret Thatcher. More than that however, she was subjected to the interplay of Franco-British lenses, for, if Thatcher had been seen in Europe as an adamant, awkward customer, she had for the most part, been regarded as a one-off freak; whereas in both French and British media Edith Cresson was portrayed rather as one of a species. The myth of the aura of the stereotypical French woman was exploited in both countries, giving rise to belittlement in patronising and ageist terms.

From the moment of her appointment as Prime Minister on 15 May 1991 she was framed in the nick-name attributed to her by President Mitterrand: *le petit soldat*. This could have had the effect of creating the tough image, let us say that of a *femme-fusil* (a more dynamic version of the *femme-fourreau/fuseau* of 1950s fashion) roughly on a par with that of "*la dame de fer*". But this reading is immediately frustrated by the word "*petit*": the tension set up in this label finds itself reworked ad nauseam in the weeks which follow, as exemplified in the following headlines.

Left-wing fighter with a splash of Chanel, (*Independent* 16 May 1991)

The little soldier grows up, (*Observer* 19 May 1991)

Le "petit soldat" au château, (*Le Point* 20 May 1991)

These ambiguities are pursued in both French and British press in terms of youth versus age, and competence versus female-provoked disorder. Our "little soldier" is, in fact, aged fifty-seven, but we are regularly reminded that for women age does not confer automatic wisdom:

> "L'histoire a déjà enregistré que Mitterrand, après avoir donné à la France son plus jeune Premier ministre - Fabius en 1984 - lui a donné donc sa première femme Premier ministre. Image **contemporaine**, pour reprendre le titre du nouveau magazine féminin auquel elle a accordé sa plus récente interview." (*Le Point* 20 May 1991)

This is already voiced in *The Independent*'s front page article of 16 May 1991:

> "The appointment of Mrs Cresson has in some ways echoed that of Laurent Fabius, who was made prime minister in 1984 [...] Mr Fabius, who was then just 37, captured the popular imagination by virtue of his youth."

We can again deduce that femininity can confer youth, but not necessarily with positive connotations. This point is also taken up in the *Independent* profile of 16 May 1991 which features a photograph of her, centre page, dancing with Fabius. This will be treated in more detail later.

The Observer (19 May 1991) after having established that:

> "The little soldier has become a general."

proceeds to undermine any credibility this might afford by saying

> "To give France its first woman Prime Minister was a gimmick which might unlock enthusiasm and goodwill long denied the Rocard government [...]
>
> In fact the excitement unleashed by Cresson's élan could reverse present trends which threaten Mitterrand with a conservative victory [...]"

Of course the Cresson venture could go very wrong. Not the "Cresson" venture surely, but Mitterrand's in appointing her.

Having attributed the caption: **A doughty fighter who has longed to get her hands on real power** to a head and shoulders cartoon featuring prominent earrings, the article hedges its bets with the conclusion:

> "Is she moving at last towards pure power, unfetted decision-making, or just a larger ambush in which she is talked out of her ideas by men smoother and more plausible than she has yet encountered? Whatever the hazards ahead, *le petit soldat* can be trusted to shake things up and not allow herself to be used as cannon fodder."

In a few short steps we have travelled from the woman marching ahead as a general, to the edible woman referred to earlier in relation to exotic fashion.

The opening words of this same profile: "Elegance and mayhem", are key to the overall gloss put on her on her appointment. She is projected almost exclusively, in quality and popular press alike, in terms of male opposition to her on two grounds a) her womanness, b) the corollory of that, namely, woman's stereotypical chaos, the wicked witch syndrome. The press, both French and British, are unsure which to foreground and generally decide on a cocktail of both.

61

Hence, her reputation as the *"parfumée"*, a nick-name bestowed on her by another predominantly male group, *les agriculteurs*, has stuck as a counterweight to the *soldat* image:

> "The French peasantry came to respect, but never to accept, the woman they dismissed as *"La parfumée"*, the scented, jewelled city dweller who nevertheless threw herself into the struggle [...]" (*Observer* 19 May 1991).

and:

> "She visited her couturier, Torrente, to choose her summer wardrobe. Her standard of elegance is so high and her taste so constant that the clothes she chose did not give her secret away." (ibid).

In contrast with Norma Major, Cresson needs no lessons here. *Le Point* (20 May 1991) takes this further:

> "Lundi dernier, avant sa nomination, elle renouvelait d'ailleurs sa panoplie (tailleurs et robes de dîner) chez son couturier préféré depuis 1981, Torrente, où on lui trouve "une taille de mannequin". Ministre du Commerce extérieur, elle clamait: "Pour décrocher un contrat, il faut harceler, faire la danse du ventre s'il le faut"."

We move from fashion model to entertainer, and back again, for the caption of the accompanying photograph is presented as a quotation of her own:

> "Aucune femme moche ne peut réussir en politique."

And the above *Observer* profile has taken this on board, implying that her physical presentation could even be a substitute for political "failings" (not her own).

> "Her leftist reputation, offset by her nationalist message and appearance of well-groomed refined prosperity, could enable her to glean support both on the Left and in the Centre which eluded Rocard."

As an antidote to the perfume and any positive connotations of the military image an enmeshing of disorderly woman and undisciplined soldier has also been carefully effected.

She is referred to variously as *"une pétroleuse"*, *"une fausse bonne idée"*, *"une sulfateuse sur la vie politique"*, and we are told *"Les sceptiques [...] craignent [...] ses foucades et ses désordres"*. (*Le Point* 20 May 1991).

This is parallelled in *The Observer* (19 May 1991) by a quotation attributed to Lipowski in 1974, when Cresson would have been forty years old.

> "I thought she would tear my eyes out, so much did she want to change the world".

Here we witness youth, violence and female (feline?) *griffes* rolled into one.

She is, then, for the most part, problematised, all possible means being exploited to detract from her calibre. What really goes on in her head is totally overshadowed by the myths which she is expected to fulfil, summed up in the taunt of an agricultural protester's placard in 1992:

> "We hope you are better in bed than in your work at the ministry." (ibid).

By contrast many French people at the time were voicing the view:"*On*

63

dit qu'elle en a ..."

The above are only some of the textual framings of Edith Cresson as she took up office as Prime Minister of France. We turn now to some of the visual representations to show how they sustain the above myths and portrayals, and how they also, in some particulars, mirror the treatment of Norma Major as analysed above.

We have already referred to the photograph carried by *The Independent* of 16 May 1991 in which Edith Cresson is dancing, centre page, with Laurent Fabius, both of them wearing formal working suits, she in pin stripes. This is unlikely to be a contemporary photograph so the choice is not innocent: it reinforces the female equals youth equation discussed above. The "serious" person on this page, in a smaller shot to the right of the article, is the now ex-Prime Minister, Michel Rocard, briefcase in hand, walking away from the previous day's cabinet, out of the photograph and out of the page, while Edith waltzes around in the centre. This is hardly a serious pose for the new leader of a government, unless she is about to lead us a dance, but it proves the adage that *"quand on n'a pas de tête il faut des jambes"*. The picture rustled up by *Le Point* (20 May 1991) for the occasion would also suggest this: we are taken back to 1985 in Shanghai where even a dog-tooth check suit and Cresson's perusal of the *China Daily* (no eye-to-camera here, of course) cannot offset the effect of the foregrounded legs, high-heeled shoes and the trace of a petticoat.

This is in direct contrast to a corresponding photograph of John Major (*Le Point* 13 July 1991) occupying two thirds of a double page spread, legs well foregrounded, but Major well ensconced in a solid armchair conveying authority, and looking to camera. A small (2" by 5") "official" shot of Cresson (*Le Point* 20 May 1991), leaning forward across her desk, flanked by the obligatory gilded candelabra style table lamps which completely dwarf her, is totally unconvincing, and indeed so small that this one example of eye to camera contact is completely insignificant.

This is somewhat improved upon in *The Observer*'s (16 June 1991) more close-up black and white shot of her in her "new office", framed, but not dwarfed, by the same table lamps and addressing the camera confidently, undermined, however, by the full page interview, incorporating central colour photograph, entitled: **France's femme fatale: Edith Cresson gives her exclusive views on politics, prejudice, power, love, sex and the unromantic English**. This is a four-year-old article dredged or stored up for the occasion and, chin on hands, Cresson watches over it with a sphynx-like smile.

She is smiling, as on almost all photographs of her, and as she smiled repeatedly during the A2 interview with her immediately following her appointment on 15 May 1991. At the end of each response to a series of predictable and often patronising questions there was a repeated lift of the head and a smile, both determined and inviting: inviting what, precisely? Berger, pursuing his thesis that men act and women appear, asserts that "Women watch themselves being looked at".[9] If we accept this, then such an interview at such a crucial point provides an optimum audience of lookers, via the mediation of camera and journalists, requiring a supreme response to this watching. We can, however, assume that Edith Cresson has had ample practice in this art of responding to the looking, and that these particular instances are typical of a behaviour pattern. The net effect, when one edits out the final moment of each response, is to produce a series of fixed smiles and head positions, reducing the dynamism of the television medium to the equivalent of a still photograph: the processes of the television medium have reduced the dynamism of the newly appointed Prime Minister to a *tête de femme figée*, much akin to the isolated heads discussed earlier in this chapter, but wearing, in place of a hat, the mask of a joker.

L'Express of 20 June 1991 did offer one brief alternative reading with its headline:

---

[9] Berger, op. cit., p.47.

Dieu descend sur terre

above a shot of Edith Cresson, flanked, however, by Mitterrand and with the byline, **François Mitterrand sonne le rassemblement. Pour ramener à lui un peuple désordonné,** offset partially by the caption, **Edith Cresson: Le Président et la gauche croient en elle.**

For a wild moment we are allowed to think that *L'Express* has had a revelation and that God is truly woman. But maybe she is merely a goddess, beside God-Mitterrand, *"à côté de lui et issue de sa côte à lui"*.

Edith Cresson is portrayed here as Mitterrand's female and political consort, *la "jeunesse" aidant*: such a portrayal, had Fabius been President, would have been impossible, since the two forms of *"jeunesse"* cannot be exploited simultaneously: for the element in the continuum from one premiership to another and from Britain to France is not the female line but male youth. Thatcher has given way to Major and Cresson is portrayed as an extension of Fabius, Rocard being a temporary irrelevance in this media picture. Cresson and Major, then, are both seen as new boys, but via different routes. And Cresson, as a boy, or rather a youth, must remain a *petit soldat*, only now coming of age at fifty-seven.

Further comparisons in this Franco-British play of consorts show that Norma is perceived as requiring increased formality in order to make a suitable consort for Major and thereby enhance his authority. By contrast, paradoxically, Cresson needs to remain feminine to male lens terms to be credible first and foremost as a woman, a condition for her credibility in politics, as the agricultural workers demonstrated, and, secondly, to provide a sufficiently "youthful" consort to Mitterrand.

Nevertheless, in order to be credible in politics she must also be seen to possess, as rumour had it, that which is unfeminine, such that if a woman is viable neither via the head nor via the feminine mystique, she may be rendered so thanks to an imaginary accretion or two. However, once this aspect is

66

exploited and woman speaks out she may put herself in jeopardy.

Cresson is now caught in a triple bind, that of *petit soldat, femme mystérieuse* and *femme qui se fait homme*.

Even acknowledging Cresson's provocative and controversial comments on Anglo-Saxon sexuality (*Observer* 16 June 1991), and on the Japanese work ethic, the media have lost no opportunity in exploiting both these "own goals" and all the myths which have accrued to her, be they representative of her as an individual or of woman as a class. The "appearance" of woman in both senses of the word is as evident here as it was in the examples drawn from 1920s and 1940s fashion. Getting ahead does not mean that a woman is credited with having an independent head, and therefore a persona separable from the male lens portrayal of the whole body, but if she is likely to be thus credited, she becomes dangerous. Becoming a player rather than an appearer is disruptive, as Cresson, herself has said:

"[...] a truly political woman is disturbing [...] in the same way as a woman artist disturbs, I think we do and we are on the right track". (*Observer* 16 June 1991)

When women travel the spectrum from *tête de femme, femme de chef, femme de tête,* to *femme-chef* they take risks. *Femme fatale* may become fated woman.

We conclude therefore, with one final media depiction of the two women whose outspokenness has, for different reasons, brought them opprobrium. Their views are not the issue here, but rather the treatment the women received.

The first of these is the Colin Wheeler cartoon of 8 July 1991 in *The Independent* depicting Major dragging a reluctant Mrs Thatcher, in the guise of a pit bull terrier, under the guillotine. This can be briefly paraphrased as : OK bulldog silences outlawed cross-breed.

Secondly we refer to an illustrated article in the 15 July 1991 edition of *The Daily Telegraph* reporting a protest in Japan at comments made by Edith Cresson. **Japanese protesters "behead" Cresson** is the headline; and the byline: **Off with her head: An activist in Tokyo beheads an effigy of Madame Cresson.** The three pictures, presenting the going, going, gone action of the decapitation "read" like a cartoon,[10] beneath which there is a photograph of Cresson on 14 July ... smiling.

The message is clear: for women who reach top office, but become an encumbrance, the media answer is symbolic castration.

---

[10] Although this sequence of three photographs may look like the work of one skilled photographer, it is in fact composed of three shots from different photographers and even different agencies, viz: AP, Reuter, and EPA respectively. Considerable trouble has been taken to reproduce in still form, and to provide a dynamic temporal dimension to, the grisly narrative of the Cresson effigy beheading: about to be struck, head smitten off, smiling head held in the protestor's hand. This provides an interesting contrast to the stilling of the live, smiling televisual images referred to earlier.

5.　　"EQUAL BUT DIFFERENT": GENDER IMAGES IN
　　　CONTEMPORARY FRENCH TELEVISION ADVERTISING

RENATE GUNTHER

In July 1991 I recorded a fairly substantial selection of French TV advertisements. From this material I eventually chose seven adverts for closer analysis, since these exemplify dominant themes and images in the representation of gender in current French advertising practices.

Before turning to the questions I will discuss in this chapter, I would like to clarify that by "gender" I mean the social construction of a whole set of physical, psychological and behavioural attributes, defined as "masculine" and "feminine" respectively. These assumed "differences" are cultural, not biological, and historically their main purpose has been to legitimise and reinforce social inequalities between men and women. This use of the notion of "difference" as a justification for inequality can equally well be extended to the areas of race and class, as the work of Colette Guillaumin, amongst others, has clearly shown.[1] It follows that any geniune concern with sexual equality needs to begin with the dismantling of the traditional masculine/feminine opposition. Given the influence of the media, and in particular of advertising, in shaping viewers' perceptions of reality, the main question I wish to address here is the extent to which French TV advertising either contributes to or sabotages this process of questioning dominant gender images. At first sight, it seems that a number of the adverts discussed in this chapter have responded to the demand for more accurate representations of social changes, in particular the changed position of women in contemporary French society. In an attempt to portray "equality" and to appeal to a new market of female

---

[1] Colette Guillaumin, 'Question de différence', in: *Questions féministes*, No. 6, septembre 1979, pp. 3-21.

consumers, these adverts appear to step across the gender divide, as men are seen in traditionally "feminine" settings, such as the kitchen, whilst women are allowed access to the "masculine" sphere of professional activity. However, these reflections of sexual equality are merely superficial token gestures, as the same adverts reconstruct highly conventional representations of sexual difference and thereby subvert the very "equality" they supposedly promote. Representations of femininity, in particular, have not changed, as a woman's identity is still seen as defined by her body, her physical appearance and her relationships with men, despite half-hearted efforts to construct a new image of "the liberated career woman". As Rosemary Betterton comments in *Looking On*: "Women may take on 'masculine' roles but they still have to be shown as attractive and desirable'.[2] Indeed, the model of "the independent woman" is often introduced in advertising as an implicit threat to her traditional counterpart, but always vanquished by the latter, whose femininity triumphs thanks to the products advertised. This constructed opposition between the "new liberated woman" and the "traditionally feminine" woman is often framed in terms of a conflict between culture and nature. The word "nature" and its various derivatives punctuates this entire sequence of adverts, where it is invariably associated with the assumed essence of femininity, the female body. The assumption underlying this nature/culture polarity seems to be that whilst social progress has changed women's roles and activities, their fundamental "nature" needs to be protected and stabilised. If "equality" is seen as a cultural phenomenon, then, "difference" is part of "the natural order", maintained intact, paradoxically, by a whole series of man-made synthetic products.

1. Sveltesse Yoghurt

A bright summer's day. A young married couple and their two children,

---

[2] Rosemary Betterton (ed), *Looking On: Images of Femininity in the Visual Arts and Media*, London, Pandora Press, 1989, p.20.

a girl and a boy, are busy picking fruit in a sun-filled orchard. Initially, the mother is seen on top of a ladder, with her husband poised just below her, gazing adoringly at her. In the next scene she is standing on the ground under a tree, holding out her skirt which her little boy fills with the fruit he has gathered. A female voiceover, whom we are invited to identify as the mother's voice, provides the commentary on SVELTESSE yoghurt. "Avec SVELTESSE, c'est son corps tout entier qu'on prend à la légère", she says, as we see the young woman being chased around the orchard and then pushed in a wheelbarrow by her husband. Meanwhile, the children are watching their parents, and the little boy comments with mock exasperation: "Elle est belle, la jeunesse".

The advert for Sveltesse yoghurt introduces one of the central themes in this selection of adverts: the reaffirmation of nature and in particular of a mythical feminine nature. In this first advert, the focus on nature suggests a return to traditional values, incarnated by the stereotypical nuclear family with the mother figure at its centre. The setting, an orchard with fruit-laden trees, immediately connotes an atmosphere of homeliness, nurturing and opulence, qualities which the viewer is invited to associate with the mother, installed on top of the ladder, looking down at her devoted husband and her two children. This first sequence of images draws on myths of "mother earth" for its construction of femininity. Femininity here is clearly equated with motherhood and "woman's nature" with procreation. The verbal and visual insistence on fruit and harvesting evokes well-established ideas about the female body and the cyclical nature of female biology designed primarily for pregnancy and childbirth. This association between the female body and the fullness of nature is underscored by a rather striking image: the young woman in the advert holds out her skirt to receive the fruit her son has just picked from a tree.

However, this initial suggestion of female lavishness is undercut by the product advertised, as the repeated emphasis is on its "lightness": "Avec

Sveltesse, c'est son corps tout entier qu'on prend à la légère", the young woman tells us and in the second half of the advert she reveals the other side of her femininity, the young mother who wishes to remain attractive to her husband. From "mother nature" she reverts back to her former role as the bashful young bride, as her husband chases her around the orchard and pushes her along in a wheelbarrow. This advert becomes the site of one of the fundamental contradictions regarding femininity in this culture, where a woman's body, after several pregnancies and births, is often no longer seen to conform to the ideal of slender youthfulness and hence sexually devalued by men. The SVELT-ESSE advert implies this contradiction, yet smoothes it over by the very product it promotes. The yoghurt reconciles the two aspects of the motherhood/sexuality opposition, making it possible for women to have children *and* to remain young and slim for their husbands. The underlying assumptions of this ad, i.e. that womanhood equals motherhood and that to be "feminine" is to be slim are, of course, never called into question, since both are framed by a scenario depicting the "eternal cycle of nature".

2. Soupline

For a few seconds we see a woman's legs emerging from a lake or pond and gliding through grass and flowers. The camera then switches briefly from the legs to the product advertised, a bottle of SOUPLINE fabric softener, as the female voiceover announces: "Voici le dernier né de SOUPLINE". The whole woman then emerges, naked, and moves slowly towards a T-shirt, presumably rinsed in SOUPLINE, which is draped over some bushes. She puts on the T-shirt, with an expression of ecstasy on her face, then picks up a fresh towel which she caresses with the same air of bliss. "Un parfum subtile comme une fleur fraîchement coupée, comments the voiceover, as the young woman in the advert smells a white flower which she then offers to another, older woman. The advert closes with a still of three bottles of SOUPLINE and the final slogan:

72

"La fraîcheur de la nature à fleur de peau".

From traditional values and family life, we move on to a sequence of images not far removed from "soft" pornography. In this highly stylised advert, the emphasis is again on the femininity/nature association, but in this instance the equation refers exclusively to a sexualised female body, a body to be looked at. Using a technique current in much advertising, the camera dissects the woman's body, so that at first only her bare legs, emerging from water and walking through grass, are visible. Her whole body, with the suggestion of nudity, then comes into focus, as she slips on the T-shirt washed in SOUPLINE fabric softener. The female voiceover, with her repetition of the keywords "fraîcheur, douceur, tendre", supplies the whole familiar array of supposedly feminine qualities, applicable by association, to SOUPLINE.

What is more interesting, however, is the image of femininity and of feminine sexuality conveyed by the young woman in the advert. Stepping out of the water like Aphrodite out of the ocean, she evokes the primeval forces of nature as well as childlike innocence. Indeed, "voice le dernier né de SOUPLINE", confirms the voiceover, as the camera shifts from the woman's legs to a bottle of the product. As in certain pornographic imagery, the woman's assumed innocence is overlaid by expressions of seductive sensuality. She is shown to be narcissistic, absorbed in her own pleasure, as she caresses her T-shirt and towel, whilst peering invitingly at the camera. Yet who is this woman looking at, or rather, who is supposed to be looking at her in front of the television screen? Other women, the potential buyers of SOUPLINE, or the ubiquitious imaginary male eye which mediates between the woman as object and the woman as spectator? As the presumed object of male desire, the SOUPLINE-woman becomes a mirror in which female viewers are asked to recognise themselves.

However, at the end of the advert, a second older woman makes a fleeting appearance, smiling tenderly at the young woman who offers her a flower. This allusion to a mother/daughter relationship seems somewhat incongruous in this otherwise overtly heterosexual scenario. In one sense it expands on the family theme already elaborated in the previous ad, but more importantly it suggests the continuity of "female nature" across generations of women, as mothers pass on the secrets of feminine softness and attractiveness to their grateful daughters. The essence of this feminine mystique is condensed in the white flower exchanged between the two women in the advert and its corollary, the bottle of SOUPLINE fabric softener.

3. Mini-Mir (1)

This advert opens with a shot of a man and a woman sitting opposite each other at a dinner table, laden with dirty dishes. The man kisses the woman's hands, suggesting the end of a romantic tête-à-tête, but the woman on a less idyllic note, points at the dishes and the task at hand: who will do the washing up? Immediately, the man leaps to his feet and offers his services. Meanwhile the woman takes her "secret weapon", a tube of MINI-MIR cleaning liquid, out of the cupboard and surreptitiously squirts it into the washing-up bowl. Throughout the ad, we see a reversal of gender roles and behaviour, as the man is shown lying on the kitchen floor, whilst the woman is sitting on the kitchen cabinet, dangling her legs and observing her husband with an expression of amused half-mockery.

This sequence of adverts contains two slots promoting the all-purpose cleaning liquid MINI-MIR. Even though the product is the same, there are some important representational and ideological differences between the two adverts, as each conveys different images of men and women and the relationship between them. I have dealt with the two adverts separately and called them MINI-MIR (1) and (2) respectively.

74

At first glance we might be tempted to read MINI-MIR (1) as an example of "progressive" advertising, attempting to transcend traditional stereotypes and reflecting contemporary shifts in gender roles: a man does the washing-up, cleans the kitchen floor and the windows, whilst his wife, concealing her secret weapon, a tube of MINI-MIR, behind her back supervises what is traditionally regarded as "a woman's job". However, far from portraying a sharing relationship between two equal individuals, the advert stages a familiar role-reversal parody, in which the man becomes the childish, submissive clown at the beck and call of his glamourous wife, who seems to be in control, both in the kitchen and in the marriage. The man is allowed to retain the illusion of his masculine expertise, as his wife calls him "un spécialiste", and mockingly praises his work as "sublime" and "merveilleux". The power relationship implicit in this advert is also suggested visually, through a reversal of the gender-specific body postures to which we are accustomed from other adverts and media images generally: the woman here assumes the dominant posture, sitting cross-legged on the kitchen cabinet, watching her husband sprawled across the kitchen floor.

Pursuing the ideology of "nature", the underlying message of MINI-MIR (1) seems to be that social change distorts nature. Gender equality within marriage conjures up a whole series of fantasmatic images of "emasculated" husbands and domineering wives. The advert derives its impact from drawing on these well-worn popular myths which oppose any challenge to dominant gender models. However, these clichés point to the contradictions inherent in the sexual ideology on which MINI-MIR (1) is based. For if the woman in the advert is assumed to hold the power, what exactly does this power consist in? It consists firstly in her secret knowledge about cleaning and washing up and secondly, in her physical appearance. Her "power", therefore, does not extend beyond the domestic/sexual sphere, as the advert reconstructs a new variation on the housewife/sex object dichotomy. Furthermore, the real nature of this ostensible feminine power is demonstrated by the image of the man in MINI-MIR (1), whose access to the washing-up bowl and the kitchen floor is seen to degrade him and strip him of his masculine dignity. Rather than showing housework as a necessary and important task, he ridicules it, implicitly caricaturing women and any other men who might be lowering themselves to this "feminine" level.

4. Plénitude

A young woman and a man are walking along. A helicopter hovers above them. The woman, laughing and clutching a newspaper, strides out purposefully, looking up at the sky, as the voiceover suggests to us her status as the "professional woman": "Moi, je vis avec mon temps, le progrès, la performance". This image is further enhanced by her outfit, a classic style trenchcoat. The man next to her is holding a camera, and in the following scene we see the woman looking at some negatives and then making a phone call. Is she a photographer, a model, a business woman? Her profession remains a mystery, as the camera swiftly moves to the next image: the woman looking at her face in a mirror, scrutinising her wrinkles and the bags under her eyes. At this point, the female voiceover is replaced by a male voice which now informs us of the "scientific" properties of PLENITUDE face cream, whilst the camera focuses on a jar of the product. We then move back to three successive stills of the woman's face, as the female voice assures us of the success of PLENITUDE in maintaining a youthful appearance: "Avec CONTOUR REGARD, les rides s'estompent. Les cernes s'adoucissent. Les poches s'atténuent".

From the domestic scene we move on to an advert which deals more directly with the modern "liberated" woman. At least this is the image which the PLENITUDE ad, for a few seconds, seems to suggest. We are presented with a few cultural signs, a newspaper under the woman's arm, a helicopter, her practical outfit plus the voiceover ("Moi, je vis avec mon temps, le progrès, la performance"), which invite us to assemble an outline of this woman as a "career woman", competent and self-assured. But what exactly is the nature of her activity, where does she work, what is her lifestyle? These questions are left unanswered, just as the general imprecision of her initial image is enhanced by the fast movement of the camera in the opening sequences and the blurred quality of the shots. It does not really matter who this woman is or what she does. "Action woman" is a vague construct, introduced very briefly only to be subverted by the familiar static image of a woman's face seen in a mirror. The shift from the first image to the second is so smooth and rapid as to be almost imperceptible. As with MINI-MIR and BALISTO, this advert could be seen as a token gesture by advertising agents to reflect the changing role of women in society. However, if this were really the case, why the sudden shift from the woman's job to PLENITUDE face cream? Why do we not see her advertising a camera, a briefcase or a computer? Because the advert is not at all concerned with reflecting social change, but, on the contrary, with undermining it in order to reinstate traditional definitions of femininity. Women are allowed to read newspapers and make telephone calls, but the obsession with physical appearance must take precedence. Thus, in our example, the active female professional is given free rein for a while, but then PLENITUDE takes over and for two thirds of the time allotted to this advert we see a woman's face demonstrating her battle against imaginary wrinkles. The message to women viewers seems clear: they may play at being independent, having careers and lives of their own, on condition that they adhere to the norms of femininity, defined primarily in terms of physical appearance. Underlying this message, there is perhaps a further suggestion, linked to the swift transformation of "action woman" into "PLENITUDE model": that this woman, whatever her professional activity may be, *needs* to maintain her youthful appearance in order to further or even retain her career. In this case, femininity is not simply an optional extra, but a necessity for survival. Finally, the very name of the product PLENITUDE evokes feminine fullness and radiance, echoing the SVELTESSE advert and implying that a woman's "real nature" lies not in her job, but in a jar of anti-wrinkle cream.

5. Balisto

Another advert depicting the "new" woman. This time her professional activity is the initial focus of the ad. She works in an office, in a position of responsibility, as she is seen checking and delegating work to her colleagues, both male and female. Her independent status is underlined by her physical movements, which suggest activity and energy. At the same time, however, she eats her way through several bars of BALISTO chocolate. After work, we see her at her dance class, again eating BALISTO. After her dance class, the young woman leaps into the arms of her boyfriend, who is waiting outside with his car. "Je me sens bien, équilibrée, épanouie", she says, thanks to BALISTO which helps her maintain her true feminine nature: "BALISTO, c'est ma vraie nature".

At first sight the BALISTO advert seems to take the attempt at progressive representations of women one step further. Here the woman's professional status and apparently independent lifestyle are more clearly defined than in the previous example. Her physical movements express vitality and exuberance and suggest that she is in control of her body. After her day at the office we see her at a dance class, again exuding an air of freedom and confidence. However, throughout the advert, this woman has been eating BALISTO chocolate. Who or what for? The purpose of the product and of the advert itself becomes clear at the end. As with PLENITUDE, the

BALISTO story of female autonomy is undercut by a return to a traditional fairytale scenario: after her dance class, the young woman is shown leaping down the steps and straight into the arms of her "Prince Charming". BALISTO, like SVELTESSE, promises "un plaisir léger", as femininity is once again equated with slimness. In retrospect, the woman's work and leisure pursuits become secondary, as the final scene contradicts, if not destroys, the carefully elaborated image of the independent woman. Her real purpose in life is to remain attractive to "her man", and it is only in relation to him that she is truly aware of her existence: "Je me sens bien, équilibrée, épanouie", she confesses, not at the office, but as he sweeps her off her feet. At the end of the day, only a male presence is seen to guarantee a woman's identity, the "nature" which must be defended at all cost, if need be with chocolate and yoghurt, against any cultural threats to gender boundaries. Significantly, the BALISTO advert closes with the statement: "BALISTO, c'est ma vraie nature".

6. NANA Bodyform

A woman accompanies a man, probably her husband or boyfriend, to a boxing match. As he gets ready for the fight, she sits down in the audience, next to an older man, whom she seems to know well. For the next few seconds she is shown to be totally absorbed in watching the match, when suddenly a NANA Bodyform press-on towel falls out of her pocket. The older man quietly picks up the towel and gives it back to the woman. She thanks him and then leaps to her feet, throwing her arms up in the air, clapping and cheering the man in the ring. The advert closes with a male voiceover: "Parce qu'être Nana est aussi naturel que ça, NANA a dessiné Bodyform".

In this advert a woman is shown in an all-male environment, as she accompanies a man, whom we assume to be her husband or boyfriend, to a boxing match. However, from the outset traditional gender divisions are clearly established. The man, stepping into the ring to fight, is the hero on whom everyone's attention is focused, whilst the woman is once again cast in the role of the supportive passive spectator. As she sits down in the audience, we notice an older man next to her with whom she is apparently well-acquainted: he might be her father or (future?) father-in-law. Even though this is one of the rare advertisements where a woman is shown looking at a man, the relationship between the viewer and the viewed simply reconfirms dominant representations of masculine and feminine behaviour. As she watches his violent display of physical power and toughness, she conveys her femininity through a series of stereotypical gestures and facial expressions, calculated to suggest her emotional nature: she alternates between screams and laughter and covers her face with her hands to express fear and shock at the spectacle in front of her. From this construction of feminine psychology and behaviour it is only one step further to the female body and biology, as we see a packet of NANA Bodyform press-on towels slip out of the woman's pocket. The older man next to her picks up the packet and hands it back to her, as she thanks him with a half-embarrassed, half-complicit smile. What exactly is the function of this man in the advert? His paternalistic attitude vis-à-vis the young woman seems to suggest that he is there to protect her, a woman alone in a traditionally male setting. Similarly, NANA Bodyform has been designed for her "protection" - against her own body. The implication of this and other similar ads is that there is something "unsafe", if not threatening about a woman's body and biology. Paradoxically, "feminine nature" seems only acceptable as long as it is controlled and mediated by masculine culture. The young woman in our advert, then, with NANA Bodyform safely in her handbag, is now free to express her "natural" emotions, clapping and cheering her man who has presumably just won the match. The ad closes with a male voiceover announcing: "Parce qu'être Nana est aussi naturel que ça, NANA a dessiné

Bodyform". What is striking, first of all, is the synonymous use of "Nana", both as the French slang word for a young woman, and as the brandname for a sanitary towel. Secondly, the word "naturel" here suggests that NANA Bodyform, far from being a manufactured and culture-specific product, is simply a natural extension of a woman's body.

7. Mini-Mir (2)

This scenario opens with a young couple standing on the backdoor step of their house, waving goodbye to the man's rugby-playing friends. "Vous avez joué comme des chefs, les gars", he shouts as they throw a rugby ball at him. Unlike MINI-MIR (1), this advert immediately conveys the "norm" of conventional masculinity and femininity. The man is tall, a physically imposing X *rugby player, whereas his wife is portrayed as a 1990s version of "the dumb blonde", complete with bright red lipstick and fluttering eyelashes. From the couple's back garden, the camera moves into their kitchen. Again we see a pile of dirty dishes, this time the remnants of a post-rugby-match dinner. The man moves into action to show his expertise at housework. The woman still holds the key to the successful completion of the task, hiding a tube of MINI-MIR behind her back. However, the man is shown to be in control of his wife, throwing a rugby ball and a clean dish at her. In the final scene, after having done the housework, the man leaps on top of his wife with the words "Pour ça aussi, je suis spécialiste", whilst the voiceover praises the qualities of MINI-MIR.*

If MINI-MIR (1), with its role reversal comedy, attempts to subvert any real questioning of existing gender models, MINI-MIR (2) firmly reinstates these models and reestablishes sexual inequality as "the natural order of things". This reconstruction of the norm derives primarily from the highly conventional representations of masculine and feminine appearance, behaviour and sexuality.

81

At the same time, however, the man's and the woman's roles and activities remain apparently unchanged. A semblance of "progressiveness" and "equality" is thus maintained, as the woman is still seen to be in charge of "the secret weapon", whilst her husband does the washing up and cleans the kitchen floor. However, the image constructed of the couple's respective gender identities is the exact opposite of that of their counterpart in MINI-MIR (1). From a serious "man's game", rugby with "the lads", the man in MINI-MIR (2) moves on to play "a woman's game", but unlike his predecessor, he does so in a "masculine" manner. Instead of lying on the kitchen floor, he hurls first a rugby ball and then a clean casserole at his wife, leaving her breathless and helpless on the couch. The word "spécialiste" in this advert is no longer used tongue-in-cheek by a woman who knows that she is really in control, but literally denotes the man's assumed dominance and expertise at all "games", whether rugby, housework or sex. The continuous play on the word "jouer" could well be applied to the relationship between the couple in MINI-MIR (2), a power game in which the man is clearly "le chef" and the woman a passive object. The progressive message from MINI-MIR (1) to (2) is that men may do "women's work" from time to time, as long as they do not sacrifice their "masculinity" in the process. In other words, men and women may be "equal", on condition that they preserve "la différence" and remain in their allotted place on either side of the masculine/feminine divide. In all the adverts I have examined, despite an ostensible blurring of gender boundaries, this dividing line is constantly redrawn by the products advertised.

6.   ADVERTISING THE FRENCH: 'DES PUBLICISTES AUX PUBLICITAIRES' (1836-1991)

MICHAEL PALMER

"God stand up for bastards". Edmund's injunction, in *King Lear*, appears to have been answered during the "décennie Mitterrand". "Les publicitaires" - Advertising Man - gained, at last, "droit de cité", a certain form of social legitimacy. The first decade of the reign of "God", "Dieu", or "président Ton-ton" opened with the successful billboard campaign - "la force tranquille", etc. - due to the self-styled "fils de pub" Jacques Séguéla: it closed, in 1990, with the publication of a book exposing "les vices de pub": *Le grand bluff* by Denis Boutelier and Dilip Subramanian.[1] The current recession affecting the advertising industry in France - as in other developed countries - and "a little local difficulty" - the investigation into certain commercial (mal)practices conducted under the aegis of le Conseil de la Concurrence, the Competition Council - should not divert attention from the sea-change that occurred during the 1980s. The overall size of total advertising expenditure - "le gâteau publicitaire" increased sharply (it represented 1.3% of Gross Domestic Product in 1989); as did the size of the TV "slice" of the cake (24.9% in 1990); admen - with Séguéla the emblematic figure - gained in social recognition, playing the "gourou" and pundit, explaining post-modern society to itself; Bernard Cathelat, of the Havas research centre, the Centre de Communication Avancée, produced - with tome upon tome on "socio-styles", and their obligatory references to Roland Barthes - the weighty documentary evidence and modish typologies of social classifications that provided the

---

[1] Denis Boutelier and Dilip Subramanian, *Le grand bluff*, Paris, Denoël, 1990.

"sérieux" such punditry presupposed.[2] Advertising, it has often been observed, is a people business. Seemingly, it does not matter that Séguéla often changes views in his public pronouncements on appropriate advertising formulae. He has the visibility, the star status confirmed by the successful 1988 presidential campaign ("génération Mitterrand"), emblematic of his generation of admen, as was Marcel Bleustein-Blanchet of Publicis - one - or rather two generations earlier.[3]

"L'arroseur arrosé": this is the continual danger awaiting attempts to analyse "les années pub" or, as the M6 TV programme would have it "la culture pub". Some recent academic analyses of advertising - by scholars with very different approaches, such as Armand Mattelart[4] and Daniel Bougnoux[5] - explore how advertising fashions a new concept of "public space". The commercial logic has subverted the public service logic. It is certainly true that admen, sophisticated lobbyists in national, European and international fora, adopt arguments used to defend the freedom of the press: free speech, they claim, includes commercial speech (i.e. advertising).[6] But, for Bougnoux, at least, there is something specious in considering the concept of publicity ("la publicité") as adumbrated by Kant and the thinkers of the Enlightenment, and which was the fountainhead of the concept of "public space" as charted by Habermas,[7] alongside "la pub au XXe siècle". Mattelart, drawing attention to

---

[2] See, for example: *Publicité et société*, Paris, Payot, 1987.

[3] Jacques Séguéla and Bernard Roux founded the agency now called R.S.C. and G. in 1969: "Bleustein", born in 1906, founded his advertising and communication group, Publicis, in 1926, and relaunched it in 1946.

[4] A. Mattelart, *L'internationale publicitaire*, Paris, La Découverte, 1989; *La Publicité*, La Découverte, 1990.

[5] D. Bougnoux, *La Communication par la bande*, Paris, La Découverte, 1991.

[6] See "Euro-media lobbying" in J. Turnstall, M. Palmer, *Media moguls*, London, Routledge, 1992.

[7] J. Habermas, *L'Espace public*, Paris, Payot, 1986.

one of the few major studies on the early history of advertising in France, points out that advertising as practised by Théophraste Renaudot in the 17th Century was philanthropic and public service in nature, the *mores* of commercial, competitive advertising, "la publicité conflictuelle", à l'anglo-saxonne", only became widespread in France (according to this account), in the 19th century. This is why we shall turn, a little later, to some mid-19th century developments, frequently associated with Emile de Girardin on the one hand, and Charles-Louis Havas on the other.

To take a long-term and, at times comparative view of the apparent ephemera that is advertising may seem specious. But it is one way of avoiding the situation of "l'arroseur arrosé". The difficulties of analysing the advertising industry in France is compounded by the welter of self-serving rhetorics of many of the actors that put pen to paper or grant their umpteenth interview. The statistics provided - even by representative trade associations or research bodies (AACC, or IREP)[8] - are, to use a euphemism, "sujettes à caution". Séguéla impishly states: "Havas lies, Publicis lies, we at RSCG lie"[9]. Such is the concern to impress existing or potential clients by appearing to be number one, or in the top five, or whatever, that agencies pick and choose among the various possible criteria used in establishing rankings. This contributes to the "opacity" that surrounds the transactions of the main actors in the advertising industry in France. Who exactly are these actors? We shall attempt to answer the question. But it's worth pointing out that the fuzziness that characterises so many terms used in the communications industry in general is a commonplace in advertising. The sands are for ever shifting - between advertising and marketing, between media and non-media advertising outlets, between the so-called "grands média" (that include "outdoors" (billboard and

---

[8] AACC - Association des Agences Conseils en Communication: IREP - Institut de Recherches et d'études publicitaires.

[9] See: "Tout sur la publicité", *L'Expansion*, juillet-septembre, 1990.

poster), radio, cinema, television and the press) and a host of burgeoning, often (but not always) recently-launched electronic media: the minitel videotex and various interactive services (TVHA or teleshopping), but also direct mail. The same term has different meanings, in different mouths, at different times, or in the same mouth in different contexts. Especially in the agency world. The "créatif" and the "media-planneur" are not always the antithetical figures they are sometimes made out to be. Frontiers are blurred. "Advertissement", the Renaissance French term, was taken on board in England, hence "advertisement/advertising". French long preferred "la réclame" and "l'annonce". In the mid-19th century, Girardin, Hippolyte de Villemessant and other newspapermen encouraged the development of classified ads: these were often referred to as "les annonces anglaises". The current vulgate would have it that France subsequently progressed from "Le puffisme" and "la réclame" to "la publicité": it was no longer London but Madison Avenue that became the Mecca of aspiring French admen - of Bleustein-Blanchet in the inter-war years, and of Séguéla and his like during "les trente glorieuses", and the (belated) advent of consumer society with its advertising trappings. But while adopting some of the language and methods of American advertising, French advertising agencies - with Havas and Publicis to the fore - long resisted attempts by major US agencies to set up shop in France, and serve the needs of US companies expanding in Europe: the agency trade association, AACC, began life in 1957 (as the CAP) as an attempt to dissuade advertisers in France from submitting to the charms of such as J. Walter Thompson and McCann Erickson.[10]

If the sands are forever shifting, there has occurred, nonetheless, we would argue, a sea-change: the French advertising industry, echoing changes occurring elsewhere, sees established actors assuming new functions, and newcomers venturing into territories traditionally the patch of such as Havas and Publicis. There are, and long have been, those who wish to place

---

[10] D. Boutelier, D. Subramanian, *Le grand bluff*, p.27.

86

advertisements, the advertisers, and a wide range of outlets - media and non-media - that advertisers use to reach their intended markets. But likewise, there has long been a jostling for position - "une guerre de positionnement" - between the various intermediaries in this process. The current concern to define the functions and territory of the main actors - advertiser, agency, advertising broker and media buyer, and the various advertising outlets - reflects a malaise that exists both within and without the industry. Advertisers protest at the suspected collusion between agencies and the media: GAN, the insurance company, complains that advertisers' money disappears in a Bermuda Triangle, with agencies, media buyers and the media agreeing between themselves how to pull the wool over advertisers' eyes. Outside the industry, the Conseil de la Concurrence, an independent administrative body given new powers in 1986, launched its 1990-91 study of the advertising industry after the recommendations of its 1988 report were largely ignored.[11]

It was in France that, during the past 20-25 years, the "centrale d'achat" radically modified existing relations between advertisers, the advertising middlemen - the agencies and the "régies publicitaires" - and the media. Bulk purchasers of advertising time and space in a range of media and non-media outlets, the "centrales d'achat" or "media buyers" (the English, shorthand, term) appear to have transformed the existing contours of the industry in France before, from the mid-1980s, expanding elsewhere in Europe. The development was spearheaded by the Gross brothers, Gilbert and Francis - nephews, but competitors, of Marcel Bleustein-Blanchet - whose flagship company is Carat Espace. The rise of the Gross group occurred as (brand-name) TV commercials made their (timid) beginnings (1968); Gilbert Gross obtained discounts for bulk purchases of ad slots on one of the (then) less successful radio stations (Europe n° 1); one of the first major advertiser-clients he secured

---

[11] On the powers of the Conseil de la Concurrene, see G. Cas, R. Bout, *Lamy droit économique*, Paris, Lamy 1989. On the 1990-91 study, see *Le Monde*, 18-19.2.1990, 7.6.1991.

was Marcel Fournier, the founder of the first hypermarket chain in France; another major client was B.S.N., the food group, whose media director was dissatisfied with the collusion between the agencies and the media to whom he allocated B.S.N. ad spend. Fifteen years later, with the advent of private sector TV in France (1984-6), the Carat group profited from the expansion of TV advertising.

The purchase of advertising time and space over a wide range of media - with the attendant negotiation of discounts, additional commissions and "opaque" commercial practices - was not novel. Georges Roquette of Havas, for one, was celebrated in the 1950s and 1960s, for his mastery of the intricacies of the arrangements whereby the agency and regional newspapers might profit from a system of additional commissions ("surcommissions"). But, as Carat expanded, the bulk purchaser of advertising took on board functions previously performed by other industry actors - the agencies, in particular. Carat expanded into media research and media planning. Some agencies fear that they may be left, at best, their creative role - the conception of the ad. campaign. "Et encore". Agencies which had disapproved of the commercial practices, and the development, of the Gross group, themselves founded their own media buying operation. Even the emblematic figure Bleustein-Blanchet, the founder of Publicis, who reacted with both anger and moral indignation when first approached by his nephew, Gilbert Gross, with a media buying proposal, has lived to see Publicis itself develop a media buying operation.

Much of this account of the growth of media buying organisations is part of current advertising lore and mythology. *Le grand bluff*, based on interviews with some 124 leading figures in the advertising world, with the trade press, are the source of what recent data can be printed or otherwise reproduced.[12] "The magic and mystery of a name": much of the current imagery and rhetoric surrounding the advertising industry in France is still reminiscent of the kind of "flou" or mix of rumour, claim and counter-claim that 150 years ago, in different circumstances, allegedly helped Louis-Napoléon Bonaparte seduce the French, and become the first President of the Republic elected by (male) universal suffrage (December 1848). Semiologists and socio-psychologists, whether or not in agency employ, have done much to advance the understanding of the *modus operandi* of advertising: working for Publicis on the dossier Renault, Roland Barthes contributed to the car manufacturer's decision to market each new model under the letter R and a number (R 16 etc.); Bernard Cathelat, the promoter of the concept of "sociostyles", has worked for Havas since the 1960s. We wish now to suggest how an historical approach may further an understanding of the mechanics of advertising in France.

It was long said of the French advertising agency world that the leading players of its "golden triangle" - located between l'Etoile (Publicis), Neuilly (Havas-Eurocom) and Issy-les-Moulineaux (RSCG) - did not have the capital resources to compete worldwide with British, American (and Japanese) advertising groups. During the past fifteen years or so, Publicis, Havas, RSCG and others have pursued European, American and international expansion strategies - with mixed fortunes, and a chequered history of joint-ventures, mergers and crossholdings, and rival take-over bids. One of the myths is that France has distinctive "creative" skills: an emblematic figure in this regard is Jean-Paul Goude - the "créatif" who conceived the 1989 French Revolution bi-centenary parade, the 1991 logo of "la Cinq", the music of the A2 book-

---

[12] Advertising industry pressure was exercised on several publishers not to publish *Le grand bluff* before Denoël ultimately printed a - slightly revised - version of the original typescript. The book proved a success, reportedly selling approaching 30,000 copies between late 1990 and late June 1991 (by comparison, George Steiner's essay, *Réelles présences*, Paris, Gallimard, 1989, aided, no doubt, by a special edition of the Antenne 2 book programme "Caractères", also sold some 30,000 copies.

programme "Caractères", and countless innovative TV and film commercials for car models. Both these examples - French ad groups' international ambitions and the creative skills of a Jean-Paul Goude - testify rather to the "global village" nature of advertising. By contrast, a distinctive feature of the French advertising industry for the past 150 years or so has to do with media brokerage, and the controversial nature of the *middleman* - or rather the many middlemen - in advertising in particular, and commercial communications in general.

Advertising sometimes "precedes" the media. In the 1630s, the *Gazette* of Théophraste Renaudot, to whom Louis XIII and Richelieu awarded the "privilege" of printing a periodical publication, was produced on the presses that printed the "feuilles volantes" of Renaudot's Bureau d'Adresses et de Rencontre. In the 19th century, printers in small provincial towns sometimes started up a weekly or bi-weekly publication to attract advertising and provide employment for their presses. In the often-quoted manifesto or prospectus, in which Emile de Girardin launched *La Presse* (1836) the "father of the modern press" proclaimed: it is for advertising to finance the press. The shortfall in revenue from subscriptions and sales was to be made up by increased ad revenue as advertisers were attracted to low-price high-circulation daily newspapers. Later commercial media - radio and television - applied, with variations, Girardin's prescription. But the search for advertising, and the *modus operandi* of the nascent advertising industry, presented difficulties and contributed to the emergence of a wide range of middlemen and brokers, "courtiers" and "régisseurs". To simplify grossly: commerce and industry were reluctant to advertise; the promoters of shady financial stock, especially in times of speculation, were eager, on the contrary, to reach the unsuspecting gull or "gogo". Newspapers, banks, credit houses and wheeler-dealer promoters complied: in the 1890s, the decade of the Paname scandal, the highest-circulation daily, *Le Petit Journal* (one million copies) was criticised for publishing dishonest ads. It replied: "my ad columns are a wall; I am not responsible for what people choose to placard on it".[13]

The Parliamentary commission of enquiry into the Paname scandal and, later, the publication of a Russian envoy's correspondence from Paris revealed the role of advertising financial middlemen in "l'abominable vénalité de la presse".[14] Newspapers farmed out their financial bulletins or reports, their advertising columns: and "la publicité rédactionnelle" - within the news/editorial content - was commonplace. This has been amply documented. As has the direct or indirect control of media - in the 1830s, 1930s or 1980s - by various financial, commercial and industrial "combines" (to use a turn-of-the-century term). The complexity of the relations between advertiser, advertising middlemen, and the media, is less well documented. Partly because Havas, the longest-established of the present major advertising groups, has not fully opened its company archives.

In appears that, as early as the 1840s, Havas secured control of the non-local advertising columns of a number of provincial newspapers.[15] Established in 1832-3 as a modest news-bureau, translating foreign newspapers and providing summaries of "foreign intelligence" for Parisian newspapers (and the French government), Havas by 1840 was respected by the Parisian press, the French government and business circles for the speed and accuracy of its reporting of foreign news. Provincial titles that wanted - but could not afford -

---

[13] See P. Albert et al., *Histoire générale de la presse française*, Paris; P.U.F., 1972, iii, pp.258-275: M. Palmer, *Des petits journaux aux grandes agences*, Paris, Aubier, 1983, pp.171-205, 298-308.

[14] ".... *L'abominable vénalité de la presse* ...." (A. Raffalovitch), Paris, Librairie du Travail, 1931.

[15] See: G. Feyel, "Correspondances de presse parisiennes des journaux de province de 1828 à 1856", in *Documents pour l'histoire de la presse nationale aux XIXe et XXe siècles*, Paris, Coll. "Documentation", Editions du C.N.R.S., 1977, pp.87-340; O. Boyd-Barrett, M. Palmer, *Le trafic des nouvelles: les agences mondiales d'information*, Paris: Alain Moreau, 1981, pp.104-108, 373-375.

Havas material (features, serialized novels, etc. as well as news-services) ceded control of their non-local advertising columns to the agency. Havas, according to this interpretation, diversified from news into advertising; based in Paris, it acted as the advertising representative of provincial newspapers. Financially weak, undercapitalised, the latter sub-contracted their ad columns to Havas: Havas discharged the functions of what, in today's language, would be called ad consultant, media broker and media buyer. At the centre of the relationship between advertiser and the advertising outlet, between, say, the department store and the regional daily, Havas, in the later 19th century, became - to all intents and purposes - the "passage obligé" for both. Later, Havas failed to establish a similarly dominant position when commercial radio began in France. Publicis profited from the occasional sluggishness of what had become, in some respects, "une administration". But Havas and Publicis between them, from (at least) the 1950s to the late 1980s, were the dominant advertising groups and profited from the variety of functions they discharged as middlemen. Today, in their capacity as agencies serving advertisers, they conceive and plan ad campaigns, and advise on the choice of media and other outlets; like the Gross group, they buy and sell ad space in bulk. They "control" (sometimes as minority partners) the advertising revenue of major media (Publicis' Régie-Presse: *Le Monde*; Havas' Information et Publicité: Radio Luxembourg, etc. They are multi-media operators and owners (Havas, for example). In 1987, a Conseil de la Concurrence report highlighted the dangers of overweening middlemen wearing so many caps: they distort competition. Havas and Publicis advise companies who pay to advertise, and advise the media who receive advertisers' money. They can change the rules of the game "at will". As the subcontractor representing the advertising interest of a given newspaper, Havas can charge a high rate to an agency competing against an Havas agency; thus the advertiser will prefer to choose the Havas agency.[16]

---

[16] D. Boutelier, D. Subramanian, *Le grand bluff*, pp.18, 354-357.

"Abus d'une position dominante": this term is used periodically when major groups in the communications industry promise to expand yet further - in politically, culturally or economically sensitive areas. In early 1987, there were "alarms and excursions" when Havas discussed with another French communications mega-group, Hachette, the possibility of a joint bid for the privatized TFI TV network: other ad agencies raised the banner of opposition, "le front du refus", against what was known - singularly aptly for an Anglo-French audience - as "Havachette". The concentration of media ownership, the expansion of multi-media organisations which themselves may be part of industrial groups (cf. TFI acquired by the Bouygues-led consortium in 1987), are *leitmotive* of the communications industry. Advertising groups in Britain and France cite the phrase dear to the (fallen) Australian tycoon Alan Bond: "get big or get out". There are reportedly some 200,000 brand names in the world: major international advertisers - "à la" Proctor and Gamble, Nestlé, Uniliver and Coco-Cola - account for a growing percentage of total advertising spend; media mega-groups - " à la" Hachette - claim they must expand yet further so as to better negotiate with multinational corporations. Advertising groups - the most undercapitalised, financially overstretched, and market-sensitive of the three (advertiser, media, and ad agency/group) know they are the weakest link in this, capitalist, chain. This partly explains the volatility, the continual jostling for position and redefinition of territories in the "people business": like the proverbial amoeba, or, in French parlance, "octopus" (Hachette, "la pieuvre verte"), ad. agencies have to expand, or else do battle, merge or disappear. Established players oppose newcomers: but Havas and Publicis, for all the anathema they they poured on the Gross group, at times found it politic to negotiate with Carat Espace: in the summer of 1991, after three years of a complex "ménage à trois", it was Carat that broke off its European media buying operation with Eurocom, the Havas company: and back in 1988 Carat had negotiated with Publicis. Eurocom in 1991 particularly

93

resented the gall of a Carat corporate advertising campaign: "we, Carat, advise the media; others - such as Eurocom, - advise the advertiser". As Carat well knows, the lines are blurred: and as Havas-Eurocom well knows, but does not like to trumpet, its group invented the bulk purchase of ad space.[17]

The "opacity" of the advertising circuit - of the exchange of moneys, of the advantages in kind, of additional commissions on the one hand, of rebates on the other - has never obscured the monopolistic inclinations of the advertising middlemen. In the mid-19th century - Theodore Zeldin reminds us -

> "Jules Mirès ... bought the *Journal des chemins de fer* in 1848 for the express purpose of getting banks and companies to pay him to boost the shares they were trying to sell. In the course of the Second Empire, he obtained control of five more similar papers; backed by the Péreires, his ambition was to create a Saint-Simonian *omnium*, which would be master of all financial advertising in the country".[18]

Polydore Moïse Millaud, an associate of Mirès, likewise dreamed, on founding the low-price, mass-circulation daily, *le Petit Journal*, in 1863, of conquering "the million" or mass-market, while other titles - "les grands journaux" - vied for the quality market.[19] "L'omnium de la publicité": such a vision has been the ambition, it seems, of many a Havas, Bleustein or Gilbert Gross.

---

[17] "Pourquoi Carat provoque Eurocom", *CB News*, 3.6.1991, pp.3-4. (In 1988 Carat Espace was bought by the British advertising and communications group W.C.R.S. In 1989, this media buying group was rebaptised Aegis: in July 1991, Eurocom held an 11% stake in Aegis, and Carat, a 27% stake. In 1989 Aegis and Eurocom planned to create a pan-European buying operation. In 1990, following a recommendation ("avis") of the Conseil de la Concurrence, the French finance minister opposed the proposed combining of the media buying activities of Carat and Eurocom in France (save for international ad campaigns on international media). The pan-European media buying operation seemed compromised.

[18] T. Zeldin, *France 1848-1945*, Oxford, the Clarendon Press, 1977, ii, p.523.

[19] Millaud, quoted in M. Palmer, *Des petits journaux aux grandes agences*, pp.171-2.

Current trends in the advertising industry recall traits of a "culture d'entreprise" going back 150 years or so. Advertising in France seems long to have been characterised by a multiplicity of middlemen, each taking their "cut" in the farming out, subcontracting process. French agencies often differed from British or American agencies. When Volney B. Palmer - no relation - set up shop in the United States in 1841 - he adopted a practice that many a fellow-agency would later follow: the agency that placed an ad for a client received a fixed commission (10, 15, 20, 25 ...%). In France, the commission was and is paid by the media, the ad. outlet, not by the advertiser; in the USA, the advertiser pays. In the nineteenth century, when Havas and the related Société Générale des Annonces - held sway, competition between agencies was based not on the quality of the advice or service they offered, but on price. They obtained discounts from the newspapers for whom they secured advertisements: the situation mentioned earlier, of provincial newspapers virtually going cap in hand to Havas, suggests how Havas, who chose and found the advertiser, was well-placed to make the maximum profit. Similarly, the control of ad space in bulk was already frequent: mastering the ad columns of a wide range of papers Havas, for instance, would try to sell advertisers package deals. This is not substantially different from what the media buyers, such as the Gross group, do today. It is the range of available media and ad outlets, the sums involved, and the number of middlemen - including media research experts - that have increased. As has the sophistication of the promotion of an ad group's corporate image.

"Des publicistes aux publicitaires": the logic behind this alliterative slogan is, we hope, now apparent. Charles-Louis Havas (1783-1858) was not a newspaperman but, in Balzac's memorable phrase, "un marchand des faits".[20] Emile de Girardin (1806-81) was both a businessman and a publicist - who added to the ire of his fellow journalists by proclaiming the "*im*puissance de la

---

[20] *Revue parisienne*, 1840.

presse".[21] He also, unlike Havas, was a showman. In 1836, after a newspaper polemic, Girardin killed the fellow-publicist Alexis Carrel, in a duel: the event was subsequently portrayed as the victory of the new, commercial newspaper industry over the old doctrinaire press. On launching *la Presse*, in 1836, Girardin called on commerce and industry to advertise. In 1845, Charles Duveyrier, a Saint-Simonian, founded the Société Générale des Annonces and did likewise. On both occasions, the public, advertisers and the press did not respond to the extent desired. From his news-agency base, Havas took over the S.G.A., and Havas operated as the dominant French news and advertising agency until 1940. It generally maintained a low profile, except when assailed by commercial and political enemies: writing in 1946, Léon Blum stated that his attempted reform of the Havas agency in 1936 was the most intractable issue that confronted him during the Popular Front government.[22] Whether preferring to avoid the limelight - as did Havas for generations and the Gross group, for long periods, or else eager to figure centre-stage - Bleustein-Blanchet, at times, Jacques Séguéla, at all times - "cela fait cent cinquante ans que les publicitaires sont parmi nous".

In the advertiser-agency-media triptych, agencies like Havas were sometimes perceived as particularly close to the French government (Havas was owned by the French state between 1945 and 1986) and, at times, to foreign interests:[23] advertisers from industry and commerce periodically protest against the collusion between agency, media buyers and the media. In the United

---

[21] E. de Girardin, *L'Impuissance de la presse*, Paris, Plon, 1879.

[22] L. Blum, "Non", *Le Populaire*, 9.8.1946. Quoted in O. Boyd-Barrett, M. Palmer, *Documents pour l'histoire de la presse nationale*, p.127.

[23] In 1904, during a period of civil unrest in Russia, Havas - which was at the time both a news and advertising agency - "minimised" the bad news from Russia: one French family in six, it has been reckoned, invested in "les emprunts russes" and neither the French nor Russian governments, which advertised in the French press via Havas, wished those investors to panic. See M. Palmer, *Des petits journaux aux grandes agences*, pp.220-228.

States, media buyers and brokers are less well-established than in France or elsewhere in Europe: ad agencies are possibly kept under tighter control by the advertisers. Integrated advertising - with the manufacturer, etc., itself controlling the entirety of advertising and marketing of its products, is more common in the United States. Proctor and Gamble, long revered (or feared) as the archetypal hard-sell and integrated marketeer among advertisers, and which is now the number one advertiser worldwide, was founded four years before Volney B. Palmer set up the first American agency, in 1841. In mid nineteenth century France, the creation of the news-and-advertising agency Havas *preceded* the success of major private-sector companies, committed to advertising mass-produced goods: no Proctor and Gamble preceded Havas. A century later, by contrast, the French food group, B.S.N., angered at agency and media collusion in milching it, the advertiser, via overcharging and additional commissions, played a significant role in the rise of the Gross media-buying group: in July 1970, B.S.N. centralised its media-buying which it contracted out to Gilbert Gross. This was probably the most important of the Gross group's clients. In 1988, after the additional fillip to the advertising market of the development of private sector TV channels, the Gross group was valued at one and a half billion francs - roughly the same as Havas Eurocom and more than Publicis. The same year, the worldwide ad spend of Proctor and Gamble was one billion dollars: in France alone, its expenditure was on a par with that of Citroën, the car manufacturer.[24]

In the continual jostling for position of the various actors in the advertising industry, we have used the images of "sea change" and "shifting sands". The growth of advertising (in real terms: as expressed in constant prices), and the occasional recession, call to mind the ebb and flow of the tide. But the abiding image is rather that of "middlemen". At present, the purchasers of advertising space in bulk - with the Gross group's Carat setting

---

[24] A. Mattelart, *La Publicité*, Paris, la Découverte, 1990, p.8.

the pace - expand into a range of related activities (media research, audience measurement etc.): the middlemen *par excellence* reflect in part the expansionist proclivities of the hypermarkets they advertise. Chainstores like Carrefour and Mammouth pressurize B.S.N. and other manufacturers whose products they stock. Just as in other, very different spheres, public and private sector companies, or government ministries compete in self-promotion, "la communication institutionnelle ou corporative". In the distributive trades, "centrale" counters "centrale": the rise of "centrales de distribution" - Carrefour opened the first hypermarket in France in June 1958 - led to the formation of "centrales de production". All these actors are, of course, grist to the advertising mill. The annual amount spent in France was still only 80 francs per inhabitant in 1970; it was 1,046 francs per inhabitant in 1989 (according to IREP).

"*Anything* can be said and, in consequence, written about *anything*". In writing thus George Steiner, who has for years been exploring, *inter alia*, the limits of human communication, recalls the centrality of language as a medium; he has much to say about the imperfections of, and necessity for, translation.[25] Writing from a very different stance, and after more than a decade of exploring the role played by intermediaries in the circulation of ideas, Régis Debray observes: " a good mediologue is a dog": to study the transmission process means sniffing in the corners, consorting with the intermediaries and vulgarisers, the brigands of thought.[26] Why, he asks of the nineteenth century, did Karl Marx succeed and Auguste Comte fail? Comte, he remarks excelled as an intermediary, thought in terms of three, of the trinity, and not of two, the binary.[27] Our third, concluding witness, Daniel Bougnoux, asks bluntly

---

[25] G. Steiner, *Real Presences*, London; Faber and Faber, 1989, p.5. See also, Steiner's *After Babel*, London; Oxford University Press, 1978.

[26] R. Debray, *Cours de médiologie générale*, Paris, Gallimard, 1991, p.61.

[27] Ibid, p.26.

"Pourquoi jamais deux sans trois?" and recalls how - in what we might term "the holy trinity" of media studies, philosophers and psychologists, Boolian algebra and telecoms engineers, each - in their varying ways - contribute to identifying the importance of "le tiers".[28]

"Tiers symbolisant" de "l'homme ludique", promoting the "valeur d'échange" above the "valeur d'usage", advertising has been invested in France in recent years with connotations over-and-above the transfer of money to plug a message. At the very beginning of their book, *Le grand bluff*, Boutelier and Subramanian ask: "tout cela est-il bien sérieux?" Part of the answer lies in their subsequent remark: "advertising flourishes in one of the most frequented of all crossroads" - politics and showbiz, business and the media, all interconnect here.[29] Yes, there is something unsavoury, like scrounging around in the dustbin to find the compromising letter in the Dreyfus affair. On a different plane, when defining the contours of the - perforce interdisciplinary - mediology whose hour, he claims, has come, Régis Debray likewise, provokingly, uses the language of "petites causes, grands effets": the anecdote is revealing, symbolic, emblematic.[30] "All desire is the desire of the desire of the other" (Bougnoux, quoting Lacan quoting Hegel ...).[31] The study of advertising, like that of other parts of the communications industry whose goals include persuasion, is at times like tilting against windmills, dealing with the Edmunds who arise from the murky shadows. Yet to identify the actors of the advertising industry in France - even more perhaps than to explore the "sens", "signifiant" and "signifié" dear to generations of semiologists - is to better understand one of the long-ignored, illegitimate and seminal, forces that shape the communications

---

[28] D. Bougnoux, *La Communication par la bande*, pp.93, 169.

[29] D. Boutelier, D. Subramanian, *Le grand bluff*, pp.9-10.

[30] R. Debray, *Cours de médiologie générale*, p.35.

[31] D. Bougnoux, *La Communication par la bande*, p.138.

industry and its modes of discourse. Studies of the "médiacratie" and the "médiaklatura" proliferate.[32] Some pay homage to Balzac.[33] Many centre on journalists as "médiateurs du politique". Independent studies of the advertising industry and its intermediary role are less frequent, and have something of a "parfum de scandale". They, too, may pay homage to Balzac, who published *chez* Girardin and was the first, it seems to "expose" Havas.[34]

---

[32] Terms of an uncertain vintage, developed by media professionals, partly in an attempt to stand back from the system of which they are a part ("l'arroseur arrosé..."). See, for example: F.H. de Virieu, *La Médiacratie*, Paris, Flammarion, 1990. For a more scholarly approach, see: R. Rieffel, *L'Elite des journalistes*, Paris, P.U.F., 1984; D. Wolton, *Eloge du grand public*, Paris, Flammarion, 1990.

[33] Y. Roucaute, *Splendeurs et misères des journalistes* (Paris: Calmann-Lévy, 1991).

[34] In 1840, in his - short-lived - *la Revue parisienne*.

7. IS ADVERTISING A CHARACTERISTIC ELEMENT OF CONTEMPORARY FRENCH CULTURE?

PIERRE SORLIN

On the subject of advertising and culture, when we attempt to define the relationships between the two terms, two ideas immediately come to mind.

The first concerns the international nature of advertising. If we except local advertising carried by free newspapers or shelf- and shop-window advertising, the advertising market is seen to be dominated by very large firms who target both a national and a foreign clientele.[1] When the R.S.C.G.[2] agency set up its Citroën campaign for the five-door SX model, the considerable investment only made sense if the photographs and film could be used in every country where the manufacturer had outlets; the choice of the Great Wall of China as a "catwalk" for the car allowed the public to immediately recognise the decor without associating the SX with one particular country; it was a timeless and universal framework, and the presence of an old wise man and of a very young boy, both making the Citroën "V", immediately symbolised the lasting quality of the brand and the "revolution" which it sought to introduce. Concerned to make its products profitable, R.S.C.G. had found a stereotype, a sign which was identifiable anywhere and by anyone. But is not a stereotype which is decodable in every country the opposite to what may be considered the originality of a national culture? In France, the best-established

---

[1] The argument in favour of the international dimension of advertising is forcibly made by Armand Mattelart, in *L'International publicitaire*, Paris, La Découverte, 1989 and *La Publicité*, Paris, La Découverte, 1990. The major ideas are compelling: the same objects are sold everywhere, their presentation is standardised, the advertising patterns become more and more stereotyped. However, advertising is not produced in the same way in France as elsewhere, and it does not address its audience according to the same rules. This is what this chapter is attempting to explore.

[2] Agence *Roux, Séguéla, Cayzac, Goudard.*

clichés concern Italy: a gondola or the Coliseum, a mixture of green, white and red, a tune from Verdi are sufficient to identify products as coming from Italy; the advertising is playing here on what the Italians themselves can only experience as a caricature: the original characteristics are abandoned in favour of portmanteau references.

At the same time, and this is my second remark, the link between advertising and music, poster-art, cinema and television is so obvious that it does not need emphasising: musical "clips", as they have developed since the beginning of the 1980s, have influenced advertising, which has had to accommodate the use of the significant image, ultra-rapid montage, and the rhythms of "pop" music which depends upon the repetition of a small number of syllables and upon only two or three notes: "t'as le ticket chic/t'as le ticket choc", or "Maggi/Maggi". The remarkably consistent series of advertising films financed by Eram shoes exemplifies these two tendencies: they are constructed upon an Alexandrine: "Il faudrait être fou/pour payer davantage", and thus parody fashionable shows, operas, reviews or films, whilst continuing to bend the music and the accompanying ballet to pop music conventions. With time, the connections have multiplied and advertising is now inseparable from the theatre, film and television.

Whilst bearing in mind this development, to which I shall return, I should like to use the term "culture" here in a very broad sense, which does not merely include creative traditions or practices. Very briefly, I would say that the culture of a country is its way of life, the totality of the activities which develop in it and of the interests which are expressed by it. In fact, I should like to attempt to show that the advertising which has evolved so much in the last twenty years is not an adjunct to production, but that it accords with certain major tendencies in French society.

A priori, advertising does not seem to have a very important place in the French economy: it accounts for less than 1% of the G.N.P. and comes far behind the industrial sectors. This is hardly surprising, but advertising is also overtaken by other activities which the statistics class as service industries, such as accountancy or management consultancy.[3] The revenue of the French advertising agencies, comparable to that of their British counterparts, is low compared with the figures for America, Japan or Germany.

Throughout the industrialised world, advertising lives both in a state of constant expansion and under a permanent threat of crisis: the permanent contraction of the employment market has had a serious effect upon the small advertisments which traditionally provide the press with its most reliable income. In comparison with their American or European equivalents, French advertising agencies, in spite of serious problems, seem to be relatively secure. Whilst most companies are merging and are open to foreign investment, advertising is still fragmented and still rejects foreign alliances in a way which recalls the most traditional methods of French business. It is difficult to provide accurate figures for all advertising agencies: lots of little companies follow demand and organise whole promotion campaigns or simply act as intermediaries, by advising firms and publishing material. Broadly, there are something like 2000 advertising companies, but if the all-purpose offices are excluded, this figure may be reduced to about five hundred. Three large companies account, together, for 15% of the market, and another twenty account for a further 25%. The dominance of the "big three" is not overwhelming, and it allows the small companies to survive. The fame of Publicis, the largest French agency, is impressive, but this impressiveness is part of the group's policy and contributes to the equation: major promotional campaigns = Publicis, which does not prevent other companies from obtaining

---

[3] The Institut d'Etudes et de Recherches Publicitaires publishes an annual *Panorama du marché de la publicité en France* which contains all the statistical data necessary for an understanding of the sector.

work.[4] The network of advertising agencies is dense and is sufficiently varied and flexible to resist foreign investment: the French market is one of those in which foreign investment is lowest, which separates it not merely from other latin countries but also from Britain and the United States. The absence of specialisation has resulted in a rather unusual division of labour: the small companies are able to target a clientèle and to define an appropriate strategy for that clientèle, but they have difficulty in controlling the distribution of their material. The purchase of advertising space, be it pages in a newspaper, advertising hoardings or hours of advertising on radio or television has thus become the speciality of a small number of companies who act as intermediaries between advertisers and the media. This division of labour, which at first sight appears illogical, has served the agencies well. With the crisis in small advertising, the media, and in particular newspapers, lowered their fees. For the clients, therefore, expenses went down, but the cost of the performance, the text, the pictures, the editing and the films remained the same. Since the beginning of the recession, in 1973, the revenue of the advertising agencies went up on average by 9% per annum in current figures, or by 4-6% in real terms over a long period. In a generally gloomy situation, this was a rare example of growth characterising a relatively stable sector. Henceforth, it is not possible to define French culture, in a broad sense, without including advertising.

Behind the figures, it is important to attempt to see the individuals. For a long time, advertising was carried out by a few agencies who paid graphic designers on a free-lance basis: it was a useful additional source of income for a few artists, but rarely considered as a profession. In my view, the most

---

[4] It could be rejoined that the agencies, whilst remaining independent, have often become federated through the presence of a common investor. The various branches of the Havas group, which are individually small, represent together 15% of the advertising market. But this is a purely financial presence. As regards recruitment, the choice of campaigns and their operation, the agencies receive no directives from Havas.

important change was the birth of a professional sector. Bearing in mind some of the reservations mentioned above (a lot of these agencies are multi-purpose), we can nevertheless, estimate the number of people working regularly in advertising at 50,000. For the most part, they are young and qualified; more than half of the permanent staff have managerial positions, earn high salaries and often change job. Some of these characteristics render the advertising sector similar to other areas in service industry, for example, banking, into which an increasing number of young graduates are recruited and where mobility is frequent. Yet these analogies remain superficial: advertising in fact presents quite specific charactersitics. In the first place, two-thirds of its employees are women, whose employment prospects are every bit as open as those of their male colleagues. In banking, on the other hand, management is heavily male-dominated, whilst four-fifths of women employees are restricted to subordinate tasks and their advancement and mobility prospects are slim. Another important point is the variety of those who are recruited. The "creative" staff, those who produce the posters and the films, are few in number (one-fifth of the total staff) and only a minority of them has received a formal artistic training. Numerically, the creative staff are outnumbered by the commercial staff, who come either from universities or from professional or private schools, who learn very rapidly by moving from agency to agency and who avoid specialising. At a time when the preparation for a career has become one of the major concerns of both government and teachers, the advertising sector is one of those rare examples of an expanding industry in which "general education", as it was termed for a long time in French schools, is still in demand. In France, as elsewhere, there is a considerable distance between the public image of employment and the lessons provided by statistics. The increase in women employees, the importance of qualifications and flexibility seem to be incontrovertible facts, whereas the statistical data reveal a dramatic mismatch between educational courses and job requirements, very limited professional mobility, a marked subordination of women and a long-term tendency to recession. Advertising remains, along with the computer industry, one of the rare areas in which the image is not misleading.

The broadening of the market, and simultaneously, of the field of recruitment are recent phenomena. Throughout the last two decades, advertising has been carried out in Europe according to three models. The German model corresponds to a huge dominance of the press, which leaves less than a quarter of the market to hoardings, radio and television. In Spain and Italy, the freedom given to the broadcast media has established a parity between newspapers, on one hand, and radio and television on the other. In England and France, the press receives more than half of the advertising budgets, but television has more than a quarter. This similarity must not be allowed to hide deep differences. Advertising in the broadcast media developed slowly in England, since the abolition of the public monopoly in 1954, whereas in France, it dates only from 1968 and has only become important with the legalisation of the *radios libres* in 1982 and the creation of private television companies in 1985. In 1970, the situation in France was similar to that which still persists in Germany, with advertising agencies maintaining quiet relations with the newspapers who, in their turn, guaranteed their financial stability through pages sold to advertisers. Paradoxically, in the years which followed this state of affairs, the competition between the press and the broadcast media reinforced the influence of the advertising agencies because it led those newspapers who wished to save their advertising budget to organise promotional campaigns (such as reduced subscriptions, prizes and free gifts), which in its turn implied recourse to agencies, and because it led the television channels to exceed their legal quotas,[5] thus allowing the agencies to

---

[5] Theoretically, the maximum is 6 minutes per hour. For the State-owned channels, the rules are even stricter. Since no penalties are applied when these limits are infringed, they are purely theoretical.

produce more programmes. As intermediaries between the production sectors and the media, the advertising companies have benefitted enormously from the deregulation accepted by the Government without enthusiasm but without any real will to resist. The upsurge in careers in advertising is the correlative to a triumphant free-market which concerns the whole society but which is particularly evident where traditional institutions such as newspapers are contested by new techniques.

The advertising sector would constitute an excellent starting-point for an analysis of the dynamism and weaknesses of the French economy. It is young and new, at least in its present form; it makes maximum use of the incoherences of the law and of the contradictions in which its clients find themselves; it regularly increases its investments and maintains limited but regular profits; it recruits, with no guarantee of tenure, a staff of a good intellectual level who accept heavy labour constraints and a virtually obligatory mobility in exchange for high salaries; it is opposed to both mergers and specialisation, benefits from its fragmentation, and adapts quickly to changes in demand. Its rear, however, is not protected; all it needs is an armistice between those who sell advertising space or, even more improbable, massive closures in the press and television, for the entire profession to be in crisis. Advertising refracts certain tendencies in the market, which was not the case in 1970. All the indicators are that it will not be the same at the dawn of the 21st century, and it is for this reason that advertising constitutes a good vantage point from which to observe French culture today.

It remains a fact that the word "culture" can equally be used in a narrow sense, which relates to a society's accepted values and their transmission. If we accept (purely hypothetically, for the time in which television sets are switched on does not necessarily correspond to viewing time) that the French spend on average two hours a day in front of their television set and watch twelve minutes of advertising, at the end of the day they will have watched between thirty and forty advertisement "spots". What have they seen and what have they retained from it?

It is possible to distinguish in the recent development of advertising, be it in the press or on radio and television, three different tendencies, Chronologically, they emerged at different periods, but none of them was eliminated by the one which followed: the models accumulated without replacing each other.

One of the major aims of the advert has been for a long time to convince. An examination of newspapers from the middle of the Twentieth Century brings out the didactic nature of the advertisements which they published: each advert sought to prove, with copious arguments, that its product was the best. In newspapers and on hoardings, the picture was purely complementary: it helped to convey a text which was making the argument. In the cinema, the voice-over dominated and advertising films copied the newsreels: the commentator explained with authority, the image created a mood and suggested a context in which the relevant object was naturally placed. Hence, the *Parisiennes*, who live in a luxurious atmosphere, love to dress up, and for that they need perfume - and *Soir de Paris* is tailor-made for them. This kind of advertising, which "speaks to you", has far from disappeared and has even shown a resurgence with the appearance of stars, from sport or entertainment, who stare at the viewers and tell them why such a product is for them.

An important change occurred when advertising, instead of attempting to inform, decided to entertain. Informing means demonstrating: "I will explain to you why product X is superior to its competitors and then you will buy it". There is an obvious risk, however, that the public will not be bothered to follow the message to the end. The entertainment strategy is based upon a completely different reaction: if the readers or viewers have experienced a moment of euphoria, they will associate it with the brand which has provided them with this pleasure and, remembering this moment of satisfaction, when they see the product, they will be tempted to buy it.

The pleasure thus experienced takes two different routes: recognition and puzzle-solving. The newspapers spotted this from the beginning of the century onwards, but were unable to fully exploit emotions which the broadcast media *are* able to manipulate. For radio and television have resources denied to the press: they exploit time, developing very rapidly the sequence *question/pause/answer,* and they can similarly exploit the image, be it in sound or vision. Advertising was transformed when it became a miniature quiz: put together the images of which at least some are recognised by everyone, and the pleasure experienced in identifying them will hold the attention of the viewers. Even political advertising has recognised this. In the advertising film which he had produced for the 1988 Presidential election, François Mitterrand (or rather, his advisers) showed eighty photographs following each other every three seconds. The viewers looked, puzzled over it, and sometimes discovered the answers; and when it was over, they compared scores. Against Mitterrand, Chirac invoked another kind of recognition, making heavy use of stereotypes: log-fires, football, walks in the country, visits to friends, an ordinary day which might be Sunday. Here the stereotypes are too obvious to be accepted at face value; they are ironic, in the same way as is the advertisement for Maggi Soups, with the husband in an apron doing the cooking whilst his wife is reading the newspaper: the reference is not to be taken literally; since Maggi soups came in packets, it takes no effort to make them, and hence the cliché of the modern husband who is a demon in the kitchen is a mockery.

—— If you can spot something, you can immediately feel intelligent. The puzzle is less gratifying, because it breeds a vague uncertainty: "why is that there?" The strength of the broadcast media is clearly that they are able to solve the problem at virtually the same moment that they raise it: it is all over in twenty seconds. Cinema advertising which produced real films of sometimes up to one minute in length was too slow to take the viewer by surprise, and in this sense television has created a new source of satisfaction. Sometimes the object is shown at the very beginning, but is made to fulfil a function which it does not normally have: "what is its purpose, then?" Alternatively, a story is told without it being obvious which product is being advertised: "what is being shown?"

Television, followed rapidly by the hoarding and the newspaper advertisement, has therefore become a playground. In terms of the culture of the viewer, this is probably a major change. Didactic advertising sets up simple associations like "health/natural foods" or "energy/sugar", which were easily remembered, particularly by children,[6] and were recycled in conversation: a fairly basic knowledge which influenced daily behaviour. Advertising which attempts to seduce provides less information and associates products with qualities or characteristics which could not reasonably be attributed to them: a little girl strokes the Dunlop tyre which has not run over her doll, the gesture is tender, but we do not expect a tyre to incite emotions. This incitement to pleasure leaves a vacuum which the viewer will fill, or perhaps try to fill, by a reversal of knowledge which comes, not from the advertiser, but from the receiver.

In the space of a few years, television has changed the positioning of the public. Yet in this there is nothing specific to French culture: the answer to the Dunlop puzzle may be found in any language. It is therefore especially with the third model that appear forms of game-playing (for we are still in the domain of games) which are strictly linked to French culture. In this, the specificity derives, not from the content, but from the expression: instead of rendering the object problematic, either functionally or essentially, the advertiser renders problematical the way in which it is shown. I can see several solutions to this problem, but obviously the classification which I am using is

---

[6] Jean Noël Kopferrer, *L'Enfant et la publicité*, Paris, Dunod, 1985.

open to discussion.

Our first puzzle depends upon the "*short-cut*", as expressed in the slogan of a private security company: "Si on entre chez vous, ça sonne chez nous". This is a double inversion: the entry *preceeds* the ringing of the door-bell, and the two actions do not occur in the same place. The sentence itself does not offer the slightest difficulty, but it does presuppose that the viewer supply the missing link. It would not constitute a problem if it did not occur in a context where the door-bell plays an important part. In the same way, the Orangina advert, in which we see a barmaid remove her uniform by a swimming-pool and launch herself into a wild dance, omits two pieces of knowledge held by any French viewer: "Orangina pétille", "Orangina rafraîchit". The riddle posed by the film exists only for whoever is able to immediately replace the words or ideas which do not appear on the screen.

At a slightly more complex level is the *double meaning*. "J'arrête, tu me suis", says an insurance company offering retirement policies. To follow implies not merely to walk behind someone (which is impossible when that person stops), but also to do like that person and, indeed, to interpret correctly what he or she says. Several layers of meaning are superimposed, which surround the sentence without exhausting its meaning. We can see a similar procedure in the famous Citroën "chevron" television advert: a herd of wild horses gallop out of a town and across the countryside, and reform gradually making the two lines of the double V of the car company. At first sight, it looks almost like an anti-advertisement: the town, narrow, closed, the domain of the mechanical, is juxtaposed with the countryside, where the urge of nature and the galloping of the horses are unfettered. Here again, we must bear in mind the effect of multiple meanings. Associations such as "la 2CV = la voiture par excellence" and "la 2CV = l'évasion" are familiar to French viewers and they alone allow the viewer to spot the message which, without them, would be a complete enigma.

The final stage is the defiance of logic. A sugar substitute proclaims: "Ça ne change rien et c'est ça qui change tout". Literally, the sentence is absurd, which makes it difficult to understand, in contrast to the previous two. Yet it is precisely because sugar substitutes change everything physiologically that we do not need to change our habits. The pleasure lies therefore in the act of inverting the order of reasoning and maintaining the two terms "rien"/"tout" in equilibrium. A mastery of the language is essential in order to discover that this logically unacceptable sentence is nevertheless correct. But linguistic ability is not enough and the puzzle cannot be solved without effort. I must therefore qualify the comparisons which I have drawn between slogans and television adverts. Even when the image is puzzling, it is probably more understandable than the text. The advert for Pliz, a furniture polish, shows a woman taking a run-up and sliding on her stomach along a very long table. There is yet a further twist: after Pliz, the table will be like an ice-rink, yet the product is not made to produce slides. Yet, even if we do not understand, we laugh: the paradox visually becomes apparent more quickly than linguistically.

Advertising people have created a mythical enemy, the "advertisement-hater". Yet advertising does not really have serious enemies, rather, it is an object of contempt and people blame it for handing out simplistic ideas and deadening the mind of the public with advertising slogans. There is no evidence that advertising conditions those who watch it. It could even be argued that advertising merely follows contemporary currents, and political propaganda would support such an hypothesis. The 1988 campaign seems to have marked a step forward in advertising in elections. Prior to 1988, posters aimed at either didacticism or feeling[7] and it was necessary to wait for certain procedures like the puzzle to become completely adopted by the viewers before unleashing them in the political arena. Advertising appears to me to indicate

---

[7] Jean-Marc Benoit, Philippe Benoit, Jean-Marc Lech, *La Politique à l'affiche. Affiches électorales et publicité politique*, Paris, Editions du May, 1986.

the development of a new form of curiosity, based upon compression, a rapid comprehension of narrative mechanisms, and attention to rhythm. To a certain extent, this derives from the fact that adverts, posters and campaigns are developed by well-paid professionals, but professionals who are also subject to bitter competition and who must use to the utmost the capacity for expression of the media which they use. In many areas, such as theatre, dance or music, advertising provides work for the artists and contributes to the testing of new forms. Advertising is a testing-ground for ideas men who have had a relatively sophisticated secondary and higher education; it is addressing a public which is equally sophisticated educationally and which is used to seeing in practices such as the short-circuit or the logical impossibility a linguistic means of expression. And this is what I wanted to suggest when using the term "culture": at the beginning of the 1990s, there is a, perhaps temporary, commonality of tone between the inventors of advertising and their audience which allows the former to play on mechanisms of meaning which are well known to the latter. Before speaking about the products which it is trying to promote, advertising speaks about the current state of language.

8. DESIGN FOR LIVING: THE FAMILY IN RECENT FRENCH CINEMA

JILL FORBES

As the "cinematic phenomenon" of 1988 *La Vie est un long fleuve tranquille* commands our attention.[1] One of its most interesting features is the significance it attaches to the family - a significance which extends both to the narrative and to the economy of production. Thus many of the comic reversals of value and fortune, both in the central tale of the changeling and in the ancillary portraits of the virtuous immigrants and feckless white trash, depend on notions of filiation, heredity and ethnicity whilst, at the same time, the film instates (or reinstates) the familial group as a production value.

In the postwar American, British, German and Italian cinemas the family often functions as a structuring element. The adulterous couple, together with the dynastic family and the conflict of generations motivate the narrative of much postwar western cinema as they do the bourgeois novel. Indeed, because of the obvious intertextual relationship between the cinema and the nineteenth century novel, the link between "a specific kind of society and a specific kind of narrative" explored by Tony Tanner in his brilliant study *Adultery in the Novel* is equally applicable to the cinema.[2] The family provides not just the conceptual and ideological framework for the action of films but also the model for the organisation of their production. The extended patriarchal family - what might be called the godfather structure - is (or has been) the basis of much film production, from the "familial" teams gathered round Fellini or Fassbinder, to Michael Balcon's Ealing "the Studios with team spirit", to the

---

[1] This paper was first read after a screening of *La Vie est un long fleuve tranquille.*

[2] Tony Tanner, *Adultery in the Novel*, Baltimore, Johns Hopkins U.P., 1979, pp.11-12.

legendary Hollywood moguls whose punitive contracts infantilised all their actors.[3] And the family as a mode of textual and financial organisation has proved its worth in masterpieces ranging from *The Godfather* to *The Leopard* to *The Marriage of Maria Braun* to *Heimat*, not to mention innumerable British examples from *Passport to Pimlico* to *Brideshead Revisited*.

It is all the more interesting, therefore, that in the contemporary French cinema one would be hard put to find the family structuring the mode of production, *dramatis personae* or moral problematic. Despite some apparent recent exceptions to which I shall return, I wish to suggest that the contemporary French cinema typically proposes a thoroughgoing and systematic subversion of the family to which it substitutes a more attractive social, economic and filmic organisation.

Although it might be tempting to see the challenge to the family as an epiphenomenon of May 1968, it can in fact be traced back to the 1950s and the films of the *nouvelle vague*. The *nouvelle vague* filmmakers flouted the familial organisation of the French film industry which, at the time, required a long apprenticeship as an *assistant* before accession to the rank of *réalisateur*. Thanks to new technologies which permitted smaller and more mobile crews and cheaper productions, hierarchical structures and restrictive practices were abandoned and the filmmaker became simultaneously writer, director, producer, editor and even occasionally star of his - and much less frequently her - own film. Thus part of what is meant by the *cinéma d'auteurs* is the explosion of fixed identities within the industry so that the originator of the film can play all the major contributing roles.

In addition to being professionally polymorphous, the *nouvelle vague* directors changed the narrative content of films and exploited new narrative

---

[3] See Charles Barr, *Ealing Studios*, London, David & Charles, 1977 p.6. Barr also quotes Monja Danischewsky: "If Mick (Balcon) was the father figure, Cavalcanti was the Nanny who brought us up" (p.40). There are innumerable other examples.

techniques. In stark contrast to the authors of what they aptly dismissed as the "cinéma de *papa*" they were young (Truffaut made his first feature film at the age of 27, Godard at 29), and their youthfulness was mirrored in the casting of their films and in the audiences they attracted, leading contemporary sociologists to analyse the *nouvelle vague* as a component of youth culture.[4] *Nouvelle vague* films typically privilege immediacy and rapidity at the expense of exposition and characterisation, situations rather than relationships, montage and jump cuts instead of the "grammar of editing" - the shot/reverse shot and the eyeline matching on which Hollywood realism is based - and in this way they create a cinema without "continuity", both in the technical sense of consistency from one shot to the next, and in the more general sense of the transmission of values and positions. In short, the *nouvelle vague* created a new aesthetic based on a particular coincidence of industrial, ideological and social circumstances unique to France and the French film industry. It is an aesthetic summed up in two seminal *nouvelle vague* films, both released in 1961, in which the change is represented as a challenge to the family as embodied in the heterosexual, progenitive couple. Truffaut's *Jules et Jim* and Godard's *Une femme est une femme* set the agenda for the decades to come, and they did so through a productive reading of Lubitsch's film version of Noel Coward's play *Design for Living* (1933).

Design for Living casts three young English-speaking artists, Gilda, Otto and Leo in the Bohemian environment of Paris in the twenties. Otto and Leo are old friends. When they meet Gilda she lives first with Otto in Paris and then with Leo in London, but when Otto returns from two years' travelling pining for both of them, she leaves for New York with Earnest whom she marries, only to abandon him when Otto and Leo arrive to spring her from her bourgeois prison. *Design for Living* parodies the bedroom farce by stressing

---

[4] See Claude Brémond et al., "Les héros de films dits 'de la nouvelle vague'" in *Communications I* (1961), pp.142-77.

Gilda's moral and social freedom: "I shouldn't feel cosy married", she says, "it would offend my moral principles". The cruelly named Earnest is seen as a father figure (he tells Gilda he was "very fond" of her mother), so that leaving him is a break with patriarchy, a bid to fashion her own life instead of designing the life-styles of her clients. But the play also inscribes a homosexual subtext by emphasising not simply Otto, Leo and Gilda's mutual interdependence but also their sexual ambivalence. Gilda "rails and roars against being feminine",[5] the threesome refer to themselves as "famous Hermaphrodites",[6] while Otto and Leo announce they "love" each other as much as they love Gilda. Indeed, when Gilda leaves Earnest for Otto and Leo it is because "I'm not different from them, we're all of a piece, the three of us".[7]

Lubitsch's film was much admired by the *nouvelle vague* directors and their successors, to the extent that Godard christened one of the characters in *Une femme est une femme* Alfred Lubitsch.[8] Both *Jules et Jim* and *Une femme est une femme* recapitulate the convention that Paris is the home of new forms of life and art since, like Lubitsch and Coward, both cast foreigners who are said to be in Paris to pursue their artistic careers. *Jules et Jim* is set in the period immediately before and after the First World War; *Une femme est une femme* is set in the Paris of the early sixties, but Anna Karina is filmed like Marilyn Monroe in *Gentlemen Prefer Blondes* in which Monroe was supposedly en route for an artistic engagement in Paris. Both films also create uncertainties about role and gender, *Jules et Jim* morbidly, *Une femme est une femme* wittily, which link them closely with *Design for Living*.

---

[5] Noël Coward, *Plays Three*, London, Methuen, 1979, p.15.

[6] Ibid., p.15.

[7] Ibid., p.37.

[8] For a plot summary see Alain Bergala ed., *Jean-Luc Godard par Jean-Luc Godard*, Paris, *Cahiers du Cinéma*, 1985, pp.205-208.

In Truffaut's film the relationship between Jules, Jim and Catherine is usually read as a drama of adultery and Catherine described as a woman in search of social and sexual freedom. Thus the characters read *Elective Affinities* and admire the new Strindbergian play.[9] But like Otto and Leo, the German Jules, and the French Jim had been friends and fellow artists before they knew Catherine, and had made a pilgrimage to Greece where they found their ideal of beauty. The narrator's voice stresses the fact that the men's friendship transcends their relationship with Catherine, so that when Jim takes up with Catherine after the war it is a way of reaching out to Jules whom she has married, while Jules tolerates Catherine's adultery for Jim's sake. The three are at their happiest when Catherine most resembles the men, especially in the famous cross-dressing sequence when she dons trousers, cap and a moustache drawn with burnt cork, and calls herself Thomas, and when Catherine kills both herself and Jim, Jules is less devastated than he might have been since their death helpfully resolves the ambivalence of his feelings by means of a symbolic fusion.

Turning to *Une femme est une femme* we find a comparable structure. The plot concerns Angéla's desire for a child - something which her lover Emile does not want. To attempt to satisfy her he accosts strange men in the street and asks if they would be prepared to impregnate her. When this fails Angéla turns to Emile's friend Alfred Lubitsch who obliges her desire. Whereupon Emile and Angéla make love in order that if there is to be a child both men should be its father.

Une femme est une femme is progammatic in the context of Godard's cinema. It is the first film in which he adopted the tricolour palette - *bleu, blanc, rouge* - to which he returned in *Pierrot le fou*, *Weekend*, *La Chinoise*, *Deux ou trois choses que je sais d'elle* and *Tout va bien*. His use of the revolutionary spectrum is always ironic and all of these films link often virulent

---

[9] François Truffaut, *Jules and Jim*, London, Lorrimer, 1968, pp.36, 71.

118

social criticism with a powerful critique of the couple. *Une femme est une femme* is also the first film in which Godard systematically explores the relationship between word and image, both in the celebrated sequence in which Angéla and Emile, who are momentarily not on speaking terms, use the titles of books to insult each other, and through the practice of contradicting or subverting what is being shown and said, by writing on the screen, a technique which is later used to good effect in Godard's video and televison work *Numéro Deux* and *Sur et sous la communication. Une femme est une femme* adumbrates the systematic disruption of Hollywood codes, seen at its most extreme in *Passion*, by disturbing what Mary Anne Doane has called the cinema's somatography, the ideal synchrony of sound and image which allows bodies to be precisely positioned in space, and it does this by techniques such as the intercalation of high shots which distance the action, or through the vertiginous contrast between Angéla's corporeal expressivity and her lack of verbal facility.[10]   Above all, perhaps, it links the rejection of the cinema's aesthetic conventions with the challenge to fixed identities of heredity and gender, first by rendering the hypothetical child's paternity uncertain and second through a glorious pun which elucidates the sententiously tautological (and hence suspect) title.   As he is finally seduced by Angéla, Emile remonstrates "Tu es infâme". "Non", says Angéla, proud of her command of gender, "Je suis une femme!".

The sexually and socially ambivalent threesome is a familiar figure in the works of many of the major filmmakers of the 1970s who consistently explore triangular relationships that represent what might be called the new geometry of desire. The most obvious example is Jean Eustache's *La Maman et la putain*, an explicit tribute to Lubitsch and a work of epic proportions which, as Philippe Garrell put it, "a presque tout dit de la génération née pendant et juste

---

[10] In this film Anna Karina's Danish accent is still very evident and her difficulties with the French language are a joky feature of the film.

après la guerre".[11] It is a film which consciously sets out to explore the Zeitgeist and finds it permeated with nostalgia and *tristesse*: "On a eu la Révolution culturelle, les Rolling Stones, May 1968, les Black Panthers, l'Underground et puis rien, depuis deux ou trois ans".[12] This nostalgia has both a political and aesthetic dimension, however. In other words it is not simply the political excitement of May 1968 and the Chinese Cultural Revolution which, in 1973 already seemed a long way off, but the fact that Saint Germain des Près, one of the principal locations of the film, is no longer the haunt of artists and writers but merely somewhere to practise *la drague*. Indeed, in casting Jean-Pierre Léaud as the male lead in a film which was part of an autobiographical sequence, Eustache also demonstrates how his own distance from Truffaut, or how the passage of time has transformed the inventive child of *Les 400 coups* into a penniless layabout whose proposals of marriage are rejected, or so he believes, because he is not bourgeois enough.

The film charts the shifting relationship between Alexandre (Jean-Pierre Léaud) and two women, the "mother" Marie, whom he lives with, and the "whore" Veronika, whom he introduces into the *ménage*. Like Gilda, Catherine and Angéla, Alexandre oscillates between his two partners, Marie becomes more "maternal" by welcoming the other two into her bed (where many of their discussions take place) and Veronika perceives that it is not so much Alexandre that she wants as Alexandre and Marie together: "Je vous aime tous les deux".[13] *La Maman et la putain* poses innumerable difficulties of interpretation to which I will return briefly but there is no doubt that it was seen as a seminal reinterpretation of the *nouvelle vague* and as an influential exploration of the new social and sexual relations.

---

[11] Philippe Garrel interviewed in *Cahiers du cinéma*, 344, February 1983, p.26.

[12] Jean Eustache, *La Maman et la putain*, Paris, *Cahiers du Cinéma*, 1986, p.65.

[13] Ibid., p.119.

120

Instead of the tragic or farcical *ménage à trois* in which the drama is provided by adultery, *La Maman et la putain* like *Design for Living*, *Jules et Jim* and *Une femme est une femme* clearly proposes an oedipal structure which differs from, and it seen as preferable to, that of the biological family because it allows roles to shift between generations and across genders. It would be impossible, not to say tedious, to list all the films in which the family is similarly challenged by means of a triangular relationship that explodes conventional socio-sexual relations, and I will simply mention what seem to me the most interesting or pertinent examples. The films of Jacques Doillon, for instance, are almost exclusively preoccupied with sexual relationships and the extreme emotions they generate. Doillon uses children to parody the married couple in both *La Drôlesse* and the appropriately named *La Vie de famille* and in other films uses substitution, surrogacy and incest to demonstrate how variable the geometry of such relationships can be. Thus in *La Femme qui pleure* the neglected wife offers herself as a sexual partner to her husband's mistress while in *La fille prodigue* a daughter sets up an extra-marital affair for her father and then seduces him herself. In André Téchiné's *Hôtel des Amériques* the affair between Hélène and Gilles is doomed because each has another "lover", though Hélène's is dead and Gilles's is his musician buddy Bernard. In Téchiné's *Le Lieu du crime* Lili escapes her stifling, provincial family and boring husband through a romantic encounter with Martin, a criminal on the run who bears an uncanny resemblance to her son, and with him creates a fantastic, alternative and implicitly incestuous family, which is the "place" of the crime in question. Similarly, in Téchiné's *Les Innocents* the various biological families depicted are all in some way impaired or unsatisfactory - one is contracted for security and children not out of love, another has a handicapped child, a third contains a drunken homosexual conductor who hates and is hated by his wife and son. Once again a new oedipal structure is created, consisting of the deaf and dumb boy Alain, Saïd the Algerian whom he loves, and Alain's sister Jeanne who is in love with Saïd, a family which is socially underprivileged and only partly biologically determined but which more closely matches the desire of the individuals concerned. Finally, most of Bertrand Blier's films involve triangular relationships - Depardieu, Dewaere and a series of women in *Les Valseuses*, Thierry Lhermitte, Coluche and Isabelle Huppert in *La Femme de mon pote*, Depardieu, Dewaere and Carole Laure in *Préparez vos mouchoirs*, Depardieu, Michel Blanc and Miou-Miou in *Tenue de soirée*. While the homosexual relationships become more explicit in the later films, culminating in the drag sequences in *Tenue de soirée*, it would be true to say that Blier is only against the couple if it is heterosexual and that many of his films are constructed in such a way that the women and particularly the mothers, are eliminated, murdered, induced to kill themselves, handed on to other men, or simply abandoned.

Why does this trope recur and what does it mean? In my view, it does not reflect, except anecdotally, the socio-sexual revolution of May 1968. First, as I have tried to show in the way Godard and Truffaut read Lubitsch, the assault on the couple began well before 1968; secondly, because the sexual revolution was not uniformly seen as positive. For Blier it encourages both frigidity in women (Miou-Miou in *Les Valseuses*) and sexually predatory females (Geneviève Page in *Buffet Froid*, all the women in *Calmos*). For Veronika in *La Maman et la putain* sex without reproduction has become pointless. [14] All the films cited were made by male directors and, it might be argued, translate a male sensibility[15] pointing to a crisis of masculinity which is also apparent in other contemporary films although it is attributed to a variety of causes, to the decline of the Communist Party and the rise of individualism in Sautet's *Vincent, François, Paul et les autres*, to affluence in

---

[14] Ibid., p.120.

[15] Coline Serreau's *Pourquoi pas?* is, to my knowledge, the only film by a woman to use this figure but it, too, questions the nature of the 'male' identity.

Ferreri's *La grande bouffe,* and to the women's movement in Blier's *Calmos.* Furthermore, it is a feature of many of these films, particularly *La Maman et la putain, Le Lieu du crime* and *La fille prodigue* that they are structured as fantasies, that is as *mises en scène* of the unconscious. But in the case of Eustache and Blier, at least, these are specifically male fantasies with an essentially pornographic structure. The point is reinforced by Eustache's *Une sale histoire* in which a man recounts his experiences as a voyeur in a ladies' lavatory and then repeats his account, and by Blier's *Beau-père* in which the twelve-year-old daughter of the narrator's recently deceased mistress insists on the narrator seducing her but when she grows up he casts around for another girl to take her place - for it is the refusal of narrative closure and the possibility of endless repetition, as much as the sexual content, which are the indices of pornography here.

One of the few post-1968 films to confront the question of the biological family directly is Godard's *Numéro deux* and this film enables us to make the link between the challenge to the family and a particular kind of film practice. In *Numéro deux* the heterosexual couple is unhappy. The husband, Pierre, worries because he sometimes imagines his wife is a man when they make love; the wife, Sandrine, feels oppressed by the binary divisions (masculine/feminine, outside/inside) which organise her life and attempts to get beyond them by hopefully intoning "numéro un, numéro deux, numéro trois". Their dissatisfaction is shared by the elderly couple, the grandparents who live with them, and it is rapidly being acquired by their children. The collective failure to transcend the oppression of the family is attributed by Godard, who appears at the opening of the film, to the fact that sexuality, politics and aesthetics are now determined by television which he describes as "une affaire de famille".

This *boutade* was no more than a statement of the truth, for by the early 1970s television finally achieved the domestic dominance in France that it had held for more than a decade in other European countries. Its preeminence caused a crisis in the film industry such that by the 1980s virtually all film production required the financial participation of television. As a result the cinema could no longer claim to be the purveyor of family entertainment and it responded by increasingly addressing specialist audiences. The *nouvelle vague*, as we have seen, addressed young people, but in the early 1970s the major innovation was the huge expansion in the production and exhibition of sex films which, until new taxes were introduced by a panic-stricken Minister of Culture in 1974, flooded the cinemas of France. The scene of anal rape in *Numéro deux*, repeated on the video monitor, parodies the pornographic cinema whilst also implying that television in some sense rapes the intellect, but it also confirms that this is the inevitable consequence of the decline of family entertainment.

Not surprisingly, there is a corpus of films made in the 1970s and 1980s which are openly nostalgic for the days of family entertainment in the cinema. Téchiné's *Souvenirs d'en France* links the history of the family with the economic history of France and the history of the cinema, while his use of stars such as Catherine Deneuve in *Hôtel des Amériques* or *Le Lieu de crime* is, as Bill Marshall has shown, both an appeal to the notion of film as spectacle and a recognition of its impossibility. Bertrand Tavernier tries to revive the "tradition de qualité" but finds it inescapably linked with death both in *Un Dimanche à la campagne* and especially in the grotesquely titled *Daddy Nostalgie*, while Truffaut signalled his total capitulation to Hollywood production values in *La Nuit américaine* in which we discover that working on a film set is just like belonging to one big, happy family. I would similarly count recent successes such as *Jean de Florette* or *Le Château de ma mère* as sentimental exercises in nostalgia for a film industry which vanished along with a particular kind of rural France, as convincing as the politician's ritual invocation of rural origins, but no more than that.

La Vie est un long fleuve tranquille is more than simply nostalgic. It should not be forgotten that the director Etienne Chatiliez first made his name in commercials for products such as *X-tra* your family soap (powder). Whatever their degree of caricature, the essential feature of the families in *La Vie est un long fleuve tranquille* is their socio-economic exemplarity. In being as typical as the families in TV commercials they confirm the curious reversal of values brought about by television whereby the socio-economic classifications of the advertising industry determine plot and characterisation in fictional material rather than the practices of art disrupting the expected patterns of our lives. Other items in the film such as the Groseilles' attempt to play *Happy Families* or the fact that the credit sequence presents the unfolding of the action of the film as though we were entering into a television screen, underscore the reversal of values brought about by television. In other words, the rehabilitation of the family as a narrative structure and the restoration of the changeling to his "true" identity, albeit one that is influenced by his sojourn with another family, suggests the demise not simply of alternative social identities but also of non-patriarchal film practices, so that *La Vie est un long fleuve tranquille* can be interpreted as a depressing indication of the ever-expanding hegemony of television both in film production and in life. Today, living is designed for and by the small screen.

9.   CARNIVAL, CONSUMPTION AND IDENTITY IN *LA VIE
EST UN LONG FLEUVE TRANQUILLE*

BILL MARSHALL

A few words of justification may be necessary for my choosing this film.
Most obviously, it is a film in which questions of identity and its construction
are foregrounded. But *La Vie est un long fleuve tranquille* was also a cinematic
phenomenon in several ways. One of the biggest box-office successes of 1988
more than 3 million *entrées* in that year alone, one million in Paris - it took
fourth place behind two other French films, Jean-Jacques Annaud's *L'Ours* and
Luc Besson's *Le Grand bleu*, and the Hollywood blockbuster *Who Framed
Roger Rabbit?*. And this from a film whose budget amounted to merely 15
million francs (*Le Grand bleu* cost 78 million), with a first-time director, no
stars except Daniel Gélin in a secondary role, and with its origin in an
ambitious but marginal production company, Téléma, headed by Charles
Gassot, which basically specialised in making commercials, having previously
wholly produced just one feature.   Indeed, the script had been refused by
various distributors, with many questioning the choice of cast (stage actors
largely new to the screen) and even suggesting Catherine Deneuve in the role
of Madame Le Quesnoy.[1] The actual realisation of the film was thus made
possible only through the support of the eventual distributor, the independently
oriented and creative Martin Karmitz, and the French scripwriter and director's
best friend, the *avance sur recettes* from the Centre national de la
cinématographie, as well as, inevitably as far as the contemporary economy of
the French film industry is concerned, a deal with a television channel, FR3, its
logo featured and *speakerines* spat on in *La Vie*.   The chord it struck in the
French public was, however, not repeated in Britain. Released in late 1989 and

---

[1] *Le Film français*, 2178, 29 January 1988, p.3.

distributed by Contemporary Films, its success has been less great here than other French social comedies of the 1980s and 1990s, Serreau's *Trois Hommes et un couffin* and *Romuald et Juliette*, or even Chatiliez' second feature, *Tatie Danielle*. The reasons for *La Vie*'s relative inexportability are not hard to discern: its painstakingly detailed examination of cultural and linguistic difference are less easily translatable than the more international categories of gender roles, race and old age dealt with in the three comedies already mentioned. And its (seemingly) non-consensual view of French society jars with two of the main types of French film that find distributors - and an audience eager to acquire this kind of cultural capital - in the UK: the postmodern conceits of Beineix and Besson (the Forum des Halles genre), or the literary and nostalgic mode of *Jean de Florette, Manon des Sources* and *Cyrano de Bergerac*, with the exportable "Frenchness" located in a mythical past, rendered all the more particular and authentic, and, paradoxically, in tune with a *national* identity, for being regional (the genre of France as theme park for the English middle-classes).

The premise - and humour - of *La Vie est un long fleuve tranquille* lie precisely in a non-unified France or Frenchness. As Pierre Bourdieu notes, the system of the social stratification of taste produces effects which tend to disguise the very existence of that system and that struggle.[2] In *La Distinction*, the habitus is seen as the source of the practices - both classifying and classifiable - in which socially positioned individuals engage in everyday life, providing them with a matrix of perceptions and assessments acquired through learning, apprenticeship, and primary socialisation in the home, and thus constituting the whole represented social world, the space of lifestyles.[3] "Distinction" is both the act of demarcation, the construction of meaning and

---

[2] P. Bourdieu, *La Distinction: critique sociale du jugement*, Paris, Minuit, 1979, p.280.

[3] Ibid, p.190.

value through difference, and also the means by which some judgements of taste can be asserted as superior, more valid, more "distinctive" than others. Thus we take part in the game and are taken in by it, and the struggles between high, middlebrow and low culture are in fact objectively complicit with one another: *on est tous embarqués*. *La Vie*, in fact, is almost like a primer for Bourdieu's work, a rendering visible of his categories through its meticulously detailed realist *mise en scène* and narrative oppositions.

The names of the two families are themselves rich in connotations: the Le Quesnoy (prestige of the article, pun on Lecanuet, the French bourgeois provincial politician par excellence); the Groseille ("le gros et le gras, gros rouge, gros sabots, gros travaux, gros rire, grosses blagues, gros bon sens, plaisanteries grasses").[4] Their social spaces, individual identities, habitus, stare across a chasm (seemingly) impenetrable to each other, although they rely on their *relation* with the other for self-definition. One of Bourdieu's fundamental demarcations is that generated by the "aesthetic disposition", the capacity to bracket off material urgencies and practical goals, in turn generated by the ability to withdraw from economic necessity. It is on the primacy of form over function, leading to the denial of function, that high or legitimate taste asserts itself. (The Groseilles' photograph of a seascape is of a beautiful thing rather than having beautiful form; the tackiness and gaudiness of their decor is part of the seeking of big effect at a small price that characterises the "taste of necessity").[5]

Thus "taste of necessity" and "taste of luxury" can be mapped out across binary oppositions such as that between popular outspokenness and highly censored language. Mme Groseille's colourful *jurons* clash with the archaisms of M. Le Quesnoy("tu vas vite en besogne", "voire"), particularly visible or

---

[4] Ibid, p.199.

[5] Ibid, p.442.

audible at their encounter, when she ironically echoes his "préférable". The family's educational capital and investment in it (a *caisse d'épargne* other than financial) means that the language of the dictation class (mocked in the final cut of the scene) is theirs and not the Groseilles', as well, paradoxically, as that of Momo's English lesson (one has only to recall Claude Duneton's *Je suis comme une truie qui doute*[6] for a confirmation of the infiltration of middle-class values into the materials and practice of foreign-language teaching). Similarly, the agitation, bluster, grimaces and gesticulations of the Groseille household clash with the slowness and impassivity which signify elevation *chez les* Le Quesnoy, particularly the father (bourgeois speech as the right to take one's time and other peoples).[7]

Food and the body are the important other sites of opposition, between quantity and quality, belly and palate, matter and manners, substance and form. At the table, the convivial indulgence of the Groseilles, the emphasis on being in the present, contrast with the ethics and aesthetics of sobriety of the Le Quesnoys, in which the meaning and primary function of consumption are denied. "Comme c'est joliment présenté!" declares Madame Le Quesnoy to Momo at the sight of a dish bedecked with a bunch of parsley and contained in the coveted silver. Bernadette's spilling of the soup thus acquires colossal dramatic status. Even the visible bottle of Ricard in the Groseille flat is explained by Bourdieu as part of popular taste, in so far as it is both strong and copious.[8] (Incidentally, the significance of the *riz au lait* at the Le Quesnoy household is more to do with the infantilisation of the sons and the denial of their sexuality/bodies than with social stratification, since it is a fairly classless children's treat). Tastes are consequently *embodied* differently, in the sheer

---

[6] Paris, Seuil, 1976.

[7] *La Distinction*, p.241.

[8] Ibid, p.211.

contrast of physicalities between most members of the two families. For the Groseille women, while there may be an ideal hairstyle, there is really no "ideal" body to aspire to, and consequently, no embarrassment or timidity with obesity. As Bourdieu observes: "la part des femmes qui ont une taille normalisée supérieure à la taille modale croît très fortement quand on descend dans la hiérarchie sociale".[9]

However, *La Vie est un long fleuve tranquille* is a narrative film, and so partakes in a dynamic structure of equilibrium and disequilibrium followed by resolution, a new equilibrium. This raises the question of value, the position taken with regard to the old equilibrium, and what sort of new order emerges after the disruption of the "middle section". As with Chatiliez' second feature, *Tatie Danielle*, in which the position the audience is invited to take up vis-à-vis the cantankerous and diabolical old woman is undecidable to say the least, *La Vie* poses many problems. The Le Quesnoy household is by the end in chaos, with their dining table come to resemble that of the Groseilles, and one son about to make a *tartine de ketchup*, but the perspective on this is by no means clear. Are the Groseilles to be seen as the repositories of some "popular" values, refusing integration into the social game and the goals it pursues, or are they complicit with it by the mere fact of taking part and consuming? How does their racism relate to this evaluation?

For some critics and scholars, popular and mass culture provide a rich potential of resistant readings to dominant or hegemonic ideological forms. One of the leading exponents of this "alternative semiotic"[10] of private resistance is John Fiske, who in *Television Culture* maps out the opposition between "ideology" and "popular pleasures" via terms such as: meanings and physical sensations, depth and surface, subjectivity and the physical body,

---

[9] Ibid, p.228.

[10] J. Fiske, *Television Culture*, London, Methuen, 1987, p.240.

130

responsibility and fun, sense and non-sense, unity and fragmentation, homogeneity and heterogeneity. For this he draws on the immensely suggestive work on dialogue and particularly carnival associated with Mikhail Bakhtin. Bakhtin's critique of the synchronic, system-based linguistics of Saussure was predicated on what he saw as the inherently context-bound dialogisation of utterances. Whereas dominant groups seek to make the sign uniaccentual and endow it with a classless and eternal character, through, say, a standard language or authoritarian discourse, the social reality of language means that we are not complete beings or isolated speakers but see ourselves through the mirror of others' words, the competing languages of society are within us. In the works of Rabelais, Bakhtin sees an expression of millennial forms of popular, marketplace, oppositional culture he calls the carnivalesque, bound up with natural cycles of change and renewal. For our purposes, we can home in on several of its characteristics:

- a valorisation of Eros, the life-force, myths of nature;
- a celebration of the grotesque, excessive body, and of the "material bodily lower stratum";
- the overturning of social power relationships;
- the valorisation of the obscene and of "market-place speech" in language;
- a rejection of social decorum and politeness;
- "the concept of an anticlassical aesthetic emphasising not harmonious beauty and formal unity but rather asymmetry, heterogeneity, the oxymoron and the *mésalliance*".[11]

Carnival therefore implies something richer than mere amusement or humour: rather, a whole transformation of the dominant representations of social relationships. Clearly, there is much that is suggestive here for the fun but also

---

[11] R. Stam, *Subversive Pleasures: Bakhtin, Cultural Criticism, and Film*, Baltimore, Johns Hopkins University Press, 1989, p.94.

the overall perspective of *La Vie est un long fleuve tranquille*. Bourdieu's focus on food, the body and language are thus "carnivalised". The degradation of the Le Quesnoy world is an overturning or uncrowning, not in terms of the actual social relationships but in a victory of the material level of earth, body and change over the high, abstract and serious, in short of joyful relativity over the bourgeois concept of the completed and atomised being. The kids and their ultimate rebellion in favour of (collective) bodily pleasures hold out the promise of regeneration and renewal. The static exchange involving Momo in fact produces dynamic change. The jocular language of the Groseilles around the dinner table that is the source of such pleasures recalls Bakhtin's description of banquet imagery in Rabelais, in which human labour ends in food, "in the swallowing of that which had been wrested from the world". No matter for now that the Groseilles' "labour" is petty criminality - at one point Momo is said to be "au travail" doing precisely that.

Elements of carnival are also present in the representation of those two central factors of social differentiation, the (grotesque) body and language. For Bakhtin, the "grotesque body ... is a body in the act of becoming. It is never finished, never completed; it is continually built, created, and builds and creates another body".[12] The protuberances of the female Groseilles denote a body that is open, transgressing itself, overcoming the confines between bodies, between the body and the world. In Rabelais, Bakhtin observes, the belly, bowels and the orifices of mouth, nose, anus, as boundaries between body and world, joyfully proclaim the openness of the self and of the future. It is thus not far fetched to see Mme Groseille, and to a lesser extent Roselyne, as the comic successors of Gargantua and Pantagruel. The repressions of "good manners" are overcome by the pleasures of bodily functions such as eating, belching, spitting (the assault on the TV *speakerine* says much for the

---

[12] M. Bakhtin, *Rabelais and His World*, translated by Helene Iswolsky, Cambridge, Mass., MIT Press, 1968, p.317.

Groseilles' capacity for resistance to dominant images and languages), having sex (the table at the Groseilles' becomes a site for sexual activity between Madame and Monsieur), and even singing (Mme Groseille's renditions contrasting here with the one moment of music and even "carnival" for the Le Quesnoy, the performance of "Jésus reviens", an incongruous juxtaposition which provides possibly the film's funniest moment). In *Tatie Danielle*, it should be noted, Chatiliez goes one better, with Tatie opening her bowels in the middle of her nephew's dinner party: in Bakhtin's reading of Rabelais, excrement is a joyful intermediary between the living body and dead, disintegrating matter that is being transformed into earth and manure.[13] The primacy of the visual is replaced to a large extent in the Groseilles' world by touch, taste and smell, as Roselyne says to Paul, "je ne me laverai pas pour garder ton odeur": in contrast, the first shot of the Le Quesnoys in the film features them washing. Even the involuntary muscle spasm of M. Le Quesnoy and Momo could be seen, as well as a comment on heredity and paternity, as a repressed memory of those aspects of comic performance in folk humour which simultaneously mimicked the acts of death, sexual intercourse and birth.[14] Similarly, the Groseilles' position in the social differentiation of language can be expressed in Bakhtinian terms, with the contrasts between the two families being expressed in terms of *heteroglossia*, a plurality of competing languages based on social position, "bounded verbal-ideological belief systems"[15] or points of view on the world, "the diverse perspectival languages generated by sexual, racial, economic and generational difference".[16] In *La Vie est un long fleuve tranquille*, we witness, not the portrayal of "reality" as

---

[13] Ibid, p.175.

[14] Ibid, pp.353-4.

[15] *Subversive Pleasures*, p.50.

[16] Ibid, p.43.

such, but the staging of the conflicts inherent in heteroglossia, a movement from the centripetal to the centrifugal. The linguistic crises provoked by the violation of social space in the film are examples of a breakdown in what Bakhtin calls *tact*, the "ensemble of codes governing discursive interaction", "determined by the aggregate of all the social relationships of the speakers, their ideological horizons, and finally, the concrete situation of the speaker".[17]

This approach is not without problems. Umberto Eco, for example, has characterised carnival as "*authorised* transgression".[18] Bakhtin himself warns against translating the folk humour of the end of the Middle Ages into the practices of bourgeois society. Satire and parody are often associated with bare negation, whereas folk humour also dealt with positive renewal. A dominant tone of *La Vie est un long fleuve tranquille* is that of irony and distance, as in the title itself and its relation to the explosion in the opening credits. Moreover, from the 17th century onwards laughter lost its universal, philosophical attributes to retreat into individuality, the mocking of private or socially typical vices, and festive life retreated into private spaces[19] (the cinema auditorium is of course in Western societies usually a strange amalgam of private and public). This is a salutary warning against the easy translations of critics such as Fiske, who can write: "In the postmodern world, style performs many of the functions of carnival. It is essentially liberating, acting as an empowering language for the subordinate."[20] Thus, Mme Groseille's changing hairstyle, however empowering it may be, would be a *direct* equivalent of the radical subversions of Rabelais's carnival. The difficulty with reading a mass media text such as *La Vie est un long fleuve tranquille* through Bakhtinian

---

[17] Ibid, pp.45-6.

[18] U. Eco, "The frames of comic 'freedom'", in U. Eco et al., *Carnival!*, Berlin, Mouton Publishers, 1984, pp.1-9.

[19] *Rabelais and His World*, pp.28, 66-7.

[20] *Television Culture*, p.249.

carnival lies partly in the fact that some fundamental aspects are missing, such as bisexuality and transvestitism, participation and the erasure of the boundary between spectator and performer, and especially the relationship to, and indeed union with, the community. In *La Vie est un long fleuve tranquille*, and in Western societies in general, there is no "community" to speak of. Indeed, the film features very little public space, apart from the transitional journeys made by Momo. The church and the hospital represent repressive order. It is no accident that only the scenes of the children at the river (with connotations of nature, transgression, generational renewal, inter-class sex), and in and outside Hamed's shop, create any sense of that public space, a point to which I shall return.

Nonetheless, apart from the Buñuel-like thrusts at religion, there is a certain undecidability about the role of satire in the film, and the position or perspective from which it is conducted. An opening is therefore left for a reading which sees a whole system being ridiculed, and so the notion of the "popular" as contained in Bakhtin provides a position from which the laughter can be understood. We might therefore say with Robert Stam, who has written on Bakhtin and film, that "The appeal of the mass media derives partially from their capacity for relaying, in a *degraded* manner, the distant cultural *memory* (or the vague future *hope*) of carnival".[21] What we have in *La Vie* is a simulacrum of the carnivalesque, eminently co-optable. The reason is that the carnivalesque elements coexist with a whole set of problematics concerning gender, and, most especially, consumer society and the identities it generates.

This is not the place to engage in an analysis of Bakhtinian theory and its relation to feminism. His theories have been seen to valorise difference within the self, and the concept of the material bodily lower stratum to be non-phallocentric, and he may even have something to say about infant socialisation

---

[21] *Subversive Pleasures*. p.92. My emphases.

and the mother as first interlocutor.[22] However, the notion of carnival does seem to elide questions of sexual difference and the power relations thus generated in society. Of course in *La Vie est un long fleuve tranquille*, these relations are interrogated by the Josette/Mavial subplot. Mavial as the town's obstetrician is in a sense the patriarchal controller of women's fertility, literally so in the case of Josette and the abortion he forced her to have. His mistreatment of Josette, punctuated by spasmodic sexual couplings connoting the mechanical rather than the carnivalesque, is finally punished by his symbolic castration, with him chair-bound, all social capital gone. The euphoria of the final scene, with a power relationship permanently reversed, is marked by the Maurice Jarre song about Paris ("Paris en colère"), that is, about a collective entity or identity, overcoming oppression. Josette's act is for all women. The mode of the subplot is decisively located in the domain not of carnival but of melodrama (a form historically linked to comedy) and soap opera, with their interrogations of women's desires and social position. Josette is both victim and then scheming villainess (positively valorised) from the moment she lifts her black widow-like veil at the funeral. This is thus almost another film from the narrative of the two families Josette's *crime passionnel* in fact sets in motion.

And yet gender relationships in the main narrative are marked by ambiguity rather than the black and white of melodrama. The impact of the revelation of true parenthood in fact centres on the two mothers, with motherhood clearly valorised and transcending the class divide. The reason for this seems to be that the mothers, the organising forces behind the two households, are thus the two organisers of consumption, and it is on patterns of consumption that the humour and, as far as it goes, the carnival of the film are predicated. The final bathos of the tin of ravioli on the Le Quesnoy table is due to the fact that the pressure of events has rendered the mother absent. As for Roselyne Groseille, she can be read either as empowered and

---

[22] Ibid, pp. 6, 22, 159-64 *passim*.

carnivalised sexual subject, using sexual conventions for her own ends in the manner of Madonna's star persona, or simply as part of a system of sexual exchange (it is hinted, though not explicitly stated, that she is on the game). And why, as far as the two switched children are concerned, was the choice made for a male child to be empowered and (upwardly) mobile, and the female child in the bourgeois household to be the one unable to face the world?

The problem lies not simply in the film's refusal in the central narrative to examine power relationships as regards gender, a lack made all the more visible for its dominance of the Josette/Mavial subplot. The film does not tackle power relations at all (outside the generations to be found within the family), and this is because the two families are constituted in relation to consumption rather than production. Given this, politics is in a stroke evacuated. It is thus much more appropriate for the Groseilles to be a *lumpen*, semi-criminal group as opposed to a working-class family with all the political traditions of the north of France as part of their culture ("des pauvres", as the film's vocabulary goes, rather than "des ouvriers"). Questions of taste and consumption, rather than of power and production, thus come to dominate.

The link between carnival and consumption made in the film renders the former term problematic. The Bakhtinian notion of the "popular", in whatever "degraded" form it survives here, was grounded in terms of the body, nature, and so on. The notion of "play" invoked, sometimes via Bakhtin, by so-called postmodernist commentators, is grounded in nothing, amounting to simply a free and supposedly "liberating" circulation of signifiers without signifieds, surfaces without depth, through style and image. It is a fine line indeed, and a fundamental problem in critical approaches to the mass media, between resistance and complicity. In these "postmodern" terms, then, the very "valuelessness" of *La Vie est un long fleuve tranquille* which is problematised and discussed in this chapter is in fact the key to its "meaning". It represents a world in which particular forms of consumption articulate particular personal identities. The encounter between the Le Quesnoys and the Groseilles simply generates new exchanges (notably the "selling" of Momo), and new patterns of consumption within both families. Or, to quote Baudrillard in *La Société de consommation*, the fate of all objects, including even identities constituted by image and lifestyle, is to become elements of exchange *in a semiotic system*: "c'est justement sur la relégation de leur valeur d'usage (et des 'besoins' qui s'y rattachent) que s'institue l'exploitation des objets comme différentiels, comme signes - niveau qui seul définit spécifiquement la consommation".[23] In this light, the flattened out, postmodern world of the withering signified[24] would indeed seem to be present in *La Vie est un long fleuve tranquille*, placing Chatiliez not so far from the worlds of Beineix and Besson. Like them, he began as a director of commercials, for products such as Eram and Free Time burgers, albeit parodically, but they gained their impact and popularity in that they were about other commercials and their rhetorics, representations of other representations. That absence of a public self, of a community, we noted in relation to carnival and the late twentieth century in the West, is in a sense resolved in the case of the postmodern consumer subject. Consumption is an act both public (the construction of a lifestyle as sign and communication) and private (an act of individual exchange). It is no accident that the quintessential public building of our era is the shopping mall. And yet, it remains highly debatable whether the relation between the two families is simply, in Baudrillard's or even Bourdieu's terms, to be understood as the absence of "real" differences and the reign of sheer differentiation in the terms of consumer society and of taste stratification: "c'est sur la perte des différences

---

[23] J. Baudrillard, *La Société de consommation*, Paris, Denoël, 1970. (Gallimard-Idées edition used, p.131).

[24] See D. Hebdige, "The Bottom Line on Planet One", in P. Rice and P. Waugh, eds, *Modern Literary Theory: a Reader*, London, Edward Arnold, 1989, pp.260-281; F. Jameson, "Postmodernism, or the Cultural Logic of Late Capital", *New Left Review*, 146, July-August 1984, pp.53-92.

que se fonde le culte de la différence".[25]

This potentially uneasy coexistence in the film between popular carnival and "postmodern" consumerism eventually encounters the film's narrative resolution, in a scene sandwiched between the chaos *chez les* Le Quesnoy and Josette's victory. The binaries of the narrative structure have presupposed at least the possibility of a third or middle term. Quite clearly, the *lumpen*, semi-criminal Groseilles and the rigidly Catholic Le Quesnoys are to be understood as Other to the vastly middle-class audience that attends cinemas in France. The two families induce both recognition and distance, the latter intensified by the ironic *mise en scène*. It is not the first occasion - one thinks for examples of the families in the serial *Chateauvallon* - that two world views that are out of time potentially prepare the way for a new consensus. In addition, we must not forget comedy's highly integrative practices, how the subversions and transgressions it contains are simply institutionalised generic requirements, how "the comic" so often implies a position of superiority for the spectator, bound up as it is with narcissism and an assertion of the ego's invulnerability vis-à-vis reality/castration, and how Freud's analysis of jokes stresses humour's power to include and exclude.[26]

This penultimate sequence of the film features Hamed the shopkeeper and Momo, and takes place first in the shop, then with Momo in transition to the Le Quesnoy home (it is punctuated by the farewell between Paul and Roselyne). Throughout the film Hamed has in fact been coded as a positive but especially "centred" character, the butt of the Groseilles' racism, "respectable" but not above a little fraud himself, hence the insurance scene. Perhaps the most significant scene in which he is involved is when his little boy's hair is dyed blonde by the Groseilles. This carnivalesque action has its

---

[25] *La Société de consommation*, p.127.

[26] S. Neale and F. Krutnik, *Popular Film and Television Comedy*, London, Routledge, 1990, pp. 3, 40, 75.

racist overtones, but is also characteristic of the film's readiness to demolish pieties. Moreover, father and son have radically different attitudes to it. This generational difference prepares the final scene with Momo. For both Hamed and Momo represent mobility and the crossing of cultural frontiers - one through migration, one through Josette's act - in contrast with the worlds of the Groseilles and the Le Quesnoys. Hamed calls Momo "mon frère", someone with whom to share a cross-cultural mint tea. Momo then sets off and reconstitutes his identify as a Le Quesnoy in the mirror by combing his hair, identity, unlike in the Lacanian mirror scene, figured here as non-unified, even a masquerade, just as the nation in the film is fragmented, represented in terms of liminality and frontiers, between the social worlds of the families, set in the far north of France. (This scene is in turn "mirrored" earlier in another transition for Momo: in contrast Bernadette is earlier shot in front of a mirror, *passively* fragmented by the wardrobe doors). The *mobility* of *Mo*mo, his brilliant mimicry evinced in the film, points the way forward to new identities based on hybridity, to a self knowingly constituted by difference and relations to others, plural and *disponible*.

Another narrative of this kind, Mark Twain's *Puddn'head Wilson*, relates the switching of two babies, one slave, one free, and through the category of the "human" condemns the arbitrary racial codifications of American society. Its mode is tragic, ending in decline from fortune to misfortune, freedom to servitude. In *La Vie est un long fleuve tranquille* a similar premise is used to suggest in comic and optimistic mode that the grounding for that stable, unitary self is no longer tenable, and, joyfully and powerfully, Momo manipulates the representative of the Law in that penultimate scene. In any case, part of the appeal of the story certainly lies in its fantasy of changing identity and biography. But what of the political implications of this? This centred third term of *disponibilité* and irony, suggested *Le Nouvel Observateur*, was a dream of cultural *métissage* for the middle-classes, for "Il y a des Groseille soixante-huitards dans le coeur des Le Quesnoy recentrés. Il y a des Le Quesnoy laïques (le peuple oui, mais derrière une vitre) dans la génération Mitterrand".[27] In this way, *La Vie est un long fleuve tranquille* is somewhat more consensual than it appears and than Chatiliez' claims in interviews might suggest. The carnival of May 1968, such as Raymond Aron described it in *La Révolution introuvable*, did indeed become the individualism of the 1980s and 1990s, and, according to some, now runs the risk of destabilising the individual subject to the point of its destruction.[28] The juxtaposition of the sometimes competing, sometimes complicit discourses of carnival and consumerism in *La Vie est un long fleuve tranquille* speak to us of the different political potentialities of both critical work on popular culture and of contemporary subjectivity in general.

---

[27] A. Schifres, "A la tienne Etienne", *Le Nouvel Observateur*, 25 March 1988, pp.42-4.

[28] See L. Ferry and A. Renaut, *La Pensée 68: Essai sur l'anti-humanisme contemporain*, Paris, Gallimard, 1985; G. Lipovetsky, *L'Ere du vide: Essai sur l'individualisme contemporain*, Paris, Gallimard, 1983.

10. FRANCE'S *MISSION CIVILISATRICE* IN AFRICA: FRENCH CULTURE NOT FOR EXPORT?

TONY CHAFER

Three main categories of justification have been offered for French colonial expansion in Africa in the last quarter of the nineteenth century. The first of these was economic in nature and sought to justify French colonialism in terms of guaranteeing France new markets for its products and the second sought to justify the possession of colonies in terms of the contribution that they were supposed to make to French *grandeur*.[1] The third type of justification offered for French colonialism was of a different nature however since it set out to justify French colonialism for the benefit it brought not only to France but also to those living under French colonialism. In essence, the argument put forward was this: French colonialism was neither brutal nor oppressive but, through its positive contribution to the materials and moral development of colonised peoples, was progressive, peaceful, "civilising".[2] The positive benefits of living under French colonial rule were that it brought an end to despotism and arbitrary rule: improved security; instruction and economic progress; in short, it meant a better life. The "civilising mission" was thus portrayed as integral to French colonialism.[3]

---

[1] For an analysis of the contribution Africa was supposed to make to French *grandeur* see in particular J. Chipman, *French Power in Africa*, Oxford, Blackwell, 1989.

[2] Cf. René Pleven in his opening speech at the Brazzaville conference in 1944: "Dans la grande France coloniale, il n'y a ni peuples à affranchir, ni discriminations raciales à abolir. Il y a des peuples qui se sentent Français et qui veulent prendre et à qui la France veut donner une part de plus en plus large dans la vie et les institutions démocratiques de la communauté française". Quoted in L. Gbagbo, *Réflexions sur la Conférence de Brazzaville*, Yaoundé, Editions Clé, 1978, p.65.

[3] Cf. J. Chipman, op. cit., p.13, comparing British and French colonialism: "In the British case, emphasis came to be based on political structures - the Westminster model - in the French instance, the message was primarily cultural - the *mission civilisatrice* - which held out

The presumed universality of French culture gave particular force to this self-appointed "mission", insofar as it also served as a justification for the policy of assimilation, with which it was closely linked. The term "assimilation" has been taken to mean different things. In its limited sense it can mean simply legalistic or political assimilation,[4] but in the broader sense it means educating colonised peoples so that they are imbued with French culture in every way: thus they must learn to speak the French language, adopt a French lifestyle and French ways of behaving and thinking. In short, when applied to Africa, it means Africans "learning to be French".[5] Essentially liberal and humanist in inspiration, the policy of assimilation was a product of the civilising mission insofar as, taken to its limit, it implied the creation of "black Frenchmen".

If this project was genuinely the aim of French colonialism and if the civilising mission is to be taken seriously, then one would expect that the diffusion of French culture through education would be considered a priority and that the colonial authorities would want to introduce full French metropolitan-style education as quickly as possible, even if in practice lack of funds meant that it could initially only be made available to a select few. In this chapter French colonial education policy in West Africa will be examined with a view to answering the question whether the creation of "black Frenchmen" was in fact a policy aim. The largest French colony in sub-Saharan Africa, the federation of *Afrique Occidentale Française (AOF)* has been

---

the promise of bringing together natives and Frenchmen into a common purpose".

[4] For an analysis of the different meanings of the term "assimilation", see M.D. Lewis, "One hundred million Frenchmen: the 'assimilation' theory in French colonial policy", *Comparative Studies in Society and History*, IV, 1962, pp.131-33.

[5] This was the title of a study of French education policy in West Africa, carried out by W.B. Mumford for the University of London Institute of Education in the 1930s, which was, in part, responsible for the widely held misconception in much of the English-speaking world that French education policy in black Africa was assimilatory: "The general impression, from conversation with the boys, is that they are French in all but the colour of their skin", W.B. Mumford, *Africans Learn to be French*, London, Evans Brothers, undated, pp.46-47.

chosen as especially appropriate for a study of official education policy since this was the only French colony in black Africa where education was under government control throughout the colonial period.[6] The period from 1903-1944 has been chosen because 1903 marks the end of the missions' control of education and the establishment of a unified, government-controlled education system in AOF, while 1944 is the date of the Brazzaville conference, which represents a watershed in the field of education as in many other areas of colonial policy, and can be seen with hindsight as marking the beginning of the period of French decolonisation in black Africa.[7] For this reason the period 1903-1944 represents the "golden age" of colonial rule in West Africa and is ideally suited to a study of colonial education policy.

Education Structures

The Government-General decree[8] of 1903, which set up the system, established a three-tier, pyramidal structure for education in AOF (see Figure 1). At the base of the pyramid were the elementary primary schools (this tier was further subdivided into "village" and "regional" schools[9]); at the next level were the upper primary schools and finally, at the top, were the federal schools, the function of which was to train technicians; clerks and lower-level administrative staff for the colonial administration and European firms; and

---

[6] In the other major French colony in black Africa, *Afrique Equatoriale Française*, most schools were mission-run during the colonial period.

[7] This was not however the intention of the participants, who included the following unequivocal statement in the preamble to their recommendations: "Les fins de l'oeuvre de civilisation accomplie par la France dans les Colonies écartent toute idée d'autonomie, toute possibilité d'évolution hors du bloc français de l'empire: la constitution éventuelle, même lointaine, de self-gouvernements dans les colonies est à écarter", quoted in L. Gbagbo, op. cit., p.70.

[8] *Journal Officiel du Sénégal*, 24 November 1903, p.678-81.

[9] Only the regional schools, situated in larger centres of population, offered the full cycle of primary education; village schools were opened in smaller centres of population where there was sufficient population to justify opening a school.

instituteurs and assistant teachers (*moniteurs*) for the village schools. Two important features of this system are worth noting here, the non-equivalence of the education pyramids in France and Africa and the lack of any secondary or higher education provision for Africans.

If we now turn to the curricula followed and the diplomas for which pupils were prepared, once again we find that they are distinguished by their non-equivalence with the French system. Elementary primary schools followed a watered down version of the metropolitan curriculum; for example, the village school curriculum consisted essentially of the basics of spoken French, arithmetic, an introduction to the metric system, some practical training and, in moslem areas, Arabic. The emphasis was on the vocational, practical nature of education, with a significant place being accorded to manual and agricultural work. The aim was constantly to "adapt" education to the African situation.[10] Partly this was a reaction against the type of education which had hitherto been provided by the missions, who were criticised for providing an education which was too bookish and academic, too "French" in nature and therefore not applicable to, or useful in, Africa. This was the main reason given by the colonial authorities for wresting control of education from the missions and placing it under official control in 1903.[11] Partly also, as we shall see, it was the product of a particular view about what was the most appropriate form of education for Africans. With respect to diplomas, all the qualifications for which pupils were prepared in AOF were local in nature and not therefore recognised in the metropole. The *Certificat d'Etudes Primaires Indigènes* was

---

[10] For a discussion of the ambivalence of the term "adapted education", see T. Chafer, "The Politics of Adapted Education in French West Africa, 1903-39", M.A. Dissertation submitted to the School of Oriental and African Studies, University of London, 1986, pp.6-9.

[11] D. Bouche, *L'Enseignement dans les territoires français de l'Afrique occidentale de 1817 à 1920*, Paris, Librairie H. Champion, 1975, p.497.

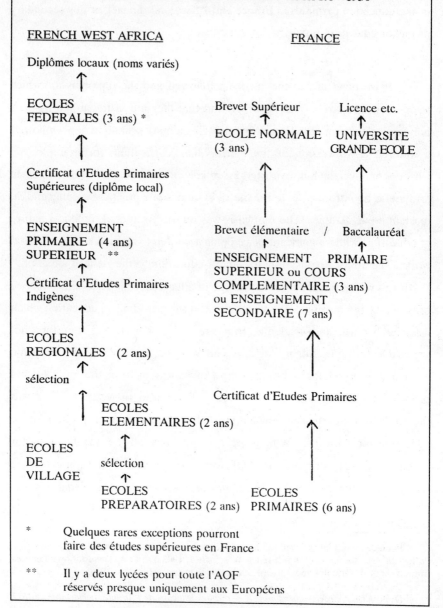

Figure 1: **COMPARISON OF EDUCATION PYRAMIDS IN FRANCE AND FRENCH WEST AFRICA - 1930**

FRENCH WEST AFRICA   FRANCE

Diplômes locaux (noms variés)
↑

ECOLES   Brevet Supérieur   Licence etc.
FEDERALES (3 ans) *   ↑   ↑
                                          ECOLE NORMALE   UNIVERSITE
   ↑   (3 ans)   GRANDE ECOLE

Certificat d'Etudes Primaires   ↑   ↑
Supérieures (diplôme local)
↑

ENSEIGNEMENT   Brevet élémentaire / Baccalauréat
PRIMAIRE   (4 ans)   ↑   ↑
SUPERIEUR   **   ENSEIGNEMENT   PRIMAIRE
   ↑   SUPERIEUR ou COURS
Certificat d'Etudes Primaires   COMPLEMENTAIRE (3 ans)
Indigènes   ou ENSEIGNEMENT
                                          SECONDAIRE (7 ans)
   ↑
                                                       ↑
ECOLES
REGIONALES   (2 ans)
   ↑
sélection   Certificat d'Etudes Primaires
   ↑   ECOLES
   | ELEMENTAIRES (2 ans)   ↑
           ↑
ECOLES
DE   sélection
VILLAGE   ↑
           ECOLES   ECOLES
           PREPARATOIRES (2 ans) PRIMAIRES (6 ans)

*   Quelques rares exceptions pourront
        faire des études supérieures en France

**   Il y a deux lycées pour toute l'AOF
        réservés presque uniquement aux Européens

146

basically just a *certificat de scolarité* which indicated that the pupil had completed her/his (usually his, since boys attended French schools far more than girls in Africa) elementary primary education and all the other qualifications awarded by French schools in AOF had no metropolitan equivalent. The reason for this is clear: if schools in Africa had awarded the same diplomas as metropolitan schools, Africans would have been able to use their qualifications to apply for posts in France and would also have been able to demand the same salaries and conditions of work in Africa as Europeans. By denying them access to French qualifications it was always possible to argue that, since they were less well qualified than Europeans, they should be paid less.

It is clear from the foregoing that the colonial authorities did not wish to introduce full metropolitan-style education into West Africa. But if this was not how they interpreted the "civilising mission", if they did not want to create "black Frenchmen", what then did they want to achieve by introducing French education into Africa?

Essentially, the French authorities pursued two separate but complementary objectives with regard to colonial education during the period with which we are here concerned. Firstly, it was to reach out to the masses and bring them within the orbit of French influence; this was the central aim of the village schools, which were renamed "rural schools" in 1930, when the emphasis on manual and agricultural work in their curriculum was also increased, in some cases reaching as much as half of the school day.[12] The second objective of French schools was to select and train the indigenous subordinate elite, loyal to France, which would staff in the first instance the colonial administration and schools and secondarily meet the needs of the

---

[12] For a study of the rural school, see D. Bouche, "L'école rurale en Afrique Occidentale Française", in *Etudes africaines offertes à Henri Brunschwig*, Paris, Publications de l'EHESS, 1982, pp.271-96.

European trading firms in Africa. This was an essential function of the school system in a non-settler colony such as AOF, where there were never sufficient European staff available to fill the lower-level posts. Using official documents and texts by French colonial educationists working in West Africa, French policy with regard to "mass" and "elite" education will now be examined.[13]

"Mass Education"

The first aim of French education in West Africa was to extend and reinforce French influence. Having completed the military conquest of Africa, the task of "pacification" was now to be completed by means of the "moral conquest"[14] of Africans. The instrument of this moral conquest was education. A 1924 official policy statement reveals clearly a key motive behind the French strategy with regard to education: "Il avait donc été créé dans les tribus, à côté des écoles coraniques, des écoles françaises d'apprivoisement... La pénétration à tout prix de toutes les races par l'école s'impose à notre oeuvre civilisatrice. En la circonstance l'école joue un rôle politique au moins aussi important que son rôle éducatif, et dans cet ordre d'idées politique et éducation se

---

[13] These terms are here placed in inverted commas because in neither case is the term strictly correct. "Mass" education had reached no more than one pupil in 40 by 1924 (*Journal de l'Afrique Occidentale Française* [JOAOF], 1 May 1924, p.311) and had reached no more than 5% of school-age children by the end of the Second World War. The term "elite" education is also misleading since it was never in fact intended that Africans should constitute a genuine elite, able to compete with the French on an equal basis for posts of direction and responsibility within the colonial administration; on the contrary, while they constituted an elite within their own society, they were always intended to be a subordinate elite vis-à-vis the French coloniser. The terms will nevertheless be used in the text from now on without inverted commas.

[14] G. Hardy, Inspector of Education in AOF from 1912-19, published a book entitled *Une Conquête morale, L'enseignement en AOF*, Paris, A. Colin, 1917. Cf. also Cheikh Hamidou Kane's semi-autobiographical novel, *L'Aventure ambigue*, Paris, 10/18, 1961, p.47: "L'école étrangère est la forme nouvelle de la guerre que nous font ceux qui sont venus ..."

148

confondent".[15] Two points are worthy of mention here. Firstly, while the use of the word "apprivoiser" is linked in the text to "notre oeuvre civilisatrice", the preceding and following sentences betray the underlying aim of French education, which is to inculcate loyalty to France, to "tame" the African and make of him/her a docile political subject. Secondly, the educational role of the school, its "civilising mission", is clearly perceived as secondary to its *political* function of reinforcing French domination.

Linked to this first theme in official statements on colonial education is the concern to avoid the production of "déclassés". Partly this was the product of an understandable desire not to waste money training more school graduates than the westernised sector of the economy could absorb, but it also had a political motivation; school graduates who passed through the European education system frequently emerged from their schooling alienated from their own society; if they were then unable to find salaried employment which they felt was in keeping with their qualifications, they risked becoming disaffected and thus a potential source of social unrest and political discontent. The way of avoiding this was seen as the adaptation of school curricula so as not to uproot Africans from their own society. This was what lay behind the concept of adapted education, which in practice meant three things. Firstly, it meant adapting education to what was perceived as the lower level of intellectual development of the African:[16] this also of course helped to justify the provision of a non-academic education with a reduced intellectual content. Secondly, it meant adapting curricula to what were perceived by the colonial power as African needs. The priority was therefore to provide an education

---

[15] JOAOF, 1 May 1924, p.311. Cf. also p.326: "Elle (l'école) doit se garder tout d'abord de heurter de front les croyances et les coutumes de l'indigène. Elle essaie de l'apprivoiser en lui inspirant confiance et en lui témoignant de l'intérêt et de l'affection".

[16] Cf. G. Hardy's seven basic principles which guided French education policy in West Africa: "Mesurer l'extension de l'enseignement aux aptitudes actuelles et réelles de l'indigène...", op. cit., p.5.

that would bring immediate improvements in Africans' standard of living, which incidentally also of course provided further justification for the emphasis on vocational training, and particularly agricultural work, within the curriculum.[17] Thirdly, with regard to girls, it meant training them to be good housewives and mothers, for example by imparting basic notions of hygiene and giving them lessons in sewing and good housekeeping.[18] In sum, adapted education was to bring benefits to Africans through improvements in their standard of living and could thus be portrayed as contributing to the civilising mission, understood here not so much as the diffusion of French culture but rather as the spreading of western economic values and methods. It also of course brought benefits to the colonisers in terms of the increased revenue-earning potential of African producers and thus helped to justify the provision of education in the eyes of a cash-strapped colonial administration.

Thirdly, education was seen as a means of integrating Africans into the cash economy and improving their agricultural productivity. The stereotype of the "lazy native" was, and remains, an enduring western image of Africans and an underlying assumption in the French approach to education in Africa was thus the idea that education should be education for work in order to "make the natives more productive". The following song, composed in 1915 for use in primary schools by Georges Hardy, the Director of Education in AOF, is evidence of this attitude among colonial educationists:

---

[17] Cf. A. Sarraut, *La Mise en valeur des colonies françaises*, Paris, Payot, 1923, p.94: "L'instruction, en effet, a d'abord pour résultat d'améliorer largement la valeur de la production coloniale...", Albert Sarraut was Minister of Colonies from 1920-24.

[18] Such an education was in fact singularly ill-adapted to women's needs in Africa, where many of them were farmers in their own right. The idea that women were first and foremost mothers and housekeepers owes more to French bourgeois prejudices than to an understanding of African realities.

"AU TRAVAIL!

Pour que notre Afrique soit riche,
Amis, mettons-nous au travail,
Remuons nos terres en friche,
Battons le fer, poussons le rail,

Refrain
Bruit des marteaux, ô bruit joyeux,
De Saint-Louis à Bingerville,
Va rappeler aux paresseux
Que seule la paresse est vile.

Moquons-nous de ceux qui rougissent
De travailler de leurs dix doigts;
Celui que ses mains enrichissent
Est plus noble que tous les rois.

Il faut que la terre d'Afrique
Sorte enfin de son long sommeil;
Qu'à l'atelier, dans ses boutiques,
Aux bougans, sonne le réveil."[19]

The emphasis in the village school was on manual, especially agricultural work. Against the background of the world economic crisis, this emphasis increased in 1930. As has already been mentioned, with the introduction of the *école rurale*, all schools were henceforth to have a *jardin scolaire* and up to half the timetable was to be given over to agricultural work. Academic standards and cultural goals - the "civilising mission" - were abandoned. The aim of the rural schools was unequivocally stated: "Il est à la fois hautement moral est franchement pratique. Pas de diplômes, pas de fausses promesses, pas d'ambitions démesurées. L'école est faite pour le village et par lui, elle répond à ses besoins... l'écolier aujourd'hui est le paysan, le pasteur ou l'artisan de

---

[19] Quoted in P. Désalmand, *Histoire de l'éducation en Côte d'Ivoire*, Abidjan, Eds. CEDA, 1983, p.413. One wonders what impact the first line of the second verse would have had in a class of fifty black children singing this song under the direction of an African teacher!

151

demain... il s'agit d'éduquer la masse pour la rapprocher de nous et transformer son genre de vie".[20] Three observations can be made at this point; firstly, the practical orientation of education is here given a moral justification; secondly, the role of schools as an instrument for the extension of French influence is underlined; and thirdly, the reference to transforming the way of life of the mass of the population here has nothing to do with the civilising mission and imbuing them with French culture, but means above all making them into better producers of cash-earning crops. From the point of view of the coloniser this also has the advantage of transforming them into taxpayers and potential consumers of French goods.

Finally, and especially in moslem areas, French schools were seen as part of a strategy for countering the influence of Islam. Initially afraid of the spread, and potential power, of Islam, the French colonial authorities sought to provide an alternative education to that offered in the Koranic schools. They soon realised, however, that they were in no position to compete and decided instead to seek a *modus vivendi* with Islam by attempting to win moslem leaders over to the French cause in the hope of indirectly influencing the people through their leaders.[21] The creation of the *médersa* was the product of this strategy and this will be examined in a little more detail in the following section.

In sum, an analysis of official pronouncements on education during this period reveals that, with respect to mass education, the civilising mission was at best a subordinate and very long-term aim and at worst forgotten altogether. Given the enormous cost of providing western-style education for all in a country as underdeveloped in western economic terms as AOF and given the

---

[20] J. Brévié, "L'Enseignement massif et l'école indigène", *Bulletin de l'Enseignement de l'Afrique Occidentale Française*, 74, 1931, p.4.

[21] See C. Harrison, *France and Islam in West Africa, 1860-1960*, Cambridge, Cambridge University Press, 1988, pp.64-65.

limited financial resources at the disposal of the colonial administration in French West Africa, this is not unduly surprising. What of elite education however? Since the numbers involved were far smaller and costs were consequently much easier to control, one might expect that the "civilising mission", in the sense of imparting of French culture to Africans through the provision of full metropolitan-style education would be more in evidence as an aim with respect to elite education. In the next section we shall examine to what extent this was actually the case.

"Elite" education

The central aim of elite education in French West Africa was to select and train an indigenous French-speaking subordinate elite, loyal to France and able to serve the colonial power by meeting the staffing needs of the colonial administration.[22] It took place in the upper primary schools, situated in the main administrative centres of AOF, and in the federal schools, which were run by the Government-General and all of which were initially situated along the coast strip of Senegal, at Saint-Louis, Gorée and Dakar.[23]

The precondition for selection into this elite was competence in the French language, but this was not of itself a sufficient condition. The other criteria for selection, once this precondition had been met, were of an economic and political, rather than intellectual, nature. The adoption of a strict manpower approach to elite education was intended to ensure that the size of the French-educated elite was geared closely to the needs of the job market. The motivation for this was however not purely economic:

---

[22] As A. Sarraut made clear: "(l'instruction) doit, parmi la masse laborieuse, dégager et dresser les élites de collaborateurs qui, comme agents techniques, contremaîtres, ... employés ou commis de direction, suppléeront à l'insuffisance numérique des Européens", op. cit., p.95.

[23] They were called federal schools because they were financed and controlled by the Government-General and recruited students from throughout the federation of AOF.

"... puisque nos moyens actuels ne nous permettent pas encore d'atteindre la masse et restreignent nos efforts à une minorité, choisissons judicieusement cette minorité. Faisons une sélection dès le début. Considérons l'instruction comme une chose précieuse qu'on ne distribue qu'à bon escient et limitons-en les bienfaits à des bénéficiaires qualifiés ...

Il convient donc tout d'abord d'inviter les classes dirigeantes à profiter les premières de notre enseignement. Aussi la scolarité revêt-elle un caractère obligatoire pour les fils de chefs et de notables... Le fils de chef et de notable, ou simplement de famille aisée, instruit dans nos écoles, fait rarement un déclassé".[24]

In other words, having admitted mass education was not a realistic objective and that there was thus a need to select those who would benefit from a French education, it was important that the beneficiaries be selected from those members of the traditional elite who were least likely to create problems for the colonial power and most likely to have an interest in becoming its political allies: "C'est sur elles que s'appuie notre autorité dans l'administration de ce pays, c'est avec elle surtout que nous sommes en constant rapport de service".[25] The higher up the educational pyramid one went, the more important political criteria, and particularly loyalty to France became.[26]

Having selected the candidates who were to be trained as members of the elite, the question arose as to what type of education and training they should receive. Once again, we find that the curricula in AOF schools were a watered-down version of those followed in their metropolitan counterparts. As

---

[24] JOAOF, 1 May 1924, pp.326-27.

[25] Ibid., p.327.

[26] For example, the form on which African teachers applied for promotion included a section entitled "Appréciation du Commandant de Cercle" [the local head of the French colonial administration] which invited him to make comments on the teacher's "1) Manière générale de servir; 2) Tenue; 3) Habitudes sociales; 4) Rapports avec les représentants de l'Administration locale", Archives Nationales de l'AOF (AAOF) 046/31.

was the case with mass education, the emphasis was on adapting curricula to local needs and to the local situation. The curricula were not therefore the same as in French equivalent institutions and the diplomas they awarded were not recognised in France. The reasons for this were twofold. On the one hand, allowing Africans access to metropolitan qualifications would have meant that they could demand equality of pay and status with Europeans. This would have put into question the very foundation of the colonial system, based as it was on the fundamental assertion of the inequality between Africans and Europeans, since there would no longer be any reason for having separate *cadres* for African and French staff, with the higher, executive *cadre* reserved for Europeans, nor would there any longer be any justification for paying Africans far lower salaries than their European colleagues.[27] Being obliged to pay Africans the same as Europeans would also have had unmanageable cost implications for the AOF public budget, which the colonial administration was obliged by law to balance.

The principal school for training the French-speaking African elite was the Ecole William-Ponty, which was situated on the island of Gorée, just off Dakar, for most of the period with which we are here concerned.[28] Reserved for boys, its three sections - for teachers, administrators and medical staff - trained most of the professionally qualified African personnel recruited by the colonial service in black Africa. It has been called the "Oxford of French West

---

[27] During this period, French staff were appointed to the *cadre européen*, later renamed the *cadre supérieur*, while Africans were appointed to a separate *cadre indigène*, later renamed the *cadre secondaire*. Pay rates and conditions of service were, needless to say, far better in the former than in the latter. Cf, also R. Schachter Morgenthau, *Political Parties in French-speaking West Africa*, Oxford, Clarendon Press, 1964, p.32: "French colonisers did not produce an obvious 'colour line', as did the British. Instead, Frenchmen drew a 'cultural line' not very different from the 'colour line'."

[28] The Ecole William-Ponty was initially called the Ecole Normale de Saint-Louis and was situated at Saint-Louis. It moved to Gorée in 1913 and was renamed shortly afterwards. In 1938 it moved again, to Sébikotane, near Dakar.

Africa",[29] but this is misleading since the curriculum of the school was certainly not comparable in either content or level to that of an institution of higher education. Indeed the diploma it awarded was almost certainly below the standard of the *baccalauréat* and may have been equivalent to no higher than the metropolitan *brevet élémentaire*.[30] The centrepiece of the curriculum was the French language. Other subjects studied included theoretical and practical morals, arithmetic, geometry, basic physical and natural sciences applied to hygiene and agriculture, the history and geography of AOF and basic notions of French history and geography, drawing, singing and manual work.[31] Even in this elite training school the importance of agricultural work continued to be stressed, at least in theory. However, there were considerable practical difficulties involved in turning this into reality because of the cramped conditions at the school and the headteacher admitted in 1912 that the emphasis on agricultural work was maintained essentially for moral reasons, to encourage students to perceive manual and agricultural work as just as important as "le travail de l'esprit".[32]

Apart from the Ecole William-Ponty the only other paths to elite status in French West Africa were the two *lycées* at Saint-Louis and Dakar. However, these were reserved almost exclusively for Europeans and in any case did not prepare pupils for the baccalaureat, but for a special colonial equivalent, the *brevet de capacité coloniale*.[33] There was also a brief experiment, introduced

---

[29] R. Schachter Morgenthau, op. cit., p.12.

[30] P. Sabatier, *Educating a Colonial Elite: The William Ponty School and its Graduates*, University of Chicago, unpublished PhD Thesis, 1977, pp.77-78.

[31] JOAOF, 1 May 1924, p.349.

[32] Headteacher's report, 1911-12, AAOF, J54/2.

[33] The *brevet de capacité coloniale* was equivalent in standard to the *baccalauréat* and could be exchanged in France, on payment of a small fee, for the *baccalauréat*. Since at most two West Africans a year obtained the *brevet*, the number who obtained the *bac* would have been even smaller since only those few who won government grants for study in France would have

in 1920, which involved sending a small number of the highest-ranking Ponty graduates to the *Ecole Normale* at Aix-en-Provence, where they followed a metropolitan curriculum. The programme was however terminated after only four years, apparently largely for political reasons.[34] Three other *écoles normales* were created, in addition to William-Ponty, in the 1930s. Two of these were *écoles normales rurales* which were created to train teachers for the new "rural schools". With the renewed emphasis on adapting education to a rural milieu, there was a clear need for a different, less academic form of teacher-training and the *écoles normales rurales* were intended to meet this need. The third, the *Ecole Normale des Jeunes Filles* was created at Rufisque in 1938, primarily in order to train teachers, although the standard was lower than at William-Ponty and additional courses were given in sewing, cooking, childcare and other aspects of housekeeping.[35] The only other route to elite status in French West Africa was the *Ecole Technique Supérieure*, which opened in Bamako in 1940[36] and from which the first students graduated in 1944.

In sum, as was the case with mass education, the aim of elite education was not to produce "black Frenchmen" but loyal servants of French colonialism. This may seem surprising, given the well-known example of a figure such as Léopold Sédar Senghor, who had received a French academic education, including following a course of higher education in France, and was considered

---

been able to exchange their *brevet* for the *bac*. Furthermore, as P. Sabatier, op. cit., pp.453-54, notes, the range of possibilities for study in France was extremely limited; by the mid-1930s, five Africans had studied veterinary medicine at Alfort, two were preparing to become military doctors, one was preparing the entry exam for the Ecole de Travaux Publics and another was at the agricultural institute in Algeria.

[34] Ibid., p.88. It seems that the French were afraid, amongst other things, of the influence that contact with radical political ideas might have on the Aix students.

[35] "L'Ecole de Rufisque est une école normale professionnelle et ménagère. Il s'agit de former de bonnes ménagères, des auxiliaires pour l'enseignement des filles", AAOF, 2G39/92.

[36] JOAOF, 14 April 1939, p.499.

a successful product of French assimilation policy. In fact, however, Senghor was the only African from sub-Saharan Africa to pursue a purely literary education on a government grant[37] before the Second World War, and government policy towards elite education was intended, as we have seen, to ensure that the example of Senghor remained exceptional.

Cultural objectives were not however completely abandoned. In the 1930s colonial educationists began to put forward the idea of creating a new, *métisse*, Franco-African culture as an alternative to assimilation. The abandonment of the idea of creating "black Frenchmen" had a sound practical justification: if Africans became too "French", they would be less effective in dealing with their own peoples as the cultural distance between them would be too great. The answer was therefore to aim to develop a Franco-African culture among the French-speaking African elite. This was to be achieved by encouraging Africans to study their own societies using the methods they had learned in French schools, thus creating a synthesis of French and African culture. However, many Africans saw this, at the time, as a way of diluting the French curriculum so as to keep them in a position of permanent subordination. This point is made, somewhat patronisingly, in an official report on the Ecole William-Ponty in 1941, the author of which then goes on to justify the concept of Franco-African culture:

"Leurs voeux allaient vers une assimilation totale: *mêmes diplômes* - que de campagnes en ce sens dans l'école, où il y eut de malencontreux essais, dans la presse indigène, dans la presse métropolitaine même - *mêmes soldes, ... même vie extérieure*, mêmes préoccupations vestimentaires ou mécaniques et, pour ceux qui étaient capables de s'en soucier, *même vie intérieure*.

Il fallait s'efforcer de leur barrer cette route qui n'était pour eux qu'une impasse, qui ne pouvait les conduire qu'à la constitution

---

[37] J.G. Vaillant, *Black, French and African. A Life of Léopold Sédar Senghor*, Cambridge (Mass), Harvard University Press, 1990, p.62.

158

d'une société sans tradition, sans règles, sans équilibre; il fallait les amener à refuser une promotion facile hors de leur propre société pour vivre au contraire avec elle, en elle, pour en être le ferment; être non plus une caricature de tête mais la vraie tête d'un vrai corps".[38]

The idea was thus the selective transmission of certain aspects of French culture to Africa, to impart to Africans those aspects of the French way of life which would help them to improve their own lives, but without uprooting them from their past, without provoking a break with their own traditions. This, the author of the report continued, was relatively easy when it was simply a question of training auxiliaries as agents of French rule: "il était à peine besoin qu'ils fussent intelligents",[39] but it was quite another matter once it was a question of training *cadres* who could teach the new ways and promote them by example among their own people. This could not be achieved through books, or solely through classes, however brilliantly executed, but only through education in the broadest sense, by means of sustained contact with carefully chosen whites from whom they would learn by talking and by example. This approach, the author believed, would lead to "l'imprégnation' française des élèves, à leur conquête morale, à la création d'une culture qui soit vraiment franco-africaine".[40] The cultural objective of William-Ponty was thus to promote the idea of Franco-African culture by training teachers who could pass on elements of French culture to their African pupils without uprooting them from their own society. The creation of two *écoles normales rurales* in the 1930s should also be seen in the context of this strategy.[41] The promotion of

---

[38] Rapport statistique annuel sur le fonctionnement de l'école William Ponty 1940-41, AAOF, 2G41/81, pp.5-6.

[39] Ibid., pp.6-7.

[40] Ibid., p.7.

[41] A. Charton, "Rôle social de l'enseignement", 1934, quoted in ibid., p.8.

the idea of Franco-African culture was not however accepted by many students, who saw it as part of a deliberate plan to keep Africans in a subordinate position by denying them access to French culture and thus the possibility of gaining equal status with the French.[42] After the war Africans were to demand, and obtain, moves towards the introduction of metropolitan curricula and diplomae in AOF.

This was not the only difficulty encountered by the colonial authorities in implementing their strategy for elite education in AOF. However much they may have wanted to avoid disrupting African society and creating *déclassés* through the introduction of French education, this was in practice unavoidable. The very fact of the French colonial presence, which introduced foreign role models, new modes of social organisation and ways of working, was itself disruptive of African society. Furthermore, education provided an alternative means of social advancement to that provided within traditional society and this in itself had a destabilising impact on indigenous society. Initially, the colonial authorities had attempted to recruit the sons of traditional chiefs and notables into French schools and train them as loyal intermediaries who would liaise between the French and their own people. When this strategy had proved inadequate because of the failure to attract sufficient members of the traditional elite to French schools, the colonial authorities who were increasingly concerned about the destabilising effect of French education on indigenous society, tried to bolster the position of members of the traditional elite vis-à-vis the French-educated elite by adopting a more conciliatory attitude towards them and enhancing their position within the colonial system.[43]

---

[42] Cf. P. Sabatier, op. cit., pp.129-30.

[43] For example, chiefs played a key role in the census, on which the administration largely based its tax demands. They also collected taxes on behalf of the French and had wide-ranging powers in the implementation of the system of justice. These functions, which they carried out on behalf of the administration, meant that the chiefs became identified with the coloniser. Giving them greater powers therefore had the opposite effect to that desired since it alienated them from their own people and undermined their position of authority within their own

The other main problem confronting the colonial authorities in French West Africa at this time was how to counter the growing influence of Islam. Having, as we have seen, given up the idea of trying to compete with the Koranic schools and in an attempt to limit the spread of Islam, the French seem to have decided from an early date to come to some sort of accommodation with Islam. A key element of this strategy was the *médersa*[44], which was conceived as an instrument of *rapprochement* between the French authorities and moslem leaders, through which the former hoped to gain some influence over the latter. In some *médersas* they even went so far as to abandon teaching in French, something which in most cases would have been considered wholly unacceptable, and used Arabic as the language of instruction in an attempt to encourage moslems to attend. The civilising mission was not entirely forgotten however, since the official texts creating the first *médersas* in French West Africa stated as one of their aims "to give an elite of young moslems proper views on the civilising role of France in Africa".[45]

The "civilising mission": Explanations for Failure

We suggested at the beginning of this chapter that the civilising mission was essentially liberal and humanist in inspiration. It has also been linked to the French revolutionary, republican tradition and the idea of bringing fraternal help to oppressed peoples.[46] It was subsequently presented by some as a justification for French colonialism. As we have seen however, the civilising mission became in practice something much more prosaic and conventional. In part it fell victim to the racial stereotype of the African as the "lazy native"

---

society. Cf. A. Auchnie, *The "Commandement Indigène" in Senegal*, 1919-47, University of London, unpublished PhD thesis, pp.395-97.

[44] The term comes from the Arabic for school, "madrasah".

[45] Quoted by C. Harrison, op. cit., p.62.

[46] W.B. Mumford, op. cit., p.27.

who had to be taught to work, although even without this racial stereotyping, there was an economic need, given the French government's insistence on the colonies paying their own way, to integrate Africans into the cash economy. Here, the civilising mission seems to have meant making Africans more "productive". Another stereotype was that of the quarrelsome native in a state of endemic conflict. In this context the civilising mission had nothing to do with education but was synonymous with the "colonial peace", with the coloniser bringing security and law and order to Africa. Finally, there was the image of the heathen, barbaric African, which served as a justification for missionaries to "civilise" Africans by converting them to Christianity.

The different interpretations of the "civilising mission" reflect the diversity of interests and of ideological and political perspectives of French colonialists. They were far from being a united, homogeneous bunch. Administrators, traders, planters, military men, teachers, missionaries, these people did not share the same interests, did not have the same ideological and political outlook and did not therefore hold the same views as to the reason for the French colonial presence in Africa. As a result they did not share the same view of France's "civilising mission"; indeed, their conception of the civilising mission was coloured by their own motivation for being there. This is partly a result of the fact that colonialism was not a central feature of French nationalism at this time; despite the rhetoric of the civilising mission, the government was not really interested in colonial questions and did not give a lead. Those colonial administrators who genuinely believed in the value of French education in Africa therefore had first of all to fight a battle against those who thought that the provision of an intellectual education of any sort, however watered down, was a waste of time because of African primitivism.[47]

---

[47] "Ceux-là (les ennemis de l'enseignement indigène en général) estiment qu'enseigner le français aux indigènes, c'est ouvrir la porte à toutes les révoltes et transformer notre colonisation en de perpétuelles saturnales", G. Hardy, op. cit., p.183.

They also had other priorities when considering the most appropriate education policy to pursue, which had nothing to do with the rhetoric of the civilising mission propounded by some politicians and colonial activists in France. They were concerned, firstly, with the question of how to balance the books. Education, like every other part of the colonial service, had to pay its way; since education could be made more "profitable" in economic terms through the creation of *jardins scolaires*, which in practice often bore a greater resemblance to farms than to gardens, it had a role to play here. Another priority for colonial administrators was to recruit loyal Africans to staff the lower levels of the administration. Finally, they were concerned with the question of how, as a tiny European minority in a non-settler colony, to maintain social and political stability.

These factors, together with the fact that many of those directly involved in France's colonial project did not share the essentially liberal perspective of the civilising mission, are a necessary part of any explanation for the failure of France's civilising mission in Africa.

It emerges from the above that the idea of the civilising mission remained a *leitmotif* of statements justifying the French colonial presence in Africa. A major problem however was that there was no consensus with regard to what the civilising mission actually meant in practice and that the meaning it was given varied according to the political perspective of those who used the term. It is also clear that the civilising mission, in the widely accepted sense of the export of French culture to other parts of the world, was not an objective of colonial education policy in West Africa. Was the civilising mission in this latter sense therefore an idea which, as one commentator has suggested, was ultimately confined largely to school textbooks, where it became part of a strategy for the creation of an "imperial mentality" among a French population which did not always accept French colonial ambitions?[48]   There is undoubtedly some truth in this, but there is also perhaps another dimension to the civilising mission. Even if it did not actually mean exporting French culture to Africa and creating "black Frenchmen", nevertheless French colonisers did want Africans to *feel* French in some way: if they did not want to produce *assimilés*, they did want to produce *évolués*. The latter were preferred because they had not made the whole journey down the road to the acquisition of French culture, they had not crossed the threshold into the danger zone where they might challenge French power and demand equality with Europeans. The aim was *rapprochement* and influence, *not* integration and it was from this that the idea of Franco-African culture largely stemmed: "... il fallait franciser les élèves sans en faire des Français".[49]

However, if France was not prepared to export its culture, there was no danger of some kind of cultural void being created in large parts of French West Africa by the disintegration of indigenous African society and cultures. The government's own census figures show that moslems had increased in number between 1924 and 1936 from 3.9 million to 6.2 million. Ironically therefore the great beneficiary in cultural terms of France's civilising mission in West Africa has been not French culture but Islam.

---

[48] M. Semidei, "De l'Empire à la décolonisation à travers les manuels scolaires français", *Revue Française de Science Politique*, XVI, 1966, p.85.

[49] P. Désalmand, op. cit., p.249.

164

11. ETHNIC MINORITIES AND THE MASS MEDIA IN FRANCE

ALEC. G. HARGREAVES

Following large-scale immigration in the post-war period, Third World ethnic minorities are now an established part of French society. Yet while often seen in news reports and current affairs coverage, in other respects immigrants and their families feature comparatively little in the mass media. As Susan Hayward has observed, "apart from the news [...], social representation on French television is almost exclusively *white* middle-class. There is no working-class soap for example. [...] So-called racial minorities are very much *not* in evidence."[1] My purpose in the present chapter is three-fold: firstly, to consider briefly the dominant images of ethnic minorities which do appear in the media, secondly, to illustrate the underlying marginalisation of the immigrant population, and finally, to offer a critical review of recent attempts to reverse this trend.

DOMINANT IMAGES

Immigration came to occupy a major position in news and current affairs coverage during the 1980s, notably with the rise of Jean-Marie Le Pen's *Front National* (FN). The relationship between these two phenomena has yet to be fully explored. Was the rise of Le Pen responsible for this preoccupation with immigration, or was his emergence actually aided by prior media coverage of the issue? Were the media right to give him a platform from which to peddle his anti-immigrant programme, or should he have been starved of what, in another context, Margaret Thatcher called the oxygen of publicity?

---

[1] Susan Hayward, "Television: a *Transparence* on Modern France?", in Martyn Cornick (ed.), *Beliefs and Identity in Modern France*, Loughborough, ERC and ASMCF, 1990, p.103, author's emphases.

While ethnic minorities were given less prominence prior to the 1980s, such media coverage as there was certainly helped to create generally negative images of the immigrant population. A content analysis by Pierre Seguret of five daily newspapers for the year 1978 found that most references to immigrants occurred in what the French press call *faits divers*, as against *articles d'informations générales*. The latter concern major public issues (politics, economics, etc.), whereas the former generally recount exceptional events in the lives of private individuals. Most of the *faits divers* mentioning immigrants in Seguret's year-long sample were crime stories, and articles where immigrants were the victims were heavily outnumbered by stories casting them as the aggressors. While attention was seldom drawn to the ethnicity of immigrants from European countries, the origins of Third World immigrants involved in criminal activities were often mentioned. The majority of the *articles d'informations générales* dealing with foreign residents concerned various types of assistance rendered by the French state or private individuals; the working lives of immigrants and their sizeable contribution to the French economy were given very little coverage. Criminals and *assistés*: these were the principal images of Third World immigrants which the average reader was likely to derive from French newspapers in the late 1970s.[2]

The most important shift in the 1980s was what we may term the islamicisation of immigrants by the French media. The majority of immigrants from Third World countries had, of course, been Muslims all their lives, but it is only during the last decade that the media have chosen to highlight this point.[3] The islamicisation of media coverage dealing with immigration has coincided with the politicisation of Islam both domestically and in the world at

---

[2] Pierre Seguret, "Images des immigrés et de l'immigration dans la presse française", unpublished *thèse de 3e cycle*, Montpellier, Université Paul Valéry, 1981.

[3] Constant Hamès, "La Construction de l'islam en France: du côté de la presse", in *Archives en sciences sociales des religions*, vol. 68, no. 1 (July-September 1989), pp.79-92.

large. Internationally, a resurgent Islam was widely portrayed as a threat to the West following the Iranian revolution of 1979. At home, growing numbers of Muslim immigrants, who until the mid-1970s had been regarded as temporary residents, decided to settle in France with their families and began to create a substantial religious infrastructure. As Constant Hamès has observed,[4] all these forces converged symbolically for the first time in the early months of 1983, when the media gave extensive coverage to strikes by immigrant workers in the French car industry. While most of their demands were material rather than spiritual in nature, in some cases they included demands for workplace prayer-rooms,[5] and the Socialist Prime Minister of the day, Pierre Mauroy, claimed the strikers were being manipulated by outside religious forces (a clear allusion to the Khomeiny regime in Iran).[6] This incident came during the final stages of the campaign for the municipal elections of 1983, in which the FN became a serious electoral challenger for the first time. Mauroy's statement typified the way in which politicians from all sides of the political spectrum vied with each other to exploit xenophobic sentiments among the electorate. By far the main beneficiary of this process has been the FN, whose anti-immigrant propaganda plays upon precisely those images of the foreign population already stimulated by the media: feared as potential criminals and pilloried as a drain on the French economy at a time of recession, immigrants from Islamic countries are held by virtue of their religious beliefs to be a fundamental threat to the national identity of France. Anti-immigrant hysteria reached a peak during the so-called *affaire du foulard*, in which three girls from immigrant families in Creil were banned from a state school because they insisted on wearing Islamic headscarves. The affair dominated the French media in the

---

[4] Ibid, p.84.

[5] The first Islamic prayer-room had in fact been established in Renault's Billancourt factory as early as 1976.

[6] *Le Monde*, 11 February 1983.

autumn of 1989, overshadowing for much of the time even the collapse of communism in eastern Europe.[7] Capitalising on this enormous media tide in December 1989, the FN candidate swept to a by-election victory in Dreux, scoring a staggering 61% of the vote.

A public opinion poll conducted among parallel samples of French nationals and Muslims resident in France during the headscarf affair showed that the two communities held dramatically different images of Islam. Whilst most Muslim immigrants saw their religion as peaceful, progressive, tolerant and protective towards women, the great majority of French respondents considered Islam to be essentially violent, backward-looking, fanatical and oppressive towards women.[8] As an equally large majority of the French say they have never had any significant personal dealings with immigrants,[9] their images of the Muslim population are clearly derived primarily from intermediary sources, the most important of which are the mass media. By focusing on exceptional cases, the press and electronic media have undoubtedly created very misleading images of the Islamic community. Newspapers, magazines and television stations splashed the findings of public opinion polls showing that the French were overwhelmingly opposed to the wearing of Islamic headscarves in state schools; the fact that Muslims in favour of the headscarf were heavily outnumbered by those who wanted it excluded from the schoolroom[10] went almost unnoticed. As the Prime Minister, Michel Rocard,

---

[7] Well over 600 pages of press clippings were collected by the Agence pour le Développement des Relations Interculturelles in its "Dossier de presse sur l'affaire du foulard islamique", 4 vols, photocopied, Paris: ADRI, 1990. For an analysis of press coverage, see Antonio Perotti and France Thépaut, "L'Affaire du foulard islamique: d'un fait divers à un fait de société", in *Migrations société*, vol. 2, no. 7 (January-February 1990), pp.61-82.

[8] IFOP opinion poll in *Le Monde*, 30 November 1989.

[9] SOFRES opinion poll in *Le Figaro Magazine*, 19 May 1990, pp.158-162; cf SOFRES opinion poll in *Le Nouvel Observateur*, 13 September 1990, pp.4-7.

[10] IFOP opinion poll in *Le Monde*, 30 November 1989.

168

observed, it was easy to forget amid all the publicity surrounding the three girls in Creil that 350,000 other girls from Muslim homes were attending school perfectly normally without any attempt to don Islamic headscarves.

Similarly skewed coverage was given to the Rushdie affair and the Gulf War. When a few hundred demonstrators marched through Paris in February 1989, calling for Rushdie's death, film of the incident was screened endlessly on French television. The fact that the demonstrators were mainly Pakistanis, and that as such they were quite unrepresentative of the immigrant community as a whole, was made less clear. The great majority of the estimated three million Muslims in France are, in fact, of North African origin; the Pakistani community numbers no more than around 15,000. In the early stages of the Gulf War, the press repeatedly reported (and often simply manufactured) speculation that Muslim immigrants might serve as a fifth column against the allies.[11] How many Frenchmen registered the findings of two opinion polls carried out among Muslims in France showing they were every bit as hostile to Saddam Hussein as they were to George Bush?[12] How many realised that television film purporting to show pro Iraqi Islamic demonstrators brandishing kalashnikovs in Algiers was, in fact, archive footage of a Hezbollah demonstration in Lebanon?[13] Small wonder, then, if Middle East terrorists, Islamic political activists and ordinary Muslim immigrants are often lumped together in a quite indiscriminate way in the minds of the French public.

---

[11] Press coverage of the Gulf War is discussed in greater depth by Antonio Perotti and France Thépaut, "Les Répercussions de la guerre du golfe sur les arabes et les juifs de France", in *Migrations-société*, vol. 3, no. 14 (March-April 1991), pp. 65-82; and by Antonio Perotti, "Les Relations de la guerre du golfe sur les relations franco-maghrébines", in *Migrations-société*, vol. 3, no. 15 (May-June 1991), pp.67-70.

[12] IFOP opinion poll in *Le Figaro*, 29 January 1991; SOFRES opinion poll in *L'Express*, 8 February 1991, pp.30-31.

[13] *Le Figaro*, 22 January 1991; *Le Monde*, 9 February 1991.

MARGINALISATION

While immigrants are often displayed prominently in alarmist news and current affairs coverage, in almost all other respects they are marginalised by the mass media. The audience for which most programmes and articles are tailored is clearly French, with few, if any, concessions made to viewers or readers from ethnic monorities. A small amount of broadcasting is aimed specifically at the immigrant community, but its positioning in the programme schedules simply confirms the marginal status of those concerned. The clearest illustration of this is religious broadcasting. Antenne 2 is required by its *cahier des charges* to put out religious programmes on Sunday mornings. The importance accorded to each religious community is clearly reflected in both the length and the timing of the various programmes. The longer the programme and the later its slot, the better served are its viewers. Conversely, the earlier they have to rise and the shorter the offering, the poorer the provision from the consumers' point of view. In 1991 a typical Sunday morning schedule on Antenne 2 has looked like this:

8.45	Connaître l'islam
9.15	Emissions israélites
10.00	Présence protestante
10.30	Le Jour du Seigneur
11-12.00	Messe

With a half-hour magazine programme followed by an hour-long mass from mid- to late morning, the Catholic Church occupies a privileged position. This is hardly surprising, granted that Catholics are much the largest religious group in France. More puzzling, however, is the fact that the country's second largest religion, Islam, is relegated to the earliest slot in the schedule. And why, with around three million adherents, does it merit only half an hour, while the country's half million or so Jews enjoy 45 minutes of air time? It is true that some weeks the Jewish broadcast lasts only 15 minutes, thereby making way for a half-hour programme aimed at Orthodox Christians. The latter are, however, far less numerous than the Muslim population, and this is true even of France's Protestants, who nevertheless occupy a regular half-hour slot the timing of which is second in convenience only to that of the broadcasts serving the Catholic community. The inequity of A2's schedules was until recently even more flagrant, with the Islamic broadcast lasting only 15 minutes, while the programme for Jews varied between 15 and 45 minutes. It was only in January 1991 that *Connaître l'islam* was extended to 30 minutes... by pushing the starting time back from 9.00 to 8.45 a.m. Instead of using the extra 15 minutes to bring the Islamic community at least fractionally in from the cold, this left the other programmes in their established slots and ensured that any inconvenience resulting from the earlier starting time would fall on Muslim viewers rather than any one else.[14]

The best known programme catering for immigrants and their families was for many years *Mosaïque*, a magazine programme broadcast on Sunday mornings by FR3 from 1976 to 1987. FR3 had been created in 1972 with the particular aim of providing regionally oriented programmes. By targeting ethnic minorities from Third World countries, *Mosaïque* could be seen as a logical extension of FR3's policy of reflecting the considerable cultural diversity found within France. However, the immigrant community was dealt with on a very different basis from that applying to France's regional minorities. Whereas the latter were served by daily programmes at peak time, *Mosaïque* was broadcast just once a week, beginning at 9.00 or 10.00 a.m. There were equally striking differences where the production and financing of the programmes were concerned. FR3's regional output was financed, like most of its programmes, by the annual licence fee paid by all television viewers in France. *Mosaïque* was neither produced nor financed by FR3 (which in fact charged a fee for

---

[14] Recent developments in religious programming are discussed by Alain Woodrow, "Ondes oecuméniques", in *Le Monde Radio Télévision*, 9-10 June 1991.

broadcasting the programme), but by government-controlled bodies financed in large part by the immigrant population. The principal funding body was the Fonds d'Action Sociale (FAS), a government agency which, since its creation in 1958, has drawn most of its funds from the social security contributions of immigrant workers.[15] Although foreign workers pay social security contributions at the same rate as French nationals, their families have always received very much smaller benefits if they remain in the country of origin. The net surplus accruing to the French treasury is recycled through FAS, which funds a variety of projects designed to assist the immigrant community. *Mosaïque* was produced by a succession of quangos, all of which were financed by FAS. Thus, while regional minorities in France were catered for by frequent programmes at no extra cost, Third World ethnic minorities paid twice over (through the licence fee and FAS) for a weekly programme shunted into what many saw as a Sunday morning ghetto.[16]

The production system of *Mosaïque* had a further peculiarity. Many items broadcast on the programme were bought from television stations based in the home countries of immigrants, which were under more or less direct government control. Combined with the close association of the French government in the overall production arrangements in Paris, this made it virtually impossible for *Mosaïque* to broadcast anything that was politically inconvenient to those in power, regardless of what immigrants themselves might wish to say or hear said on their behalf. Very little was done to seek out or train new production or on-screen staff from within the immigrant community itself. As passive consumers of the programme, immigrants were implicitly stereotyped in the familiar role of *assistés*.

---

[15] On the structure and funding of FAS, see Michel Yahiel, "Le FAS: questions de principe", in *Revue européenne des migrations internationales*, vol. 4, nos 1-2 (1988), pp.107-114.

[16] For a more detailed discussion of *Mosaïque*, see Catherine Humblot, "Les Emissions spécifiques: de 'Mosaïque' à 'Rencontres'", in *Migrations-société*, vol. 1, no. 4 (August 1989), pp.7-14.

Yet there was no shortage of talent, particularly among the younger generation. Raised and educated in France, the children of immigrants often had skills and expectations far beyond those of their parents, most of whom had been illiterate when they emigrated to take up poorly paid manual jobs. From the late 1970s onwards, the younger generation began to take matters into their own hands with a variety of initiatives in both the printed and electronic media. The year 1979 saw the creation of *Sans Frontière*, a newspaper run by and for younger members of the immigrant community. Two years later, when the newly elected Socialist administration began liberalising the air waves, ethnic minorities were quick to set up local radio stations, the best known of which was Radio Beur, based in the suburbs of Paris. Such initiatives ran mainly on a self-help basis, and their audience was confined mainly to the immigrant community. In this respect, they remained on the margins of the mass media. It is only very recently that programme-makers of immigrant origin have played a significant role in productions destined for a mass audience.

IN FROM THE COLD?

An early attempt at breaking out of what many saw as a dangerous ghetto was made by the staff of *Sans Frontière*, who decided to wind up their newspaper and replace it by a new, glossy-covered magazine designed to appeal to mainstream French as well as ethnic minority readers. The new magazine, *Baraka*, failed to attract this wider audience, and collapsed a few months after its launch in 1986. Agence Im'Média, a multi-media news agency set up by young journalists of immigrant origin in 1983, has proved more resilient, but remains on the fringes of the most powerful media institutions. In 1989, the agency secured a contract to supply regular items for *Rencontres*, a new FAS-funded magazine programme for ethnic minorities broadcast by FR3. The contract was not renewed the following year, however, and while the agency still contributes occasional pieces to *Rencontres* and other programmes, it has very little control in setting the overall agenda; rather, it is called in to plug odd gaps, particularly where the ethnic minority origins of its personnel give it access to people or places which French reporters have difficulty in covering.

A few professionals from Third World countries have entered the mainstream of French television. Rachid Arab is a staff reporter with Antenne 2, while Nadia Samir is a continuity announcer with TF1. Both are of Algerian origin. Young Algerians have also played key roles in the first television drama series which have given serious attention to the immigrant community. Leaving aside occasional supporting roles and one-off programmes, it was not until 1990 that Third World ethnic minorities acquired a significant presence in the fictional output of French television. In May of that year, Antenne 2 broadcast the first episode in a four-part mini-series entitled *Le Lyonnais*, starring Kader Boukhanef as a young cop named Selim Rey. Although Selim is of mixed Franco-Algerian descent, he was born and raised in Lyons, and as the title implies, he is portrayed essentially as a local lad who just happens to have a darker-than-average skin. Beyond the customary thrills and spills of a detective series, the unspoken objective of *Le Lyonnais* is clearly to reassure French viewers that there is very little difference between themselves and the immigrant community. Selim's role as an unyielding and astute defender of the law cuts directly across the stereotyped image of immigrants as criminals. While this makes a welcome change, it does little to advance the understanding of minority cultures. Apart from periodic visits to the Kabyle restaurant run by Selim's mother, where liberal doses of couscous are somewhat ostentatiously consumed, we hardly enter the world of Maghrebian immigrants at all. As *Le Lyonnais* was conceived and produced by an all-French team, this is perhaps hardly surprising.

Programme-makers of immigrant origin played a much more significant role in two other series which hit the screen in 1990. The first of these was

174

Sixième gauche, a 50-part soap opera broadcast by FR3. The other was *La Famille Ramdan*, a 40-part situation comedy co-produced and screened by M6. *Sixième gauche* was co-written by Henri de Turenne, a well established journalist and documentary producer, and Akli Tadjer, the son of an Algerian immigrant couple. It focusses on the relationship between a French family and their newly installed neighbours, who are of Algerian origin. Through this relationship, the series aims very clearly at creating a deeper mutual understanding across the ethnic divide. The minority community occupies a still more central role in *La Famille Ramdan*. Here, an Algerian immigrant family is unequivocally the star of the show, with French friends and neighbours consigned to secondary roles. Unlike *Sixième gauche*, the basic idea of which was initiated by Henri de Turenne who then sought out a co-writer from the immigrant community, *La Famille Ramdan* is also unique in having been conceived from the outset by two young men from Algerian immigrant families, Aïssa Djabri and Farid Lahouassa. In principle, *La Famille Ramdan* was therefore the best placed of all these programmes to bring an ethnic minority out of the cold and into the mainstream of French television. In practice, the institutional framework within which Djabri and Lahouassa had to work forced them into numerous compromises, and the finished product resulting from their labours was in many important respects at variance with their original ambitions.[17]

Their first problem was to find a television station which would even entertain the idea of an ethnic minority sit-com. In 1988 they founded a small company, Vertigo Productions, with the aim of selling the idea to a French channel. On the advice of Françoise Verney, an influential broker in the French media world, they complemented the Ramdan family with a number of

---

[17] In the analysis which follows, I am indebted to Aïssa Djabri and Farid Lahouassa for placing at my disposal pilot scenarios and other unpublished documents relating to *La Famille Ramdan*.

secondary characters (all of them French) designed to help the average French viewer to identify more easily with the series. The project was nevertheless turned down flat by TF1, A2, La Sept and Canal Plus. In the summer of 1986, M6, a voracious consumer of bought-in drama series, was planning for the first time to co-produce a situation comedy of its own, and was on the look out for suitable ideas. The channel was attracted by Vertigo's proposal, but laid down a number of conditions. As Vertigo was a small, completely unknown outfit, M6 stipulated that a more experienced company be brought in as a third co-producer. This was IMA Productions, whose successes to date include the soap opera *Salut les Homards*. M6 was also very worried by the working class feel of Vertigo's scripts, and insisted that the Ramdan family should be made less proletarian so as to make it easier for viewers to identify with them.

The original scripts were based very closely on the personal experiences of Djabri and Lahouassa, who had been brought up by poor, uneducated Algerians in and around Nanterre, where they had gone through the classic housing cycle of immigrant families: from *bidonvilles* to *cités de transit*, and eventually on to HLM estates. At M6's behest, the Ramdan family was transplanted from a working-class HLM estate in Nanterre to a spacious and comfortable apartment in the 11th arrondissement of Paris. In his original incarnation the father, Driss, was, like the great majority of Algerian immigrants, an illiterate and unskilled factory worker. In the revised version, he is a taxi driver and, like his wife, Nedjma, he can read and write effortlessly in both French and Arabic. We are not told how they acquired these quite exceptional skills. Their French friends and neighbours, who were initially too working-class by M6's standards, now consist essentially of Patricia, who works as a secretary in a fashion magazine, Serge, an advertising executive and the teenage Pierrot, who alone retains a perceptibly proletarian edge.

Whereas the parents consistently occupied centre-stage in the original project, they are often displaced in the final version by their eldest son, Mehdi, a newly qualified doctor. The first episode to be broadcast focuses on the opening of his surgery, just one door along from the family apartment, and the whole of the remainder of the series is presented as a series of recollections which come to him while being psychoanalysed. This device, which was suggested by one of the mainly French team of writers brought in to script the bulk of the series, is somewhat ambiguous. At times, it genuinely serves to provide insights into the personal and cultural conflicts experienced by Mehdi. More commonly, however, the psychoanalyst functions less as facilitator for Mehdi's meditations upon himself than as a prop for story-telling and explanations which are fairly transparently aimed at the television audience. Frequently, the psychoanalyst all but disappears, leaving Mehdi recounting his experiences directly to camera. Here we have a striking visual representation of the underlying forces at work in the radical transformation of *La Famille Ramdan* from the original concept of Djabri and Lahouassa into the final, broadcast version.

In reshaping the project, M6 was preoccupied above all with maintaining and increasing its audience, which was assumed to be predominantly young, middle-class and French. As Lahouassa recalls, this was not how he and Djabri had originally conceived of the series:

> "M6 nous a dit au départ qu'il fallait viser les femmes avec leurs enfants dans les foyers où il y a deux téléviseurs, où le père regarde ses émissions alors que la mère vaque à ses occupations, genre télé dans la cuisine, ou télé dans la chambre pour enfants. Voilà le public - nous, on ne savait pas trop ce que ça voulait dire. Nous, on trouvait qu'avec notre concept il y avait une façon de trouver un autre type de spectateur, qui n'a qu'une télé, qui est content de la regarder en famille, comme dans les familles immigrées. On pensait que c'était possible."[18]

---

[18] Interview with Farid Lahouassa, 21 January 1991.

The channel evinced no interest in this potential immigrant audience. The modifications imposed by M6 were cast in the image of its target audience, whose expectations were assumed in many ways to replicate those of the channel's own production staff:

> "Lorsqu'un diffuseur rentre sur un concept, il se l'approprie, il prétend devoir amener ses connaissances, son expérience et tout. Malheureusement, ce sont des gens qui ont fait leurs études aux Etats-Unis. Je n'ai rien contre ça mais quand il s'agit d'un autre milieu, encore plus lorsqu'il s'agit d'un milieu populaire immigré, cela rend complètement caduc leur apport, ce qu'ils peuvent nous amener pour améliorer ce concept. Ce qu'ils peuvent, c'est de le déplacer vers eux-mêmes, vers ce qu'ils connaissent eux-mêmes, c'est-à-dire leur milieu bourgeois, en créant des personnages comme Patricia, secrétaire dans un journal de mode, Jean-Noël [Serge], publicitaire, et une famille Ramdan qui n'habite plus en banlieue, mais dans le 11e arrondissement, des quartiers où ils peuvent aller, où ils peuvent voir et croire qu'ils les connaissent. Ils n'ont jamais mis les pieds dans les cités populaires, ils ne connaissent pas la vérité d'une des grandes composantes de l'immigration en France, c'est-à-dire son enracinement dans les banlieues."[19]

These changes squeezed out of the series not only many of its proletarian qualities, but also much of its ethnic charge. The bourgeoisification of the Ramdans carried with it a level of acculturation which far surpasses that of most first generation immigrants. When they are not reading psychology books, fashion magazines or *L'Equipe*, Nedjma is out taking body-building courses at a nearby gym while Driss is boning up on the classics of French literature in order to impress a cultivated woman taxi driver who has caught his eye. Very little of this seems at all typical of Maghrebian immigrants. Both parents are Muslims (Driss's abstinence from alcohol serves as a regular reminder of this), and in some episodes this leads to conflicts with their

---

[19] Ibid.

children, who are more secular in outlook. In these and indeed all the other episodes, however, everyone is agreed that in the final analysis the harmony and well-being of the family outweighs any other considerations.

La Famille Ramdan is in this respect faithful to the classic values of television sit-coms. A typical example is the episode entitled "Le Père Noël chez les Ramdan", in which the younger son, Alilou, longs to share in the fun of Christmas like his French schoolfriends. Everyone except Driss is willing to have a Christmas tree in the apartment, and the father finally succumbs to Nedjma's entreaties. "On garde notre religion, c'est bien", she tells her husband. "Mais tu connais les enfants. Si tu leur enlèves Noël, pour eux c'est une punition et ça va devenir des adultes malheureux et ils n'aimeront pas leur religion parce qu'ils vont croire qu'ils ont été punis à cause d'elle". While acceding to this logic, Driss remains worried that their children may become too French. Nedjma replies: "Je préfère que mes enfants deviennent de bons Français que de mauvais Arabes. Mais ce que je veux en tout cas, c'est qu'ils soient heureux - c'est tout!" Nedjma's "common sense" is bound to endear her to French viewers. The mark of that good sense is double-edged: her commitment as a mother may in one sense be felt to transcend the ethnic divide, but the strength of that commitment is actually displayed by Nedjma's willingness to bracket off her Arab origins.

Like Selim in *Le Lyonnais*, the Ramdan family is reassuring from the point of view of French viewers because "they" turn out to be just like "us". One cannot help feeling, therefore, that in helping to bring them into the mainstream of television braodcasting, French producers have obliged ethnic minorities to jettison so much baggage that they end up travelling very light indeed. It would be easy to blame the ethnocentrism of those concerned, and this may well be a significant factor, but the experience of Djabri and Lahouassa also has something to do with the very blunt nature of television as a cultural medium. Precisely because it is a commercially-owned *broad*casting medium, one of only six terrestrial television channels in France, M6 has to aim for the biggest audience it can get. New technologies such as satellite and particularly cable television are now making it possible to talk in terms of *narrow*casting i.e. transmitting programmes aimed at very specific minority audiences. Since 1989, immigrants subscribing to cable television in a few French towns, such as Mantes-la-Jolie and Roubaix, have had access to an Arabic-language channel transmitting a diet of programmes from Moroccan television.[20] For the moment, however, these remain exceptional cases. Most viewers in France are served solely by half a dozen terrestrial channels competing against each other for the biggest possible national audience. This effectively forces television companies to aim for a somewhat mushy middle ground, which in turn almost inevitably condemns minority cultures to the outer fringes of the medium.

---

[20] See "Les Limites de l'ouverture", in *Le Monde Radio Télévision*, 24-25 February, 1991.

12. *LA FRANCE DU TIERCÉ* : HORSE RACING AND POPULAR GAMBLING SINCE 1954

PHILIP D. DINE

The idea that sport functions as a barometer of social change would nowadays be widely accepted. However, while few commentators on French society would doubt the validity of historical studies of the principal modern sports of football, rugby and cycling, the social significance of the much longer established tradition of popular gambling on horse-races has generally been overlooked. Why should this be? In fact, the principal reason for this thematic orientation is the far more easily discernible cultural fecundity of these competitive sports in comparison with more traditional sporting spectacles. As a result of this, researchers have tended to concentrate on questions like the close correlation between changes in patterns of work and leisure in the late nineteenth and early twentieth centuries and the emergence of new, technologically dependent, sports like cycling. They have recognised the obvious scope for sociological, and particularly ideological, analyses of sporting movements such as the vogue for gymnastics in the period between the Franco-Prussian conflict and the First World War. They have studied the historically and geographically specific appeal of various modern sports in France, such as football in the industrial north and east, and in the Rhône basin, rugby in the rural south and west.[1] This academic trend has been accompanied by an ever more intense mediatic preoccupation with the "star" exponents of modern sporting disciplines. Although readily understandable in itself, this general tendency to focus attention on the primary participatory and spectator sports

---

[1] See R. Holt, "Ideology and Sociability: A Review of New French Research into the History of Sport under the Early Third Republic (1870-1914)", *International Journal of the History of Sport*, vol. 6, No. 3, December 1989, pp.368-377.

has militated against a proper appreciation of one particular sporting spectacle, namely horse-racing. As Richard Holt has pointed out, this omission is all the more regrettable given the strong links which have long existed and which continue to exist between horse-racing and popular gambling.[2] It is as an attempt partially to remedy this situation that the present chapter is conceived.

The fact that horse-racing's role as a medium for popular gambling should have been overlooked so systematically in France itself may further be attributed to a deeply entrenched bias against genuinely popular culture within the French academic and administrative establishment. As Bernard Préel has argued: "Image d'Epinal contre image d'Epinal comment ne pas préférer celle d'une incapacité de notre technostructure à prendre au sérieux le loisir et surtout un loisir populaire qui ne se drape pas dans une pose culturelle?"[3] In the particular context of horse-race betting, this institutional prejudice may be voiced in the language of various brands of puritanism. More usually, however, the foundation for the effective denial of French horse-racing's social significance is to be found in a more or less unstated "hierarchy of leisure". It is this élitist conception of socio-cultural worth which continues to enable French social commentators blithely to ignore a leisure market of over 8 million consumers spending 34 billion francs in 1990.[4] At the pinnacle of this hierarchy are the familiar manifestations of high culture, whilst lower down the scale of values come various sports. Within this general category, it is necessary to distinguish between fashionable "anti-cardiac" sports like golf, squash, tennis

---

[2] R. Holt, *Sport and Society in Modern France*, London, Macmillan, 1981, p.14.

[3] B. Préel, "1989: an 1 des nouveaux loisirs?", in M. Verdie, *L'Etat de la France et de ses habitants*, Paris, La Découverte, 1989, p.104. Préel's remarks specifically concern the failure of the initial, consciously "French" form of the *Loto sportif*. See also R. Spitzbarth, *L'Economie du jeu et du sport hippiques*, unpublished doctoral thesis, Université de Nancy II, 1981, pp.39-42.

[4] These figures are taken from G. de la Brosse, "La Cinq gagne le tiercé", *Le Monde*, 30 Novembre 1990, p.24.

and even jogging, and those longer established sports imparting lower social status, such as football, rugby and cycling. However, near the bottom of the socio-cultural heap is, by common consent, recreational gambling on horse-races; though not, of course, participation in the sport as owner, trainer or even jockey. Thus regarded, horse-race betting is very commonly, but quite erroneously, lumped together with participation in lotteries and other such games of chance. This general failure to appreciate its socio-cultural specificity may not be altogether surprising, but it is by no means inevitable. Central to any real appreciation of modern French horse-racing is an understanding of the rise of one particular form of bet since its invention in 1954. However, properly to comprehend the contemporary dominance of the *tiercé*, it is necessary to give a brief account of the historical association of horse-racing and popular gambling in France. For, as Zeldin correctly insists: "Horse-racing started, like cycling, as a rich man's sport, but in this case, popularisation came from its success in opening up quite exceptional opportunities for gambling".[5]

Like industrial and agrarian revolutions, organized horse-racing came late to France and in large part in response to dramatic developments on the other side of the Channel. Racing in Britain had become systematically codified after 1750, when the Jockey Club was established, with its five "classic" races being instituted over the period 1776 to 1814. In contrast, the French Société d'Encouragement pour l'amélioration des races de chevaux en France was not formed until 1833. Nevertheless, it rapidly established its own set of classic races, on the English model, in the decade which followed. This rapid codification of French racing put it in a strong position to benefit from the new political and economic conditions of the Second Empire. It was in this period that racing began to receive central and local government support, most obviously evidenced in 1856 by the decision of the Ville de Paris to grant the

---

[5] T. Zeldin, *France*, 1848-1945 (Vol 2): *Intellect, taste and anxiety*, Oxford, Clarendon Press, 1977, pp.690-691.

Société d'Encouragement an area of land between the Bois de Boulogne and the Seine for a new racecourse (Longchamp), and the same municipality's institution of a Grand Prix de Paris of an unprecedented value, no less than 100,000 francs, in 1863. Under this state tutelage, French racing took off, with French horses starting to win important English races from the mid-nineteenth century onwards. In 1865, the famous Gladiateur achieved the still unequalled feat of winning not only the Grand Prix de Paris, but also the English "Triple Crown" of the Two Thousand Guineas, Derby and St. Leger. In an age of increasingly belligerent nationalism, it was only perhaps to be expected that this fine animal should be considered "[une] véritable gloire nationale", a status enshrined by a statue erected at Longchamp on his death in 1876.[6]

International success of this kind goes some way towards explaining the popularization of horse-racing under the Second Empire. In this, it was well ahead of the rest of French sport, which, as Richard Holt has demonstrated, remained overwhelmingly traditional until the social watershed of the *Belle Époque*. Of course, the lower-class paying spectators were, from the outset, spatially segregated from the owners, trainers and fashionable race-goers. Nevertheless, large numbers of such spectators were flocking to both Longchamp and the older Paris tracks like Vincennes some thirty years before association football, rugby union or even cycling began to displace the old communality of the *fête populaire* with its traditional games.[7] However, the real key to horse-racing's phenomenal growth lies precisely in the link with popular gambling highlighted by Zeldin. Horse-racing and gambling, have, in

---

[6] P. Arnoult, *Les Courses de chevaux*, Paris, PUF, 1962, pp.28-33. See also T. Morris, and J. Randall, *Horse Racing: Records, Facts and Champions*, London, Guinness Books, 1990, p.22, where it is noted that "Gladiateur earned the nickname 'Avenger of Waterloo' when he became the first French-bred winner of the Derby in 1865". Jules Vallès, a critical contemporary commentator on Gladiateur's victory in the 2,000 Guineas noted the Newmarket crowd's violent response to the French horse's success. J. Vallès, *La Rue*, Paris, Les Editeurs Français Réunis, 1969, p.192.

[7] R. Holt, *Sport and Society*, pp.1-14, "Sport in its Social Context".

fact, only rarely been separated throughout the history of sport, and in France the first races were organized by and between owners, specifically for the purpose of betting on the outcome. Such wagers remained a largely aristocratic pastime, however, as did large-scale gambling. The mass of Frenchmen were meanwhile provided with an alternative outlet for their gambling instincts:

> "The state used to organize lotteries during the *ancien régime*, with great success. [...] However, because the system was full of abuses, it was abolished by the Revolution, but it was soon re-established, simply to bring more money in. During the Restoration some 50 million francs were staked annually, but in 1836 the state lottery was once again abolished, this time on the ground that it was immoral. Though many lotteries were subsequently organised for specific purposes ... it was not until 1933 that the national lottery was re-established to become an indispensable institution."[8]

It is a particularly rich irony of history that the French state should have decided to abolish the national lottery at the very time when the recently established racing authorities were undertaking the wholesale restructuring of their sport. The newly codified racing programme provided the perfect medium for the popular gambling instincts frustrated by the abolition of its primary competitor. At this time betting was conducted on the Paris courses very much as it was, and indeed still is, in Great Britain, with private bookmakers shouting the odds for prospective gamblers and, needless to say, for themselves. However, the criticism which had first been levelled at racing before the Revolution - "parce qu'elles [les courses] occasionnent l'altération des fortunes et font déserter les ouvriers de leurs ateliers"[9] - was to be

---

[8] T. Zeldin, *France 1848-1845, II*, p.691.

[9] Contemporary pamphlet cited by R. Spitzbarth, *L'Economie du jeu et du sport hippiques*, p.19. See also J. Dunkley, *Gambling: a social and moral problem in France, 1685-1792*, Oxford, Voltaire Foundation, 1985.

renewed in the 1880s. The court's repeated prohibition of horse-race betting was finally enforced by Goblet, the minister of the interior of the day, in 1887. Predictably, race-course attendances plummetted, with the sport seeming on the verge of collapse. Belatedly it was recognized by the authorities that gambling constituted an indispensable part of racing's attraction to the paying spectator, and in 1891 legislation was passed to legalize the racing authorities' operation of the *pari mutuel* system of betting on-course (the *Pari Mutuel Hippodrome* or PMH as it would become known).

It was the enduring ambivalence of the French state's attitude to gambling which gave rise to this historic compromise on horse-race betting. For, if the authorities were understandably keen to generate revenue through taxes on gambling, they were very wary of being seen to encourage *l'enfer du jeu*. So, whilst the ruling body of British racing, the Jockey Club, unashamedly proclaimed its attachment to racing in its entirety, its French equivalent sought from the outset to avoid public association with anything other than "l'amélioration de la race chevaline". As Roland Spitzbarth explains:

> "La forme moderne que prennent les courses aux 16ème et 17ème siècles en Angleterre, aux 18ème et surtout 19ème siècles en France leur fait remplir simultanément trois fonctions: épreuve de sélection, spectacle, support de jeu de hasard. Si la compatibilité entre ces trois fonctions ne semble guère troubler les anglo-saxons, il apparaît que la mentalité française conduit à une critique constante de la fonction 'jeu de hasard'."[10]

It is against this background that the decision to outlaw British-style fixed-odds bookmaking in favour of a state monopoly run on the *pari mutuel* principle may be understood. Although simple enough in itself, the distinction between these two systems is worth spelling out. In fixed-odds betting, the organiser of the wager is the bookmaker, who, like the bettor, stands to win or

---

[10] R. Spitzbarth, p.23.

lose personally as a result of the outcome of the relevant race: the bookmaker is wagering against the bettor, as it were. In contrast, the *pari mutuel* system is a form of betting in which those who have backed the winning horse divide among themselves the total of the stakes on the other horses (less a percentage to cover the cost of management): in this case, each bettor is wagering against every other bettor. This system was introduced by the French state - and has subsequently been adopted by several others - for two principal reasons: it yields the most net revenue in the simplest administrative manner; and it is held to be morally preferable in that, with the management having strictly no interest in the outcome of races, it offers the consumer greater protection against corrupt practice.[11]

With the official abolition of bookmaking in 1905, the racing authorities' enviable position as both organizer and beneficiary of on-course gambling was further consolidated. The huge economic potential of its legal monopoly was very significantly extended in 1930, with the establishment of the *Pari Mutuel Urbain* (PMU). With a system of agents quickly put into place throughout the country, a vast new clientèle was almost overnight introduced to the attractions of horse-race betting; a situation which was at least as pleasing for the government, which taxed the PMU's operations, as it was for the operators themselves. The vast majority of the PMU's new outlets were located in cafés, and remain so to this day; an institutional link which was undeniably a factor in the phenomenal pre-war success of the PMU, given "the triumph of the café as 'the preferred context' for social life" in the earlier part of the twentieth century.[12] So, although there may never have been as many *Cafés du Turf* as there still are *Cafés du Sport* scattered across *la France profonde*, the social

---

[11] See J. Dowie, "The Ethics of Parimutuel Systems" (paper for the Eighth International Conference on Risk and Gambling, London, 1990), especially pp.1-2. See also the same author's "Consumer Protection in Betting" (*ibid*). Spitzbarth, pp.23-29, draws useful attention to the impact of moral considerations on the framing of the 1891 legislation.

[12] R. Holt, *Sport and Society*, p.155.

identification of horse-race betting with the back room of the local *bistrot* remains beyond doubt. Indeed, this institutional and cultural linkage is at once the PMU's greatest strength and its most serious weakness in a period of dramatically shifting patterns of leisure activity.

The amount of money staked on horse-races rose steadily from 169 million francs in 1892 to 2,567 million in 1938.[13] In 1939-40 the onset of war and the German occupation inevitably halted this progression, but PMU receipts had, paradoxically, returned to pre-war levels by the following year and continued to rise dramatically throughout 1942 and 1943. 1944 and the liberation saw only a minor fall (-11.1%). Steady expansion was the pattern throughout the rest of the 1940s and it was only in the following decade that stagnation began to set in. The person charged with remedying this situation was André Carrus, a young and exceptionally inventive *polytechnicien*. Carrus sought to attract a fresh public to horse-race betting, and was able to do so thanks to his brilliant invention of *le pari tiercé*. The aim of this bet is quite simply to pick in the correct order the first three finishers in the designated race - traditionally run on a Sunday - with a consolation return being paid for the right numbers "dans le désordre". However, the scale of its success and its subsequent importance for the entire French horse-race industry are difficult to overstate. Forsans has accurately described the institution of the *tiercé* in terms of a "bouleversement" of the established structures of the French turf.[14] The extent of this genuine revolution may begin to be appreciated with the aid of a few statistics:

> "Ce jeu [le pari tiercé] ... est une extension du pari couplé. Son succès se résume à quelques données. Créé en 1954, il draine,

---

[13] These figures are taken from Zeldin. Those which follow are from Spitzbarth, supplemented by material from C. Hill, "French providing a profitable lead", *The Times*, 7 February 1989.

[14] D. Forsans, *Le Tiercé, racket ou divertissement?* (Domène, Sogirep, 1971), p.77.

dès 1962, 50% des mises engagées au pari mutuel urbain. Cette part est portée à 65.7% en 1965 puis se stabilise autour de 60% ... alors que le nombre de courses supports du pari tiercé n'a jamais dépassé 3% du nombre total des courses donnant lieu à pari mutuel hors des hippodromes."[15]

The exponential rise of the *tiercé* in the decade following its inception (an average annual increase in receipts of 65% in this period) was replaced in subsequent decades by a broadly stable situation in which, today, some 8 million French punters bet over 34 billion francs annually. Of this, over 3 billion francs are deducted and returned to the racing industry for prize money and administration. The mechanism for this industry support is the *prélèvement légal*, a deduction periodically laid down by decree and just under 30% of turnover in 1987. It is from this deduction that the state also takes its cut, currently equivalent to 3% of income tax or just over half as much as the tax on alcohol. Whilst other multiple bets have been introduced in an attempt to emulate the success of the *tiercé* - such as the *quarté, quarté plus, quinté, quinté plus* - none has come near its impact and it continues to dominate not only the finances but also the collective consciousness of the racing industry in France. As one leading British journalist has commented:

"I have never ceased to be astonished by the importance they place on the *tiercé* in particular. Sometimes it seems as if the whole racing and trotting industries are geared to serving its interests. [...] Challenge it in any way and the French shake their heads gravely, as if you were challenging the traditions of the Revolution in a republican club."[16]

---

[15] R. Spitzbarth, p.78.

[16] P. Hayward (racing correspondent of *The Independent*), correspondence with the author, 10 October 1990. It should be noted that trotting is today considerably more popular, and more profitable, than either flat racing or steeple-chasing in France.

The industry's financial reliance on this particular form of wager clearly goes some way towards explaining its and the state's reverential attitudes towards it. Moreover, this prime generator of revenue for both the state and the racing authorities is, notwithstanding the relatively high cost of the PMU, simple and cheap to administer. Also undoubtedly attractive to these two prime beneficiaries is the fact that the *tiercé* is an exclusively off-course bet. One can gamble in this way in one of the cafés, bars-tabacs, and even some newsagents and general stores which make up the PMU's 6,800 outlets, but one cannot bet on a *tiercé* at the racecourse where the *support* itself is being run. For an industry rooted in class distinctions that continue to be reflected in on-course spatial segregation, the attractions of completely avoiding physical contact with the great mass of *joueurs* is obvious. Whilst for a state historically loath to encourage or to be seen to encourage gambling as such, substantial revenue can be generated from this "divertissement" without the spectre of *l'enfer du jeu* being raised. As a 1960s Marabout guide to the subject jauntily put it: "tiercéiste oui, turfiste non!".[17] So, whilst French courses may be amongst the best appointed and the least expensive in the racing world, they are amongst the worst attended. Racing, in marked contrast to Great Britain and many other countries, is not a genuine spectator sport in France. This is true not only of on-course attendance, which has even started to worry the Société d'Encouragement, but also of television coverage, which is extremely limited, and devoted almost exclusively to the four minutes each Sunday required to decide the outcome of that day's *événement*.

It is tempting, at this point in the discussion, to observe that France is not a profoundly "horsey" society in the way that Great Britain most certainly is. This, in spite of the fact that participation in equestrian sport is, with

---

[17] M. Poulet, *Le Tiercé: les règles d'un jeu hippique moderne*, Verviers, Gérard et Cie, 1964, back cover. The same guide observes that "le pari tiercé est un amusement dominical, au même titre que le football, la manille ou la pétanque" (p.10), and that "la plupart des amateurs du tiercé n'ont jamais mis les pieds sur un hippodrome" (p.12).

considerable financial assistance from the PMU, very definitely on the rise. For in France there is no real equivalent of the social consensus surrounding what is genuinely "the sport of kings" in this country. Royal Ascot, "Glorious" Goodwood and other big meetings go far beyond the racing world in their social impact. As do specific races, with the Derby and, above all, the Grand National constituting genuinely national institutions. In Britain even the horses themselves have been adopted as stars and media celebrities, with steeple-chasers in particular receiving enormous public acclaim (consider, for instance, Arkle, Red Rum, or, more recently, Desert Orchid). Only the Prix d'Amérique, France's premier trotting race comes anywhere near generating this type of widespread interest. Interestingly, it is possible to find rare examples of the use of racing as a theme in high French art, with Proust and, of course, Degas to the fore. Yet, there is nothing like the same fascination with the racing world manifested in popular literature; indeed, a Dick Francis *à la française* is virtually inconceivable. The particular appeal of the *tiercé* is not to be found in any great public affinity for watching horses race, in short, but in other socio-cultural factors. One of the very few French commentators to have given serious consideration to this particular leisure activity is Paul Yonnet, and his persuasive analysis is regularly drawn on in the discussion which follows.[18]

Like Fourastié in *Les Trente Glorieuses*, Yonnet argues that the post-war period saw a major restructuring of all areas of French society. His particular focus leads him to seek evidence of this modernisation and "massification" in the apparently insignificant leisure practices of contemporary France. The *tiercé*, he argues, is one of several radically new mass practices which have been systematically ignored or dismissed by previous social commentators; a fact which he regards as an indictment of academic sociology, particularly that informed by Marxist social criticism. Rejecting the familiar dichotomy between

---

[18] P. Yonnet, "Tiercé: les nouveaux dimanches de la démocratie", in the same author's *Jeux, modes et masses: la société française et le moderne*, 1945-1985, Gallimard/NRF, 1985, pp.15-90.

191

respectable *jeux d'intelligence* and not so respectable *jeux de hasard*: a gratifying but misleading distinction which is rendered all the more rigid by the abiding cult of reason of a nation which fondly imagines its collective psyche to be characterised by Cartesian rationalism – he sets out to show that the *tiercé* is not only rational but also creative and, moreover, authentically "modern". It is not the case, then, that, to paraphrase the best-known French commentator on gambling, "le coeur [du tiercéiste] a ses raisons que la raison ne connaît point". Indeed, it is precisely the rationality of the *tiercé* which distinguishes it from both gaming and lotteries. For, whilst betting, and, crucially, winning, on the outcome of horse-races may appear to the outsider to be purely a matter of luck, the fact of the matter is that the *tiercé* is not a game of chance. This is borne out by the strikingly non-arbitrary pattern of this form of betting: punters fare considerably better at predicting the actual results than would be possible if they were working on the basis of chance alone. Of course, as in all sports betting there must always remain an unforeseen and unforeseeable element at play, all the more so given the overwhelming use of handicaps with large fields as the *supports* for the *tiercé* and all similar *événements*. However, this essential element of unpredictability should not be equated with a complete absence of predictability. Central to the appeal of the *tiercé* is the cult of *le pronostic*, and prognosis is only possible because of the following factors: a) races are non-repetitive, each is unique; b) races are historically linked, with the results of previous races being relevant to the outcome of later ones; c) betting is on living things rather than just numbers, meaningful signifieds rather than meaningless signifiers. As Yonnet explains:

> "Dans les jeux de hasard (mais non dans les anciens rites de hasard), les numéros se présentent pour ce qu'ils sont, transitivement: de purs signifiants, formes abstraites, émincées, vidées du moindre contenu. Au loto, à la loterie, 1 est 1, 2 est 2, indéfiniment. Pas aux courses, où le numéro déborde de signifié: le 2 du Prix de Diane (*tiercé* couru le 11 juin 1978 sur

l'hippodrome de Chantilly) n'est pas le 2 du Prix Major Fridolin (*tiercé* couru le 25 juin 1978 sur l'hippodrome de Longchamp). Tout distingue les chevaux qu'ils désignent: le nom, le sexe, la couleur, l'âge, les gains, les performances, le poids porté, la distance à parcourir, la place à la corde dans les stalles au départ, les aptitudes, les origines, le jockey, l'entraîneur, le propriétaire, les adversaires, la dernière côte, la dernière place, la chance qu'on leur prête, etc. Le 2 du loto est une coquille vide, un dehors scellé à la nomination, prisonnier de sa pauvreté, le 2 du Prix de Diane déborde de son corps - dont il change gaiement au hasard des engagements de course -, il n'est que contenu, éclaboussement d'images, champ d'interprétation."[19]

It is this possibility of interpretation, of predicting future events on the basis of past experience, which lies at the heart of the *tiercé*'s appeal and which points to its essential modernity. For, unlike the gambler at roulette or the purchaser of a lottery ticket, the *tiercéiste* is not merely a passive observer of random results. He is not, of course, an actor, he cannot influence the outcome of the *événement* in question; however, neither does he merely await it. He is, by definition, physically removed not only from the event but also from the scene of it; as such, he may be an essentially off-course "spectator", even a *voyeur*, but he is nevertheless an extremely active and, crucially, a genuinely creative one. In marked contrast to both the common view and that of many academic commentators, the predicting of horse races is not a mindless act, but on the contrary a very "mindful" one. This "jeu de stratégie différée", as Yonnet calls it in the terminology of games theory, draws on the uniquely human faculties of simulation and representation in an attempt to reduce the unknown factors in the betting equation to a minimum.[20] The raw material for this admittedly inexact science - perhaps, it would be better to call it a

---

[19] Ibid, pp.31-32.

[20] Ibid, pp.33-35.

"studied art"[21] - must always be information. Indeed, the study of "form" is only possible because of the availability of specialist information in the press, and we are not simply thinking here of *Paris-Turf*, the French equivalent of *The Sporting Life*, but also of a whole range of periodicals devoted exclusively to the *tiercé*. Most revealingly of all, however, we must also take into account the impact of the rise of this form of bet on the traditional press. No weekend edition of a provincial newspaper would be complete without a special section devoted to the *tiercé*, nor for that matter would popular national dailies like *France-Soir*. And let there be no suspicion that this mass practice is a media-led phenomenon; on the contrary, the new bet was greeted with general media scepticism in 1954, and appropriate media coverage for a long time lagged behind public interest and was only eventually generated in belated response to it.

This rare impingement of the *tiercé* onto the wider cultural consciousness hints at the existence of a distinctive social grouping: "*La France du tiercé*", the demographic reality of which may be confirmed statistically. With the help of material gleaned from IFOP and INSEE surveys, Yonnet is able to provide "une morphologie spécifique de la collectivité qu'ils [les tiercéistes] forment". We thus discover that the make-up of the national lottery's 20 million is virtually indistinguishable from that of the population as a whole as regards age, sex and socio-professional category. This fact could be said to make the lottery a genuinely national game, albeit one played generally in a rather

---

[21] This term was suggested by a Chief Constable of Manchester, as recorded by R. McKibben, "Working-class Gambling in Britain, 1880-1939", in the same author's *The Ideologies of Class: Social Relations in Britain 1880-1950*, Oxford, Clarendon Press/OUP, 1990, p.124. Both Holt (*Sport and Society*, p.10) and Zeldin (*op. cit.*, p.692) underline the intimate connection between the emergence of mass sporting practices and the rise of the popular press. Yonnet, for his part, provides an interesting appendix on divergent approaches to the prediction of racing results: "Du bon et du mauvais usage des statistiques", (pp.84-90). His findings are confirmed by my own research in the Bibliothèque Nationale, which revealed the existence of a wide variety of patent betting systems, ranging from those claiming mathematical or scientific validity, through astrology and hypnosis, to the mysterious"*hippo-radiesthésie*".

194

infrequent and even dilettantist fashion. "A l'inverse, le tiercé s'adresse à une clientèle très différenciée, à la fois socialement (ouvriers, employés et cadres moyens), sexuellement (les hommes plutôt que les femmes), et par l'âge (concentration dans les âges d'activité); il est l'objet d'une pratique régulière de masse, dont l'importance augmente avec la fréquence. Aussi les tiercéistes forment-ils une communauté ludique séparée: il y a une 'France du tiercé', il ne peut y avoir une 'France de la loterie nationale'".[22]

This picture of a distinct group of working-class and working-age males regularly betting on the *tiercé* leads us naturally to consider other behavioural aspects of this "France du tiercé". How much do they bet? What do they hope to win? Indeed, is profit their primary motivation? If we are to be in a position to answer these and other such questions, it is first necessary to dispel a number of myths propounded by outsiders, whether conscious opponents of gambling or not. The first is that of *l'enfer du jeu*, that is to say the melodramatic representation of gambling as the road to family ruination. In fact, working-class gambling on horse-racing is demonstrably neither pathological nor compulsive. To borrow an image from Ross McKibben, working in the British context, Dostoevsky's gambler is as like the average client of the *café-PMU du coin* as chalk is like cheese.[23] An unpublished IFOP survey carried out in 1967 revealed that 80% of the 7 to 8 million regular *tiercéistes* bet only 3F (the then minimum stakes; it stands at 6F today) each time they played; 13% bet 6F, 11% from 9F to 12F, and a mere 2% bet more than 30F on the weekly *événement*. Moreover, the individual better's very limited financial commitment is accompanied by an extreme sensitivity to the cost of his weekly game, as the sharp fall-off in receipts which followed the 1st

---

[22] Yonnet, p.46. The figures which follow are also from Yonnet, and are confirmed by Spitzbarth.

[23] McKibben, p.118. Yonnet quotes Mgr Etchegaray, Archbishop of Marseilles, as a representative of the familiar outsiders' view of popular gambling: "'Que de foyers où le salaire, la retraite du père passent entièrement au P.M.U.!'" (p.43).

January 1976 increase in the minimum stake (from 3F to 5F) demonstrates. Thus, the rise and rise of the *tiercé* has depended very much on the horizontal expansion of the number of *tiercéistes*, rather than on a vertical increase in the size of individual bets.

The small scale of individual betting on the *tiercé* goes hand-in-hand, again in contrast to both the mythologised *tiercé* of non-participants and the reality of state-run lotteries, with justified hopes of a modest but surprisingly regular return on investment. The anticipation of huge gains is not, and cannot be, the basis of regular participation in the *tiercé*. The young couple who dream in Georges Perec's *Les Choses* (1965): "d'héritages, de gros lot, de tiercé" typify this misunderstanding.[24] It is symptomatic that they never actually buy a lottery ticket, still less make the necessary effort required to back a combination of three horses in the *tiercé*: their fantasy could only be maintained, at least for any time, by the non-*tiercéiste*. For, as Yonnet points out:

> "Le tiercé s'analyse, en effet, comme le contraire d'un jeu sélectif: en trente ans d'existence, il a été touché par plus de 175 millions de gagnants... En 1971, par exemple, le P.M.U. a payé environ 13 millions de mises unitaires gagnantes; compte tenu du nombre estimé de tiercéistes (7 à 8 millions), il est vraisemblable que cette année-là, à peu près chaque parieur a trouvé au moins une fois la combinaison exacte: 'Tout le monde a gagné, gagne ou gagnera au tiercé [Pierre Jotreau]'. On dit d'ailleurs d'un faible rapport qu'il est touché par 'la France entière'."[25]

Whereas the *loto* may sell itself, just like the British football pools, on the basis of its real ability to effect a radical transformation of the lives of a few selected individuals, the *tiercé* is characterised by modest pay-outs to large

---

[24] G. Perec, Paris, *Les Choses*, Julliard/J'ai Lu, 1965, p.76.

[25] Yonnet, pp.38-39.

numbers of players and thus has no real impact on the social hierarchy. This comment inevitably begs the question of the famous *tiercé* on the 1957 Prix du Président de la République, a steeple-chase run at Auteuil. This race produced a theoretical dividend for the correct three numbers *"dans l'ordre"* (20, 18, 19) of 32 million francs. With no single winning ticket, the result was a still substantial pay-out for the 29 runners-up with the right three numbers *"dans le désordre"*. The enormous potential return made the *tiercé* front page news for the first, but by no means the last, time, and thus brought this still new and little known bet to the attention of a much wider public. However, it had little discernible impact on the already regular and rapid growth in the volume of money staked. This is not to underestimate the undoubted cultural significance of this particular *tiercé*, however. As Yonnet puts it: "... l'écho rencontré par le 'Président' dans les média marquait l'irruption sociale du tiercé, qui devenait un phénomène collectif".[26]

The specificity of the *tiercé*'s social role will become more apparent if we now pay further attention to the particular ludic community constituted by the estimated 7 to 8 million regular *tiercéistes*. Without wishing to encourage national stereotypes, it is tempting to conclude that this minimally structured community of equals, retaining both a high degree of heterogeneity and a complete freedom to desist from participation, represents a uniquely French form of sociability. Where the early industrialisation and urbanisation of Great Britain produced the ideal conditions for the rise of football as a mass spectator sport, the human geography of France, with its still rural and small-town heartland, has encouraged the emergence of much looser, but nevertheless very real, forms of sport-based association. Not for the French, then, the characteristic psychological and intellectual regression of the football crowd, a homogeneous mass of strongly committed and variously belligerent club and national supporters, but rather the "free association" of such uniquely French

---

[26] Ibid, p.38.

sporting spectacles as the Tour de France. That this variously fleeting event should annually draw over 10 million spectators whilst a football club like Paris Saint-Germain is unable to attract more than a few thousand regular home spectators is evidence of this fundamental "otherness". It is, moreover, no coincidence that the PMU should this year have been one of the cycle race's principal sponsors. Truly national in impact and with 43% of all spectators in the key "employés, ouvriers, artisans" category, the Tour constitutes the perfect *support* for the PMU's publicity.[27] Both the Tour and the *tiercé* are, we would argue, manifestations of what Yonnet terms "une collectivité individualiste et pacifique" or "une anti-foule", in which the members may remain anonymous but never dissolve into the mass. With this observation we are introduced to "... l'étonnante liberté polymorphe des pratiquants du tiercé, and it is to this multi-faceted freedom that we must now give some consideration.[28]

To begin with, and as just suggested, the *tiercéiste* is free of both human leadership and guiding ideas like local particularism and national chauvinism. In this, incidentally, he is not only contrasted with the football supporter, but also with the followers of the great majority of star-based modern sports. In addition, his free-time activity is practised in a way which is itself uniquely free from social constraint:

> "...la communauté ludique des tiercéistes apparaît également comme une société d'anonymes. Le tiercéiste, pour jouer, n'est pas tenu d'avoir une histoire. Il est l'individu qui, pour une matinée, se dégage des identités, du marquage social. Il abandonne les estampilles quotidiennes, ignore les cachets faisant foi de sa personne, il échappe aux coordonnées, se libère des contraintes professionnelles, administratives, économiques, politiques et familiales. Il flotte dans une étrange liberté gazéifée: ce faisant, on pourrait presque dire qu'il se neutralise

---

[27] Figures for the cycle race's audience are taken from 1991 publicity material supplied by the Société du Tour de France.

[28] Yonnet, pp.44-57.

comme acteur social. Ne compte plus pour lui qu'une seule histoire: celle de la course et des compétiteurs."[29]

This brand of freedom may readily appear scandalous to the politicised and the politicising. Indeed, several leading public figures have publicly declared their hostility to the *tiercé*, including notably François Mitterrand, although wisely not in his present lofty incarnation. However, the real attraction of this *liberté tiercéiste* for the "average" citizen is beyond doubt, as anyone who has ventured into the PMU on a Sunday morning can testify. This particular form of sociability is, like all others, accompanied by its own rituals: the role of social drinking is only the most obvious of these and, although of undoubted importance, may consequently be overestimated in the French context. In reality, it is only part of a more complex procedure involved in the selection of the vital three numbers. One of the most infamous and untypical of *tiercéistes* - Patrice des Moutis or "Monsieur X", the shadowy figure at the centre of a string of alleged frauds in the 1960s - is, nevertheless, represented as profoundly typical in this respect:

> "Assis à une table basse, les manches de son polo grenat retroussés, le nez plongé dans un monceau de journaux hippiques, il se livrait à un exercice que six millions de Français pratiquent le samedi soir: l'étude de la course du tiercé. Le 'papier'."[30]

Whilst the coffee table and the elegant clothes might more usually be replaced by a *bistrot* counter and the *bleus de chauffe*, this image of a national

---

[29] Ibid, p.50. Compare McKibben's comments on popular gambling's constitution of "... a whole system of knowledge, which, unlike bourgeois systems of knowledge, was, at least potentially, open to all working men" (p.123).

[30] R. Lesparda, *La Maffia du tiercé*, Paris, Editions et Publications Premières, Paris, 1970, p.24.

Saturday evening preoccupation is an accurate one. By the same token, the sociable preparation of the betting tickets or *bordereaux* is very much a dominical institution in contemporary France. The relative complexity of this procedure - *pliage, inscription, encochage, dépliage* - has been significantly reduced in recent years by the computerisation of the PMU's operations. Nowadays, it is a simple matter of marking the required combination on a computer-readable printed card. Indeed, it is now possible to bet with the PMU by *Minitel*, but the trip to the local café to fill in the tickets purchased there, to have them registered and time-stamped, and, above all, to discuss that day's *événement* with like-minded individuals, remains very much a part of the routine and the abiding attraction of the *tiercé*.

Both partisans and critics of the *tiercé* are agreed that this form of betting constitutes a national institution. As one historian of the French turf puts it: "... l'engouement pour le pari tiercé revêt en France le caractère d'un véritable jeu national".[31] This is a view shared by a Communist critic of the bet: "Le tiercé est une institution tellement ancrée dans les moeurs françaises qu'il n'est pas question de la supprimer".[32] It is as such an institution that the *tiercé* has been affectionately ridiculed in the B.D. adventures of "Superdupont", "le seul super-héros 100% français!", who has also saved for future generations of French citizens such distinctive institutions as Camembert cheese and the Tour Eiffel. In what may, in the light of Ladbrokes' recent challenge to the PMU's monopoly, be seen as a prophetic battle to save the *tiercé* from a hostile foreign coalition known as "l'anti-France", "le Français volant" appeals to his compatriots' sense of national duty:

"Je m'adresse à tous les Français turfistes et non-turfistes à qui je donne rendez-vous dimanche prochain pour la grande journée

---

[31] E. Sabatier, *Chevaux, courses et jeu*, Paris, Crépin-Leblond, 1972, p.136.

[32] C. Picant, *Dossier T comme tiercé*, Paris, A. Moreau, 1979, p.205.

nationale du tiercé! Ensemble, nous miserons pour la France!
Pas d'abstention! Tous unis pour le tiercé national!"[33]

In fact, the most telling aspect of this wickedly accurate depiction of the *tiercé*'s role in French social life is the reason for the fictitious national day devoted to it in "*Opération tiercé*", namely, to make up a shortfall in the national budget. The real French state's use and abuse of the *prélèvement légal* will not be discussed here, however, so let us simply note that whilst the *tiercé* may not be accompanied by the nationalism associated with football and other modern sports, it nevertheless constitutes a "proof of Frenchness", in much the same way as does the drinking of wine.[34] Thus regarded, this dominical manifestation of French *citoyenneté* invites comparison with other, more formal, expressions of citizenship.

It is revealing to note that Yonnet's essay on the *tiercé* is subtitled "les nouveaux dimanches de la démocratie": "new", that is to say, because the freeing of Sunday from the traditional rural constraints of work on the one hand and religious observance on the other marks a crucial phase in the economic and social restructuring of modern France. Like the 40-hour week and paid annual holidays instituted by the Popular Front, the generalised extension of the century-old Sunday holiday into the modern weekend on the Anglo-Saxon model is a milestone in this continuing process. Indeed, it is "l'évidement du dimanche, sa naissance au loisir moderne" in the years following the Second World War which accounts for much of the *tiercé*'s success.[35] For, if the general increase in both leisure time and the money needed for spending on it made possible a new freedom, it also made possible

---

[33] Lob and Gotlib, *Superdupont: t.4 'Oui nide iou'*, Paris, Editions Audie, 1983, pp.17-23 (p.17 for the principal quotation).

[34] See R. Barthes, "Le Vin et le lait" in the same author's *Mythologies*, Paris, Seuil, 1957.

[35] Yonnet, p.71. See pp.66-73 for the full argument.

a new boredom: "'Que peut-on faire le dimanche?'".[36] It is no coincidence that the best known example of the specialist periodicals spawned by the *tiercé* should be called precisely *Weekend*. The launch of the new Sunday bet was perfectly timed to coincide with the emergence of a vast new leisure market, as religious observance gave way to bored affluence.

The dominical expression by millions of French citizens, at a nationwide network of state-run offices, of their choice of candidates for a brighter future must, inevitably, evoke both the *gestuelle* and the *langage* of the electoral process: *Aux guichets, citoyens!*, as it were. However, this parody of the expression of popular suffrage in a parliamentary democracy must not be taken too seriously.[37] The real extent to which any working-class voter might genuinely confuse the irreducible roles of *tiercéiste* and elector is surely extremely limited; to think otherwise would seem to betray something like a contempt for such electors. Indeed, being aware of your real inability to influence the outcome of events at Longchamp or Vincennes does not, at least to this observer, seem to constitute evidence of a subliminal consciousness of the individual's irrelevance to the permanent social conflict which underlies political elections. The genuinely democratic aspects of the *tiercé* are to be found elsewhere, I would suggest, in the strikingly unselective pattern of returns on investment which has already been noted. This phenomenon was, in fact, consciously encouraged by the racing authorities through the statutory limitation of individual stakes on any one *événement*. As André Carrus himself explains:

"La grande séduction du tiercé, c'est que chacun peut y jouer.

---

[36] Ibid, pp.71-73.

[37] In particular, I should wish to part company with Yonnet when he claims that the superficial resemblance between the two mass phenomena points to a profound depoliticisation of the *couches populaires* so attached to the *tiercé*. Indeed, to insist overmuch on the bet's *"simulacre du suffrage"* seems very like an example of that academic *"ouvriéro-intellectualisme"* so regularly castigated by Yonnet himself (pp.8-12, 23-26 and 59-63).

Mais pour qu'il conserve le caractère démocratique qu'il avait lorsque nous l'avons lancé, il faut que chacun ait des chances comparables d'y gagner."[38]

Altogether more persuasive, however, is Yonnet's general conclusion about the profoundly scandalous nature of the *tiercé* and the *tiercéistes* in contemporary French society:

"Le tiercé ne propose pas au parieur une conquête (personnelle ou sociale), il ne lui assigne aucun but prestigieux, il ne l'entraîne pas vers les cimes, il ne permet pas le dialogue avec les dieux. Aucune tentation luciférienne ne le traverse: c'est un jeu antiprométhéen.

[...] Jeu sans prétentions, facteur d'inertie sociale et personnelle, le tiercé s'établit à l'écart des contraintes sociales, idéo-politiques, et des exigences statutaires. [...] [C'est] un jeu profondément, pacifique. Et c'est là peut-être sa dimension scandaleuse: le tiercé est un *jeu apollinien* dans une société tout entière acquise aux finalités agressives, à la compétition économique et sociale, aux ambitions prométhéennes.[39]

So, *Le Monde* will undoubtedly continue to provide the specialist information required by those seeking personal aggrandisement through speculation on the *Bourse*, but it is unlikely that we will ever see a *supplément tiercé* appearing under its banner for the benefit of those tempted by a more modest form of investment. Of course, its readers are extremely unlikely to play the game in any case. Here again, we see the difference between the British and French situations; no British quality newspaper would dream of

---

[38] Cited by Lesparda, p.85.

[39] Yonnet, pp.73-74. Compare however, J. Lorcey, *Les Scandales des courses et du tiercé*, Le Havre, P. d'Antoine, 1978, p.13: "...les courses donnent au joueur le sentiment profond qu'il va faire usage de sa science pour éliminer le hasard. [...] Je l'avais dit! crie le turfiste heureux. Pendant un instant, il a tenu (ou cru tenir) les événements dans sa main: il est devenu l'égal de Dieu!"

dropping its daily racing pages. So, if it is true, as we hope to have suggested, that, to quote a highly critical journalist from *L'Humanité*, "le monde du tiercé est bien un microcosme de la France du Ve République", then we are unlikely ever to learn much about that world in the august pages of *Le Monde* itself.[40]

What then of the future? Despite occasional local difficulties - such as the June 1991 lightning strike by jockeys, which halted the *tiercé* and thus lost the state 25 million francs in approximately two and a half minutes[41] the French racing industry remains in a very healthy position, thanks in large part to the continued success of André Carrus's celebrated invention. As with every goose that lays a golden egg, of course, there will always be the risk of overexploitation. The abuse of the *prélèvement légal* to make up fiscal shortfalls is one obvious example of this permanent temptation; the proliferation of *tiercé*-style bets is another. As, indeed, is the introduction of *tiercé*s on weekdays, a development regarded by Léon Zitrone no less as an "heretical" threat to the bet's quintessentially dominical character.[42] Nor must the internal competition from a buoyant national lottery and its new games - like Tac-o-Tac, Tapis Vert, and perhaps most importantly, *le Loto sportif* - be overlooked, without for all that overestimating the limited nature of this threat

---

[40] See the appendix on *Le Monde*'s contemptuous attitude to the *tiercé*, in Yonnet, op. cit., pp.75-77. This attitude is reflected in the humorous tone of the recent article cited above (n.4).

[41] See: G. Petitjean, "Courses: des milliards sous la botte", *Le Nouvel Observateur*, no. 1393, 18-24 juillet 1991, p.6.

[42] L. Zitrone, *Mon tiercé*, Monaco, R. Solar, 1966, p.98. "Pour moi qui déteste les jeux de hasard et qui estime que les gagnants doivent être découverts par réflexion et par calcul, le Tiercé en semaine est une hérésie: aucun turfiste ne dispose du temps de réflexion nécessaire pour étudier, sur son journal favori, les chances des concurrents". It is worth recalling, perhaps, that Zitrone has long been known as the voice of both the *tiercé* and the Tour de France.

to the *tiercé*'s very specific consituency.[43] As for the external challenge made to the PMU's continued monopoly by the real "*anti-France*" of Ladbrokes and the other British bookmakers as 1992 approaches, the recent European Commission ruling against the French government would seem to be considerably less harsh than had been feared.[44]

Far more dangerous is the insidious threat posed to the *tiercé* by changes in French patterns of work and leisure. The PMU's institutional link to the *bistrot*, for so long a source of strength, is increasingly being seen as a liability.[45] The decline of *le zinc* could well mean that the *tiercé* goes the same way as the *gros rouge, beret basque* and 2CV. These are stereotypes admittedly, but reflecting a genuine socio-cultural specificity nevertheless. The *tiercé*'s broad church is one of several contemporary antidotes to the age-old disparateness of the French nation, much like the Tour de France, which glorifies that disparity and, as Roland Bathes demonstrated, raises it to the level of the modern epic.[46] For long the *chasse gardée* of continental Europeans, the tour has now become a truly world-wide competition and thus a global

---

[43] See: P. Delannoy, "Loteries, progression fulgurante du loto", in J.-Y. Potel, *L'Etat de la France et des ses habitants*, Paris, La Découverte, 1985, pp.128-130. Compare G. Mermet, *Francoscopie: les Français: Qui sont-ils? Où vont-ils?*, Paris, Larousse, 1985, pp.299-300, "Les jeux de hasard ou la fortune du pot". Also of interest is D. Stoneham, "A Pari-Mutuel Society", *Pacemaker*, February 1977, pp.87-88.

[44] See: G. Petitjean, "Un book contre le PMU", *Le Nouvel Observateur*, No. 1393, 18-24 juillet 1991, p.9. This article explains the European Commission's ruling against the French government, which must suspend only 50 million francs of its annual fiscal aid to the PMU, rather than the 1.5 billion francs demanded by Sir Leon Brittan, the commissioner responsible for intra-European competition. The PMU's continued monopoly would itself seem to be in no doubt. See also, P. Hayward, "Betting 'war' in Europe", *The Independent*, 15 February 1990.

[45] R. Holt, *Sport and Society*, p.131: "Since the Second World War the old culture of the café has been eroded by the affluence of the nuclear family, with its televisions and private cars. The young now prefer the new spectator sports".

[46] R. Barthes, "Le Tour de France comme épopée", in *Mythologies*. Compare Holt, *Sport and Society*, p.11: "In the Tour de France urban and rural populations alike found a *fête nationale* which actually coincided with the new Bastille Day celebrations". The Tour itself dates from 1903.

televisual commodity. Its future consequently seems assured. The *tiercé*'s unique brand of sociability may, in contrast, no longer be required in the France of the final decade of the 20th century. Its long-term future is particularly problematic to the extent that the post-1945 "massification" of French society may be more or less equated with the Americanisation of western Europe, as a whole; a process which seems sure to continue apace in the wake of the terminal collapse of the competing social model in the East. The geographical and historical specificity of the *tiercé* has so far been at the root of its great strength; only time will tell whether this particular form of French "otherness" will survive the next forty or so years.

13.   **THE EVOLUTION OF THE CULTURAL STATUS OF THE COMIC STRIP: AN ART FORM IN SEARCH OF RECOGNITION**

THIERRY GROENSTEEN

In October 1989, I left my post as editor of the specialist journal *Les cahiers de la bande dessinée* to become Scientific Advisor at the Centre National de la Bande Dessinée et de l'Image (CNBDI, Angoulême), an organisation which was at that time still quite small. If I open this brief account with an autobiographical detail, it is only to emphasise a fact which was inconceivable twenty years ago: thanks to the joint agreement of the President of the Republic and his Minister for Culture, France now has a Centre National whose task is to preserve and protect the comic strip. The State therefore officially recognises that the comic strip is part of French national heritage and as such should be included in cultural policy. Naturally, such a policy would be misunderstood and politically untenable if it were not supported by a general consensus.

To say that the comic strip goes back a long way would be an understatement. Although it is recognised as an art form in its own right (the 9th), it was until recently decried, maligned, criticized and disregarded. Why did this change come about? After having answered this question, I will give my own analysis of the present situation and of the work I feel still has to be done before the true worth of the comic strip is recognised.

Before the war neither politicians, schools, universities nor the media paid much attention to the comic strip. At that time there were no specialist bookshops or critiques available. In fact, the comic strip had no cultural identity at all. The only value it did have was a socio-economic one, since its lack of official recognition contrasted with an enormous general popularity. Since the strip cartoon represented virtually their only access to the visual image, young people in France, whether they were working- or middle-class, avidly bought each week "picture magazines", the most significant of which sold several hundred thousand copies. We should, however, consider two basic points. Firstly, the French "bande dessinée" was rarer than and of inferior quality to its American counterpart, the "comic", and other foreign strip cartoons. Secondly, and more importantly, French comic strips were only for children; and when foreign versions not intended for children were translated into French, they were in effect subsumed into children's literature since they appeared in young people's magazines.

The very words "bande dessinée" had not yet come into the language. The first written record we have found features in a contract belonging to Opera Mundi (a Press Agency), dated 17th December 1940. However, it was not until the mid-fifties that the term became widespread and 1960 before it came into common parlance. It was only in 1968 that it was first attested by dictionaries.

The first people to take an interest in the comic strip were neither those with a penchant for literature or the plastic arts, but educationalists and politicians, united in their crusade to control children's minds. On July 16th 1949 Parliament voted in a law concerning publications aimed at young people. This law, still in force today, even if it is much less rigorously applied, introduced a new offence into French legislation: "moral corruption of the young". This is not the place to go into the details of the law, nor to analyse the various reasons for its adoption, the most important of which was the desire for moral protection of the young. It should, however, be noted that it was a law which not only sought to condemn racism, the vindication of crime, violence and eroticism but which also sanctioned episodes which were not true to life, pictures seen as ugly, clumsy or vulgar, humour considered distasteful - in short, a law which exercised genuine power over aesthetics.

The campaign which denounced the harmful effects of the comic strip started at the end of the 1930s and was still much in evidence in the 1950s. I will merely cite two of the most famous diatribes here.

Firstly, there is that of Louis Pauwels, today director of *Figaro Magazine* and previously inventor of the concept "sida mental" ("mental A.I.D.S."), which proves a certain continuity in his thought. On the 30th December 1947, Pauwels wrote in an article on the subject of comic strips in *Combat*:

> "J'ai sur ma table, aujourd'hui, tous ces journaux. Je viens de les regarder un à un. J'ai les yeux broyés. Je sors de là comme d'un très poisseux cauchemar. J'ai le sentiment d'avoir été, pendant deux heures, aspiré par les plus sales bêtes sous-marines, engourdi, voulant crier et ne pouvant pas, plongé dans la terreur fixe, enfoncé dans le barbouillis cher aux psychanalystes, tournant, la tête en bas, dans le remugle des sourds désirs, des envies de viols et de tortures... On m'avait dit, depuis longtemps, que la plupart de ces journaux, étaient bien tristes à voir. On m'avait mal renseigné. Ils sont ignobles."

Sartre's journal *Les Temps modernes* devoted no less than three articles to the subject, all extremely negative (1946, May 1949 and October 1955). The second, published two months before the law was passed, was translated from the original American and was called "Psychopathologie des comics" in which George Legman wrote:

> "Les comic books ont réussi à donner à chaque enfant américain un cours complet de mégalomanie paranoïaque, tel qu'aucun enfant allemand n'en a jamais suivi, une confiance totale dans la morale de la force brutale, telle qu'aucun nazi n'a jamais pu le rêver... (...) Que les éditeurs, les dessinateurs et les auteurs de comics soient des dégénérés et des gibiers de potence, cela va sans dire, mais pourquoi donc des millions d'adolescents admettent-ils passivement cette dégénérescence?"

There is a wealth of similar quotations, such was the number of hysterical outbursts against the "comic" press. With hindsight, this seems to us to be relatively innocent and certainly much less likely to traumatise an individual than certain television programmes currently shown at peak viewing times.

In the midst of this almost universal condemnation, a few dissident voices made themselves heard, especially in top cultural journals such as *Critique* (no. 117, February 1957) and *Le Nef* (no. 13, January 1958) in which Edgar Morin wrote: "Il y a souvent plus de poésie, d'audace imaginative, d'humour dans la presse enfantine que dans la presse pour adultes. Je gémis à penser que l'enfant qui lit Vaillant, Tintin, Mickey, lira plus tard nous savons bien quoi."

The first books to tackle the subject are monographs devoted to popular comic strip stars: *Le petit monde de Pif le chien* by Barthelemy Amengual (1955) and *Le Monde de Tintin* by Pòl Vandromme (1959). Amengual, however, managed to get published in Algiers. In 1956, Grasset published a biographical essay on Christophe, author of *La Famille Fenouillard* and the *Sapeur Camember*, by François Caradec, a pataphysician and future member of Oulipo. Caradec was however unable to find a French publisher for his comic strip anthology from its origins to 1940, a work which served as a model for the genre. It appeared in Italy in January 1963 under the title *I Primi Eroi*.

As has often been related since, the text which was to trigger off the original movement for the study and revival of the comic strip was the article by the Genevan Pierre Strinati "Bandes dessinées et science fiction. L'âge d'or en France (1934-1940)", which appeared in *Fiction*, no. 92 (July 1961). This article provoked such a mass of letters to the editor that a "Club des bandes dessinées" was formed in May 1962 at the suggestion of a correspondent.

The Club's board of directors included Francis Lacassin (President), Alain Resnais, Guy Bonnemaison, Jean-Claude Forest (artistic director) and Pierre Couperie (archivist). Other active members would include Pierre Strinati, Remo Forlani, Evelyne Sullerot, Pierre Pascal (a Bordeaux bar owner who was to become a long-term director of the Salon International d'Angoulême), Jean-Claude Romer and Jacques Lob. Amongst the sympathisers who would participate in or even support different activities: Boileau and Narcejac, André Froissart, Marcel Brion of the Académie Française, Umberto Eco. Finally, a "sponsorship committee" was formed at the end of 1964. Originally including Jean Adhémar, Jean Chapelle, Federico Fellini, Pierre Lazareff, François le Lionnais and Paul Winkler, it extended its membership the following year to Edgar Morin and René Goscinny. Apart from a very small number of comic strip authors (Forest, Lob, Goscinny, i.e. one single cartoonist and two caption writers), the majority of the membership belonged to the world of literature and cinema, to the press and to the universities, a balance which, still today, seems relatively fair. In any case, this collection of such eminent personalities refuted all popular prejudices which made out that comic strips could only attract the support of cretins, perverts and morons.

Giff-Wiff, the Club's newsletter, was launched in July 1962 but would fold in March 1967 after 23 issues of which the last four were published by Jean-Jacques Pauvert. This joint campaign to support a much maligned art form was openly nostalgic. The opening sentence of the first edition of Giff-Wiff read thus: "Les illustrés disparus dans la débâcle de 1940 avaient laissé chez leurs lecteurs une nostalgie qui, curieusement, semble être devenue de plus en plus obsédante au cours de ces dernières années". The Club's objective was therefore to uphold the memory of bygone days, particularly by reproducing past issues.

Moreover, the period with which the members of the Club were concerned was quite narrowly defined, starting in 1934 (the launch-date of Paul Winkler's Journal de Mickey) and ending in 1942. This coincides exactly with the time when French magazines were being dominated by comic strips of American origin. The fact that these comic strips have since been so glorified that they have all been labelled as belonging to the golden age of the genre can be partly justified by their genuine qualities but more importantly stems from the beginning of a new generation. A survey published in nos 3-4 revealed that most of the Club's first 300 members were born between 1926 and 1934. Now in their thirties, they had fond memories of what they had read as children, unaware of what had been written earlier (like the wonderful work of Töpffer and Christophe or Caran d'Ache's playlets) and, in the majority of cases, had failed to keep up with the contemporary scene. The most sought-after series which were to be republished were *Flash Gordon* (alias Guy l'éclair), Buck Rogers (Luc Bradefer), Mandrake, Popeye, Tarzan etc. Although notably different from the others, *Futoropolis*, by the French writer René Pellos, can rather surprisingly be included in this category.

Following Alain Resnais' suggestion, the Club was officially rechristened CELEG (Centre d'Etude des Littératures d'Expression Graphique) on 5th November 1964. This change of name was apparently motivated by a desire for respectability upon which the comic strip was still a long way from being able to pride itself.

Francis Lacassin pointed out the new aims of the Club during its General Meeting of 7th July 1963. Henceforth, there were to be two main objectives: a) the defence of the strip cartoon, as much against the prejudices and criticisms which it suffered as against certain editors themselves, who were accused of undermining the integrity of aesthetic quality of the strip cartoon by clumsy technical interference; b) to define the "aesthetics of the comic strip". Thus the supportive and innocuous activities of a group of comic strip lovers was beginning to look like a subtle campaign.

It would be impossible to mention here all the initiatives and public events organised by Celeg. It reprinted classics and started foreign sections, jointly organised the first Salon International which took place in Italy in March 1965 and was the inspiration behind a series of television programmes

212

broadcast on the ORTF's second channel in April 1967 (*Les mille et un héros de la bande dessinée*). The press reported this "long haul" favourably, and public opinion (or at least that of the Parisian intelligentsia) seemed to have changed so rapidly that in 1967 Lacassin stated his belief that the strip cartoon was becoming fashionable and the last bastion of snobbery.

It was to be a rival organisation, Socerlid (Société Civile d'Etudes et de Recherches des Littératures Dessinées, formed in November 1964 by five Celeg dissidents) that was to develop this wide-spread interest, if not recognition, by organising exhibitions. The largest was to be *Bande dessinée et figuration narrative*, held at the Musée des Arts décoratifs in the Spring of 1967. Its catalogue was the first French work to compile a synthesis of the comic strip phenomenon from a historical, sociological, thematic and aesthetic point of view, thanks to the use of knowledge and concepts which today seem rather dated.

The collection of 48 issues of the journal *Phénix*, published between October 1966 and Spring 1977, remains further proof of Socerlid's intense activity. Compared to *Giff-Wiff*, it had already become a second-generation publication. Priority was given to European production. It was mainly in *Phénix* that the famous trio of cartoonists became established: Hergé, Edgar P. Jacobs and Jacques Martin who were respectively entitled to twelve, nine and five articles each and who were henceforth known as the Masters of the "Brussels School". Thanks to this network of correspondents, the journal offered useful insights into the world-wide cartoon scene. It eventually published new works by top artists such as the Italians Crepax and Pratt, the Argentinian Breccia and the French Mandryk and Druillet. If *Phénix* was never to have any serious competition, its specialist publications, often with quite an amateur status (known as "fanzines") nonetheless continued to thrive from 1966 onwards.

The crucial development at this time was the emergence of the adult strip cartoon. The way had partly been cleared by a number of serials published daily, especially those in *France-Soir*. But the most significant steps forward must be attributed to the members of Celeg. The first liberated heroine, *Barbarella* (1962), was created by Jean-Claude Forest. Edited by Remo Forlani, the magazine *Chouchou*, whose existence was to be unfortunately brief (14 issues in 1964-5) was a forerunner of the "new press" to come. Finally, we have René Goscinny to thank for Astérix, whose success started to reach mythical heights in 1965. By this time there was sufficient evidence that a comic strip destined for all readerships could be interpreted at different levels.

Astérix, the little Gaul, made the front page of *L'Express* on 19th September 1966. His success benefitted the weekly *Pilote* of which he was the star and Goscinny the editor. Developing with its readership and adopting the slogan "the magazine which likes to think", *Pilote* was to be the driving force behind the evolution of the French comic strip. Its most notable contributions between 1968 and 1972 came from Giraud, Druillet, Gotlib, Bretécher, Reiser, Cabu, Fred, Mandryka, not forgetting *Lucky Luke* or *Achille Talon*. Later they were to be joined by F'Murr, Tardi, Bilal, Lauzier, Régis Franc etc. Open to all new aesthetic and narrative ideas, *Pilote* was the real melting pot of the modern French cartoon. In it the strip cartoon did not simply become "for adults", it became fundamentally and irrevocably *an* adult art form. This transformation mainly came about through a greater appreciation of the author who was sometimes even made into a star, and was no longer regarded as an obscure and almost anonymous puppeteer pulling his hero's strings.

I will now give a briefer overview of recent times, only mentioning the most significant events in the search for recognition initiated in the sixties.

1970 - The Ecole des Loisirs published *La bande dessinée peut être éducative* by the educationalist Antoine Roux, a treatise which marked the beginning of a return to favour of a kind of literature which had been hitherto

214

banned in schools.

1971 - At the Sorbonne, Francis Lacassin became Professor of the History and Aesthetics of the Comic Strip. *Le Nouvel Observateur* was the first sizeable general publication to introduce a regular slot on the comic strip. New comic strips themselves also became established with the arrival of Claire Bretécher in 1973 and Reiser in 1981.

1972 - Pierre Fresnault-Dervelle's book *La bande dessinée, essai d'analyse sémiotique* (Hachette) triggered off a whole series of University research publications.

1974 - The creation of the Salon international d'Angoulême to be held annually.

1978 - Les Editions Casterman launched the monthly review (*A Suivre*). In his leader, the editor in chief, Jean-Paul Mougin wrote: "Avec toute sa densité romanesque, (*A Suivre*) sera l'irruption sauvage de la bande dessinée dans la littérature".

1979 - On October 4th, the first auction took place of Comic strip albums and illustration plates at the Hôtel Drouot. The cartoon thus made its official entrance into the art market. The Grand Prix des Arts Graphiques was created and was to be awarded annually by the Ministry for Culture. Out of the first ten prizes awarded, six went to the creators of strip cartoons.

1983 - The death of Hergé (Georges Remi, born in 1907) provoked a whole stream of tributes of the sort that had only previously been granted to the greatest figures of our century. Jack Lang announced a fifteen point plan for the comic strip, which included the creation of the Centre National de la Bande Dessinée in Angoulême. The CNBDI was to be opened in 1990.

It may appear today that the comic strip has won its battle. On the one hand, it seems to have blossomed on an artistic level by achieving total freedom of expression. On the other, it can be regarded as having been accepted in

215

cultural circles for what it is, that is to say a fundamentally original means of communication and one of the greatest media forms of the twentieth century. A few reactionaries and doubting Thomases may now and then launch a rearguard action against it, but the important fact remains that the comic strip has won its rightful place in schools, universities, the media, public libraries and museums.

There is a lot of truth in this statement except as far as the media are concerned, a point to which I will return. With Belgium, France has certainly become one of the two countries in the world where the comic strip and those involved in its production are highly revered. However, this eulogy must be qualified. I will firstly make three points on which to reflect.

1. The 1949 law has been cited, and the banning of certain editions in the 1980s has given it even wider scope in its application. In all the written accounts as well as in everyday life, the whole of the comic strip genre continues to be classified under young people's literature. The absurdity of such a position is easily confirmed by a rapid analysis of what is actually being published.

2. The comic strip was supported for fifteen years by a growing readership and by a subsequent increase in sales. But since 1983, a record year for publications, sales and turnover, the market has entered a period of recession. Comic strips are no longer fashionable; they have lost their originality (about 30% of 15-19 year olds never read any, as revealed by the latest survey by the Ministry for Culture *Les Pratiques culturelles des Français*). This trend can be explained partly by the emergence of new leisure activities (cable television, theme parks, video games, compact discs) which have captured a share of consumer spending.

3. But another factor in this comparative fall from grace is overproduction. With an average of two collections published every day (not forgetting cartoon strips in the press), editors have swamped the cartoon fan

216

with a whole host of titles whose quality too often leaves much to be desired. Large stores limit themselves to selling "dead certs", i.e. series most likely to sell, and specialist bookshops (of which there are about 150 in France) are often financially unable to champion quality and - even worse - originality. Far too many collections fail and are sold at a knock-down price very soon after their appearance on the bookstalls.

The state of crisis which the French cartoon has been experiencing for a few years now (an economic and identity crisis but also doubtless a creativity crisis) can be interpreted in several ways. Jean-Luc Fromental, caption writer and driving force behind the editorial scene, sums up the opinion of part of the profession (doubtless a minority) when he writes:

> "Dans une confusion typique entre l'aspiration à la maturité et la tentation de la légitimité, la bande dessinée a sacrifié tout ou partie de sa formidable liberté. (...) La reconnaissance, les honneurs sont des contrôles. Les distinctions sont des procès. En acceptant un ordre qui n'était pas le sien, la BD a gravement hypothéqué ses spécificités. (...) C'est parce qu'on n'attendait pas d'elle qu'elle dise quoi que ce soit qu'elle a pu tant en dire au moment de son essor. (...) Sa naïveté, sa prétendue innocuité étaient les conditions de sa pertinence, c'est-à-dire de son impertinence..." (in *Les Cahiers de la bande dessinée*, no. 73, janv.-fév. 1987, p.76).

Has the acceptance of the comic strip by powerful cultural bodies harmed the finished product? Can the Centre National d'Angoulême be considered the graveyard of a defunct art form? I do not believe so, nor do I foresee this situation occurring in the future. It is my belief that recognition must be extended further. It is precisely because this development begun thirty years ago has not been carried through to completion that instead of acceptance there is now much ignorance concerning the comic strip.

If the media carried out its true rôle of mediating and informing, as it does for literature and the cinema, the public would be less confused and discouraged by this random overproduction, and authors would be less tempted to move into painting or the cinema (as more and more of them are doing). The truth is that in the press, as on television and radio programmes, there is no regular, incisive information given about new publications which are worthy of coverage. For four years I personally attempted to remedy this in my *Le Monde* articles, before resigning, sickened by the apathy of the editorial staff.

Since the *Cahiers de la bande dessinée* ceased to be published in 1990, there has been little or no popularising criticism, nor any intellectual criticism from a specialized standpoint. On the other hand, there are dozens of magazines devoted to the cinema, from the most general to the most elitist. Moreover, it is enlightening to compare critiques of the 7th and 9th art forms. Why did the comic strip only become a subject for study and research in the 1960s when the cinema has been discussed for almost as long as the genre has existed? Why, from Eisenstein to Godard, have so many great film directors written about their art form when cartoonists have remained silent? Why is the cinema studied in all major French universities while the comic strip is totally neglected?

The wide-spread acceptance of the comic strip is partly an illusion. In reality, it has not really penetrated the bastion of humanist "high culture", that of the Fine Arts devoted to the ideal of the Sublime, nor has it gained a place in the "New Culture of the Media", that of cinema, fashion, advertising and video clips. Comic mania remains a phenomenon on the fringes of old and modern culture and one which has not really created its own cultural identity: the illustrious past of the comic strip remains largely unknown and out of reach.

Militancy in the 1960s gave rise to many pseudo-debates on the subject of the comic strip and it sometimes encouraged strange forms of idolatory. it can be more or less criticized for its obsession with a certain type of American comic strip (of an epic and fantasy type), its search for historical and cultural roots (from Lascaux to Bayeux) which had in reality no connection with it, and

218

its obsession with the fetish of collections in its most perverse form.

The comic strip is still searching for a true identity. It will take a while before the three preconditions are satisfied: a change in our definition of culture, a deepening of our knowledge and a more accurate evaluation of the specific terminology of an art form which goes beyond the boundaries of traditional intellectual pursuits.

14.   IDENTITY AND ICONOGRAPHY: FRENCH WAR MEMORIALS
       1914-1918 AND 1939-1945

WILLIAM KIDD

This chapter examines ways in which the "monuments aux morts" can be considered both as reflecting socio-cultural traits and as constructing identity by giving representational form to basic constituents of place, name, memory and values. Using illustrations drawn from Stirling University French Photographic Archive,[1] it also analyses some of the ideological and iconographical continuities and discontinuites between the first and second conflicts. Before addressing these issues, however, I propose to draw a number of parallels between my subject and Thierry Groensteen's chapter on *la bande dessinée* which, though ultimately spurious, help to highlight the conceptual and judgemental difficulties inherent in our terms of reference, culture and social identity.

The first and most reductive analogy lies in the cartoon-like simplicities of memorials assimilating the "poilus" of 1914-18 to Vercingetorix (the Loire) and "nos ancêtres les gaulois" (Barbizon, Seine-et-Marne), a theme also recalled in the Gallic cockerel which graced so many of them. Then there were the Clochemerlesque "querelles de clocher" about design, cost, location which the memorials engendered, the inter-village rivalries, the wheeling and dealing of memorial artists and salesmen, and, finally, the predictable cast of characters at the inauguration: local politicians, clergy, moustachioed veterans, *sociétés de gymnastique*, chorales, etc. Captured for posterity on postcards and calendars,

---

[1] I wish to record my thanks to staff, students and friends of the department who have contributed items to the archive since its inception in 1987. L. Adair, A. Leishman, M. Bretenoux, P. Minne, J. Monaghan, A. Smith and J. Wood deserve a special mention for illustrations used in this chapter, as do my colleagues Miss H. E. Beale, Mr A. H. Blyth and Dr B. C. Swift, my head of department, Siân Reynolds, for financial and support and Senior AVA Technician Ron Stewart for the slides he prepared.

the history/story of the memorials represents a rich potential for tragi-comic caricature whose reality is piquantly underlined in Christian Bachelier's description of the ways in which "la commémoration des guerres" not infrequently became "la guerre des commémorations".[2] As a focus for ceremonial, memorials belong within national rituals of identity, have an ideological dimension which the particular circumstances of the Second World War complicated but did not create.

A more directly pertinent series of reflections arises from the extent to which, like *la bande dessinée*, war memorials could be considered to have been "un art en quête de légitimité". One might have imagined that the sacrifice of one million four hundred thousand Frenchmen between 1914 and 1918, the grief of their families, and the collective consciousness of the survivors would more than legitimize the monuments erected to their memory in some 36,000 metropolitan communes. In fact, *qua* art, these memorials have had an extremely bad press. From sources as different as Giraudoux, Bernanos and the *Revue du Touring Club de France*, the comments elicited are depressingly consistent with Jean Dutourd's expressed contempt for "cette éclosion unique de navets dans l'histoire de la sculpture et dans l'histoire de France",[3] and Jean-Marie Dubusscher's irreverent evocation of "l'hexagonale implosion de l'art patriotic-tumbulaire".[4]

Doubtless, their very number and ubiquity has contributed to this view. But when A.J.P. Taylor observed twenty-five years ago that the memorials erected in different European countries to the dead of 1914-18 "present a

---

[2] *La mémoire des Français, Quarante ans de commémorations de la seconde guerre mondiale*, Paris, Editions du CNRS, 1986, p.63.

[3] *Les Taxis de la Marne*, Paris, Gallimard, "Le Livre de Poche", 1956, p.202.

[4] "A l'ombre des monuments aux morts", in *Entre Deux Guerres (la création française entre 1919 et 1939)*, sous la direction d'Olivier Barrot et Pascal Ory, Paris, Editions François Bourin, 1990, pp.13-25, p.14.

curious picture of popular taste, which has never been studied",[5] he did so precisely because they are not examples of "high art". Commissioned and paid for by local communities - a pro rata contribution was available from the state, subject to prefectoral approval, usually after scrutiny by the departmental Direction de l'Architecture et des Beaux Arts - they were sometimes built by local sculptors or stonemasons. Discounting, on the one hand, the very small number of works of artists of distinction such as Bourdelle, Maillol or Réal del Sarte,[6] and, on the other, the simple stone obelisks with no or little supplementary adornment which formed the largest proportion,[7] the most common memorials were factory-produced cast-iron or bronze variations on the helmeted and great-coated French infantryman striking a heroic, martial pose, advancing with fixed bayonet or the flag, or vigilant in victory, often with a German *Pickelhaube* underfoot. Charles Pourquet's *Résistance*,[8] or Eugène Bénet's *Combattant Victorieux* from the Fonderies Durenne were especially popular; my illustrations of the latter are from Capy (Somme), and Saint-Martin-de-Boulogne (Pas-de-Calais), but it is found from the Côtes-du-Nord to the Jura, and the Vosges to the Aveyron.[9] Another model, found in the Auvergne, is exemplified by the stone soldier at Saint-Hippolyte, near Châtelguyon (Puy-de-Dôme). Some of these variants are more primitive than others - Pourquet's was sometimes painted in a garish, semi-luminescent "bleu horizon" - and serial commercialism has rarely gone hand in hand with artistic

---

[5] *From Sarajevo to Potsdam*, London, Thames and Hudson, ("Library of European Civilization"), 1966, p.56.

[6] See Annette Becker, *Les Monuments aux morts. Patrimoine et mémoire de la grande guerre*, Paris, Editions Errance, 1989, p.152.

[7] Antoine Prost, *Les Anciens combattants et la société française, 1914-1939*, Vol 3, Paris, Presses de la Fondation Nationale des Sciences Politiques, 1976, p.42.

[8] Annette Becker, *Les Monuments aux morts*, p.18.

[9] Antoine Prost, *Les Anciens combattants et la société française*, p.46.

refinement. But the fact that such memorials were chosen from a manufacturer's catalogue belies their uniquely public-and-private significance for those who chose them. How, and by whom, is their "artistic" quality and aesthetic appropriateness to be measured? Whose culture? Whose identity? To the question-begging observation that "le poilu résolu et volontaire de Pourquet serait ridicule si l'auteur n'avait été, dans le style académique, un 'bon' sculpteur",[10] one could be forgiven for preferring the Burgundian Henri Vincenot's candid admission that in choosing "un stèle de granit tout simple (...), l'urgence nous avait sauvés du mauvais goût", the "urgence" in question being the village's desire not to be beaten by its neighbour.[11] Michel Ragon, I believe, got it about right when he distinguished between memorials by established artists, which, he argued, would have degenerated into tourist attractions, and the work of "tâcherons statuaires [qui] se sont transformés en sculptures populaires correspondant au goût de la majorité des populations".[12] And he continues:

> "Leur esthétique est certes une retombée de la statuaire académique florissante au Père-Lachaise. Mais ils expriment aussi le goût du mélodrame, du beau geste, de la chanson cocardière. Ils sont un peu image d'Epinal et opérette, catalogue de la Manufacture des armes et cycles de Saint-Etienne, dessus de cheminée de salle à manger populaire. Ils témoignent donc d'une culture plébéienne et petite-bourgeoise. Notamment par ce goût de l'accumulation que l'on retrouve aussi bien dans les loges de concierges que dans les jardins ouvriers: récupération d'obus placés en clôture, lourdes chaînes."[13]

---

[10] Ibid, p.46.

[11] Henri Vincenot, *La Billebaude*, Paris, Denoël, 1978, p.98.

[12] Michel Ragon, *L'Espace de la mort. Essai sur l'architecture, la décoration, et l'urbanisme funéraires*, Paris, Albin Michel, 1981, p.122.

[13] Ibid, pp.122-123.

A further and final analogy with "l'art de la bande dessinée" could be drawn in the gap between the scholarly vogue currently enjoyed by the memorials, and the layman's perception of them. Antoine Prost's pioneering work, partially re-issued in the mid-80s,[14] has generated an increasing, though still too limited number of valuable local studies.[15] Annette Becker's richly illustrated volume and the collective survey of the Second World War experience conducted for the Centre National de la Recherche Scientifique and the Institut d'Histoire du Temps Présent in 1986, influenced by Maurice Agulhon's work on Republican imagery and symbolism, have given "les lieux de mémoire" a greater resonance and public profile. But to those unfamiliar with the now abundant literature on the subject, and particularly the layman (and woman), the reaction most readily elicited is still: "les monuments aux morts? Quel rapport? En quoi cela vous regarde-t-il?" The implication is not that the memorials are of no interest, but surprise that objects so transparently familiar might be the focus of intellectual enquiry and iconographical analysis, an "appropriation" to which we must plead guilty, though with mitigating circumstances.

The mitigating circumstances are, of course, that like other artefacts, memorials reflect sociological and ideological realities of their times, and have a documentary value which transcends without necessarily betraying their original intentionality. Like other public monuments, they simultaneously derive meaning from, and confer meaning on, their physical environment, urban or rural, alpine or coastal, secular or religious. The memorials form part of a

---

[14] Antoine Prost, "Les Monuments aux morts. Culte Républicain? Culte Civique? Culte Patriotique?", in *Les Lieux de Mémoire* (I: La République), sous la direction de Pierre Nora, Paris, Gallimard, 1984, pp.195-225.

[15] Studies now exist of the Aisne (David G. Troyansky), Bouches-du-Rhône (Bernard Cousin and Geneviève Richier, Rémi Roques, Christiane Massonnet), the Loire (Monique Luirard), the three Breton departments (Jean-Yves Coulon), and the Vendée (Florence Regourd). The most recent addition to the list is Yves Pilven Le Sevellec's study of the Loire-Atlantique (see below).

décor which is lived in or used: by the *forains* who erect stalls around them, by locals asked for directions to them and who, because they are so much part of their "espace quotidien", sometimes have to think for a moment; by the railwayman's widow who proves a mine of information on the local Resistance; by the priest, pleased but intrigued that the local memorial should interest a foreigner; by the *employé de mairie* who turns out to be the *porte-drapeau* of the local *ancien combattant* association, still angry after twenty years that the "new" memorial makes no reference to Algeria, a war, in his view, not merely a police operation by a discredited colonialist régime. The examples are true but anecdotal and belong therefore to "la petite histoire". But since each and every one was occasioned by an enquiry about the war memorial, and because the latter provide a way into the interlocutor's memory and perception of events, they take us into the "histoire des mentalités" which the concepts of social and cultural identity pre-eminently suppose.

This can be demonstrated from the way the memorials enshrine certain words and phrases which have passed into the language, to become part of the collective identity of a certain "France populaire". Disembarking at Calais in the early sixties, when cross-Channel steamers were not yet car ferries, I overheard this retort from a railway porter to one of his colleagues who dared to complain that he was blocking the gangway with several items of luggage held coolie-style on a leather strap: "t'étais à Verdun, toi? Alors ta gueule!" The difference between this classic "put-down" and its Anglo-Saxon equivalent - "listen mate/son/Jimmy - I was at Sidi Barrani/ Cassino/ Falaise. O.K.?" (delete as appropriate) - is not the latter's more exotic choice of location (usually World War II, moreover), but the unstated "ils ne passeront pas!" of 1916 which, before passing into the lexicon of the Spanish Civil War in 1936 ("no pasarán"), became the "ils n'ont pas passé" on "Le Mort-Homme" at Verdun, and found with variants elsewhere. Likewise, that other resolute watchword of 1916, "on les aura", gave rise to the self-congratulatory "on les a eus" of 1919, inscribed on memorials such as the one at Saint-Georges-de-Didonne (Charente-Maritime). Though vastly outnumbered by non-militaristic expressions of grief, sacrifice and remembrance, such memorials give a basic linguistic consecration to identity in its historic oppositional sense of "them" and "us".

Identity, individual or collective, is however more than mere opposition to the "Other". At Argelès-Gazost (Hautes-Pyrénées), a schoolboy figure scales the front of the monument as if climbing a wall to write a village's epitaph "à ses héros morts pour la France"; the last word - "FRANCE" - dominates the others in size. There is no additional statuary, realistic or allegorical, and no further embellishment of the main face, which functions as a space on which the message is inscribed. Fifty years before the mysteries of the "texte lisible/texte scriptible", this schoolboy was already "writing", permanently re-writing, the identity of the country, asserting its unity from the diversity of its far-flung "communes". Unlike some memorials in the same region, notably in the adjoining Pyrénées-Atlantiques, there is no local geographical specificity here. And for reasons to be explored later, collective regional memorials ("A la Résistance finistérienne", "Aux Picards martyrs de la Résistance"), are characteristic of 1939-45. The vast majority of 1914-18 edifices admit no intermediate entity between "le pays" (i.e. "la commune"), and "le pays", France.

The child's literacy also represents the lasting legacy of the Republican "lois scolaires" and the devotion of a generation of "instituteurs", some 30,000 of whom were mobilised, of whom half were killed. On the memorial at the Ecole Normale de Meurthe-et-Moselle, pupils add a victor's wreath to the "tableau d'honneur" of their "maîtres au sacrifice fécond". At Beauvais, a uniformed teacher tells it like it was to a group of children,[16] and at Bohain (Aisne) a pupil's open book reads "République Française. Dans la paix par

---

[16] Annette Becker, *Les Monuments aux morts*, p.48.

226

l'Etude et le Travail".[17]   With the elimination of illiteracy, the war and the four million letters and cards sent each day from and to the men at the front marked a watershed in the writing habits of ordinary French men and women: "L'acte d'écrire, jadis réservé aux circonstances exceptionnelles de la vie (actes notariés, contrats, faire-part officiels), conserve dans sa quotidienneté quelque chose de sa solennité d'origine (...) on voit pour la première fois, et massivement, que les productions des poilus les plus jeunes sont les véritables travaux pratiques de l'école de Jules Ferry".[18]   Self-expression via education is of course the culture at its most basic and most profound, but the war made the exceptional into the commonplace.   Dehumanised by the military "matricule", in constant danger of obliteration during their months at the front or in "no man's land", physically distant from home and family, writing home and signing their names was one of the few ways the soldiers had of re-asserting individual identity.   The child writes the names, the place, for those who did not survive.

The popularisation of photography, of "l'image", was also reflected in the advent of war.   The photographs of men sent to the front were sometimes all that remained afterwards.   Gaston Bonheur informs us that the sepia-tinted portrait of his "instituteur" father, "disparu corps et âme dans les sinistres horizons de Sainte-Menehould",[19] was displayed in the classroom at Belvianes (Aude) he left in August 1914.   After the war, they figured on the memorials themselves, adding a face to the name.   Developing an observation from Philippe Ariès's *L'Homme devant la mort*, Yves Pilven Le Sevellec writes that "les photos émaillées des morts de la guerre, probablement les plus anciennes

---

[17] Ibid, p.48.

[18] Gérard Bacconnier, André Minet, Louis Soler, "Quarante millions de témoins", in *Mémoire de la Grande Guerre. Témoins et Témoignages*, sous la direction de Gérard Canini, Nancy, Presses Universitaires de Nancy, 1989, pp.139-169, p.139.

[19] Gaston Bonheur, *Qui a cassé la vase de Soissons? (L'album de famille de tous les Français)*, Paris, Robert Laffont, 1963, pp.25-26.

images de ce genre, mettent le portrait à la portée des milieux populaires".[20] Examples here are from two geographically distant and ideologically diverse communes, Colembert in the Catholic Pas-de-Calais (the memorial is in the cemetery, and topped with a cross) and Tanneron in the Radical Var (the memorial is a statue of "la République").

The sense of active continuity and remembrance expressed by the child at Argelès-Gazost is less common than that represented by the child and "poilu" at Le Lude (Sarthe), with its injunction "Souviens-toi", and the statues of grieving mothers and children, typical of Breton departments but found quite abundantly elsewhere. The fine granite memorial at Saint-Malo (Ille-et-Vilaine), or the less severely wrought, more "sentimental" group at Grammat (Lot), are good examples of the type, to which I shall return in due course. The irony of this cult of "l'enfance" is of course that production of children was precisely the area in which France's vulnerability vis-à-vis a defeated but soon to be resurgent Germany was most marked. This anxiety was not new: alarm bells had been ringing since the census of 1891, and the pre-war "loi de trois ans" reflected its military dimensions; after 1919, it influenced birth control legislation (1920) and was reflected in the memorials themselves: the allegorical-realist group at Brioude (Haute-Loire) of a "poilu" shielding a mother and infant and which bears the legend "défense du foyer", is open to a natalist interpretation whose other manifestations included André Michelin's series of illustrated battlefield guides, launched in the early 1920s, proceeds from which were to be assigned to the Alliance Nationale pour la Réproduction.[21] Natalism was also a theme of memorial inauguration speeches, as in the observation by the major of Saint-Sebastien-sur-Loire in

---

[20] Y. Pilven Le Sevellec, "Les Monuments aux morts de la Loire-Atlantique" (IIème partie), *Visions Contemporaines*, No. 4, mars 1990, pp.7-131, p.29.

[21] Antoine Champeaux, "Les Guides illustrés des champs de bataille, 1914-1918", in *Mémoire de la Grande Guerre. Témoins et témoignages*, pp.341-354, p.346.

1924 that "la meilleure façon de comprendre la leçon des tombes, ce sera de nous pencher sur le berceau".[22] The historic failure of demographic policy in the 1920s and 1930s is well-documented, but that's another story.

A final characteristic of Argelès is that in completing the word "France", it also attempts to draw a line under fifty-one months of war; the same idea is found on other memorials such as Salin de Giraud (Bouches-du-Rhône), in which a female figure garlands the monument to the victors; there is no grief here but a community's gratitude, though for a contemporary commentator the triumphalist position of the soldier might be thought to express male dominance over the female no less than France's victory over Germany. It is true that memorial statuary frequently had a "sexual" symbolism exploited by writers such as Bernanos and Nizan,[23] and which, in more sentimental or explicit form, was already a feature of popular post-card art of the war years.[24] It is also true that the portrayal of women as survivors, mourners, wives and mothers, or, alternatively, as allegorical figures, scarcely reflects the complex reality of their wartime role as workers and breadwinners. My point here however is rather to stress that captured in stone, the gesture of finishing the memorial remains by definition an unfinished gesture, and, seen from the perspective of 1939, expresses something of the historical ambiguity of the memorials themselves.

The France which emerged victorious but blooded from four years of conflict was still a predominantly agricultural country whose peasantry accounted for almost half (45%) of those mobilised (8 million), and 538,000 of the 1,397,800 dead. Defence of "la patrie" was also defence of "le patrimoine",

---

[22] Quoted in Y. Pilven Le Sevellec, p.107.

[23] See William Kidd, "Figures in a landscape: literature and the 'lieux de mémoire'". *Modern and Contemporary France*, No. 43, October 1990, pp.28-36.

[24] See Marie-Monique Huss, "Virilité et Religion dans la France de 1914-1918: Le Catéchisme du Poilu", in *Belief and Identity in Modern France*, edited by Martyn Cornick, published by the Association for the Study of Modern and Contemporary France and the European Research Centre, 1990, pp.115-133.

of the "territoire" the "terroir", and if urban-industrial motifs are not absent from the memorials - the miners' lamps at Décazeville and Montceau-les-Mines, for example - rural and agricultural ones predominate: in addition to the aforementioned cockerel, a patriotic symbol since 1830, some obelisks are adorned with a sword and/or a sheaf of corn, nicely suggestive of the rural origins of so many of the fallen and the grim harvest of death, but also in the cycle of sacrifice and renewal encapsulated in Péguy's "Heureux ceux qui sont morts dans une juste guerre, Heureux les épis murs et les blés moissonnés" (Pontchâteau, Loire-Atlantique). Maxime Réal del Sarte's well-known "Terre de France" series at Compiègne and Saint-Jean de Luz are of a distinctly Catholic and Maurrassian inspiration.[25] By contrast, Ceres, the cornucopic Goddess of rural plenty which like "la Semeuse" has graced the coinage for the last century, and forms a central part of the iconography of Republicanism, is among common allegorical female figures. Echos of that rural revolutionary-patriotic tradition, also embodied in the opening lines of "La Marseillaise", are found on many memorials dedicated "aux enfants de [la commune] morts pour la patrie", or whose unstated text is "aux armes, citoyens". The flag-bearing female figure behind the soldier in the monument at Bozouls (Aveyron), a relatively "naive" work artistically speaking, is but one expression of the Republican "Liberté"; the terse "on ne passe pas" on the plinth seems to convey a sexual as well as a military interdiction. At Saint-Aygulf (Var), the more conventional group of winged sword-bearing woman leading two soldiers into battle, one of them in colonial infantry uniform, belongs unambiguously to the tradition of Delacroix's "Liberté guidant le peuple" towards the barricades in 1830 and Rude's "Départ des volontaires", reproductions of which were also a feature of primary classrooms.[26]

---

[25] Annette Becker, *Les Monuments aux morts*, pp.24-27.

[26] Gaston Bonheur, *Qui a cassé la vase de Soissons?*, p.31.

In addition to rural leftism and provincial republicanism, traces of patriotic anti-militarism can also be discerned. The memorial arch at Nîmes (Gard) is flanked by figures in civilian garb representing a generation which obeyed the call to arms but took leave of wives and families as free men, as citizens and not as mere soldiers. The striking memorial at Vic-Fezensac (Gers) portrays a bereted peasant farmer conspicuously not in uniform shouldering his rifle, and, standing behind him with equally steadfast gaze, his spouse, a rifle over her shoulder, her hands on the plough. Annette Becker writes of the memorial at La Côte-Saint-André (Isère) that it is to her knowledge "le seul qui représente une femme au travail";[27] the woman-in-waiting at Vic-Fezensac, ready to assume her husband's task, is surely one to add to that short list. Moreover, despite the background presence of a basilica-like church and a bell tolling in the heavens (the tocsin, presumably), this memorial seems more to anticipate the iconography of the Spanish Republican militia of the 1930s than to echo the "levée en masse" of Jaurès's citizen army or the more traditional imagery of "le soldat laboureur". But this example, from a department long refractory to the advances of Radical Republicanism and which in 1919 voted preponderantly for the right and centre-right,[28] invites us to beware of ascribing a too one-dimensional ideological significance to the memorials, or of discounting the weight of local factors. Saint-Gilles-du-Gard produced a striking "Mater dolorosa", unusual in a historically Protestant, Masonic and Radical department.[29] In "Plodémet-le-rouge" (Finistère),

---

[27] Annette Becker, *Les Monuments aux morts*, p.81.

[28] See François Goguel, *Géographie des élections françaises sous la Troisième et la Quatrième République*, Paris, Armand Colin (Cahiers de la Fondation Nationale des Sciences Politiques 159), 1970, pp.16-57; Maurice Agulhon records no Republican monuments in the department before 1914: *Marianne au Pouvoir. L'imagerie et la symbolique républicaine de 1880 à 1914*, Paris, Flammarion "Histoires", 1989, pp.413-424.

[29] See Madeleine Rébérioux, *La République radicale, 1898-1914*, Paris, Editions du Seuil, 1975, pp.42-43.

mayoral fief of three successive generations of the Radical Le Bail family from 1877 to 1951, the tension between religion and secularism is reflected in the memorial, located between the Church with its "calvaire" and the Mairie, and portraying "un bigouden se découvrant au pied d'un menhir".[30]

The monument at Redon (Ille-et-Vilaine) shows a spectral female figure, angel of victory, grieving spouse or mother, pointing to the list of the fallen and a plaque bearing verses from Hugo's "Hymne aux morts" (from the *Chants du Crépuscule*). Part of this poem figures on the memorial at Nîmes, whilst the couplet "Gloire à notre France éternelle! Gloire à ceux qui sont morts pour elle!" was used widely, sometimes attributed, sometimes marked by the author's initials only (Fressin, Pas-de-Calais), and sometimes unattributed (Thueyts, Ardèche). Antoine Prost has argued that the use of verse written to celebrate the dead of the Revolution of 1830 by France's greatest nineteenth-century "Republican" poet is further evidence that the memorials express an ethos of secular patriotism, but evidence from the Loire-Atlantique proves this to be a considerable overstatement.[31] Arguably, by 1920 a poem written in 1831 by a writer "pantheonised" in 1885, was sufficiently remote from its origins to be invested with different meanings by different groups. If in the Republican Aude "L'Hymne aux morts" was an integral part of the celebrations of the 11 November, "la grande-messe du culte des morts"[32] a primary school text-book illustration used by Michel Giraud shows the same couplet, from "L'Hymne à la France" (sic), alongside examples of phonetic spellings: "ch dur = k", as in "E*ch*o", "*Ch*rétien", and "*Ch*rist"...[33] Its use in the memorial at Fressin

---

[30] Edgar Morin, *Commune en France. La Métamorphose de Plodémet*, Paris, Fayard, 1967, p.23. This memorial is one of several by René Quillivic. See Becker, pp.73-74 and 112.

[31] Prost, p.44. Cf Le Sevellec, pp.112-3.

[32] Gaston Bonheur, *Que a cassé la vase de Soissons?*, p.330.

[33] Michel Giraud, *Raconte-moi, Marianne, ce qu'a fait la République. Les 36000 jours des 36000 communes*, Paris, Editions Jean-Claude Lattès, 1984, p.81.

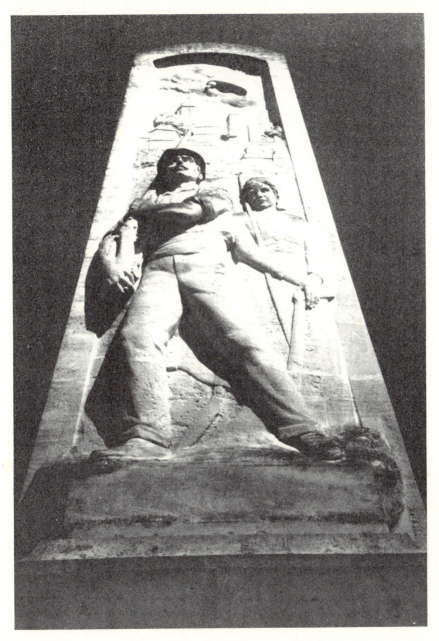

Figure 1. First World War Memorial, Vic-Fezonsac (Gers)

Figure 2. Resistance Memorial, Finistère

reinforces rather than attenuates the essentially religious significance created by the positioning of the dead "poilu" immediately below the redeeming crucifix on the exterior wall of the church. This memorial, which bears a cross as well as a sword and the words "sursum corda", was inaugurated on 16 May 1920, date of the canonisation of Joan of Arc, also remembered by a statue inside the church. "Elevé par souscription publique locale", it is a good example of how local identity sometimes coincided with forms of popular piety, a point demonstrably true also in newly-liberated Alsace-Lorraine where, because the "lois concordataires" were never revoked, explicitly confessional memorials are commonplace. Fressin, incidentally, was well-known to Bernanos, who spent many of his pre-war summers there, and to which he returned on a number of occasions between 1919 and 1923; a regular worshipper at the church, details of which occur in his first novel *Sous le Soleil de Satan* (1926), he is curiously silent about this memorial, so emphatically unrepresentative of those which he denounced in his writings.

At least, however, in 1914-18, the enemy had been identifiably German, and the endless lists of those who died in four years of fighting along a static front stretching from Switzerland to the Channel did so for the sacred soil of their village if not for that of the "patrie". The names of the 92,000 French troops killed in six weeks of "Blitzkrieg" in May-June 1940 (there never was a front, except perhaps in the minds of the General Staff), could usually be recorded by the addition of a plaque to the existing memorial, while the ensuing civil war between Vichy, the Resistance and the Occupying forces, the cycle of atrocity and reprisal which marked the years 1941-44, and finally the Liberation in 1944-45, gave the conflict a fundamentally different character. Not only were families and villages sometimes divided, those who chose active resistance (as opposed to mere "attentisme" or non-militant sympathy) were a minority within a minority, numerically insignificant in the population as a whole. Usually grouped in small isolated units living off the land and moving from place to place, the road-side where they fell was a more obvious location for a memorial than the main square, town hall, or church of a village to which only some (or none) of them belonged. If the memorials so erected are thereby more profoundly resonant "lieux de mémoire" than their 1914-18 predecessors, the lack of a precise community locus was also one reason why overarching departmental or regional commemoration suggested itself after 1945. Finally, to the old problem of commemorating the dead of different traditions (Catholic, Protestant, Jewish), were now added the divisions within a Resistance movement made up of Gaullists and Communists, Socialists, Radicals, left and right-wing Republicans, Christians and non-Christians, and numbering in its ranks anti-fascists of other nationalities, victims sometimes of French no less than German inhumanity. In ideological-representational as well as military-representational terms, many of the previous models were wholly inappropriate.

Some of these problems were acknowledged, directly or indirectly, in a circular issued by the Interior Ministry on 12 April 1946 in response to "un certain nombre de délibérations de Conseils municipaux tendant à l'érection de monuments destinés à commémorer le souvenir des sacrifices accomplis durant l'occupation et de la libération du territoire: militaires et membres de la résistance morts pour la France, fusillés et victimes de la barbarie allemande.[34] Within the pre-existing statutory framework, part of which went back to legislation passed in 1816 and after World War One, the creation of "plaques commémoratives individuelles" presented relatively little difficulty; responsibility for these was devolved onto the local agencies, though the express intention of ensuring that they were executed "avec le caractère de noblesse qui

---

[34] Reproduced in "Extrait de la Jurisprudence municipale et rurale", nos 5 et 6, Mai-Juin 1946" (four pages), p.1. I am indebted to the municipal archivist of Fremyng-Merlebach (Moselle), for access to this and other documentation.

234

s'impose"[35] also afforded an opportunity for political control by the imposition of standardised specifications which included material (usually marble), colour, dimensions, size, number and type of wall fixings, height of location, etc. The commemoration of foreign nationals killed in France, or in French service, which for practical purposes meant the Resistance, was more problematic since it normally required the agreement of the country of origin. Since in many cases this was Franquist Spain, it is doubtful if the usual diplomatic protocols were observed, but prefectoral approval continued to be required under the provisions of the "droit commun". Clearly, however, it was collective "monuments commémoratifs" of the type discussed in this paper which proved most problematic for the authorities, as evidenced by the attempt to reconcile the need to harbour scarce material and labour resources required for national economic reconstruction with the political imperative of respecting what is somewhat coyly called the "le caractère indispensable et sacré de ces manifestations destinées à glorifier la participation majeure de la France dans la défense des grands principes qui sont le génie de notre civilisation" - the mythification of "la France résistante" is already present here. That an iconographical, and hence ideological, implication was also present is confirmed by an end-note from a contemporaneous (March 1946) issue of the *Revue du Touring Club de France* recalling the mistakes made after 1919, and rejecting mass-produced models "dénués de toute valeur artistique (...), des allégories traduites en marbre ou en bronze, suivant des formules banalisés (sic) par un trop fréquent usage", in favour of a return to suitably regional versions of the traditional (and uncontroversial) "Lanterne des morts" scarcely used since the previous century. Though manifestly the writer's own preference, the use of this statement in the circular undoubtedly betokens official approval. To what extent do memorials to the dead of the Second World War reflect these concerns and the changing nature of the conflict?

---

[35] Ibid, p.3.

Seen from the front, the stone obelisk and cross at Naves (Haute-Savoie), is a typically World War One edifice expressing the village's "reconnaissance à ses enfants morts pour la France"; the side panel acknowledges the gratitude of "la Résistance espagnole" to three of its members killed at Glières on 27 March 1944 "pour la France et la Liberté". The roadside martyrdom of two FTPF (Francs-Tireurs et Partisans Français") "tombés glorieusement dans une embuscade" is marked by a broken column at the edge of the D51 at Tourtour in the Var. Eleven members of the FFI (Forces Françaises de l'Intérieur) are recalled where they fell, in a crossroads shrine, sandwiched between an elderly "calvaire" and a new 'phone box, on the boundary of the Gard and the Ardèche; above the legend "ils sont morts pour leur sol, ils sont morts pour demain", which echoes the "lendemains qui chantent", the dead are listed by rank, name, pseudonym and age; among them, "Caudron, René, dit Serge, 22 ans; Domanski, Jean, dit Bougie, 19 ans; Morales, Fernand, dit Camaradet, 42 ans; Villaroya, Amédée, dit Aragon, 35 ans"; the list includes two whose ages were unknown. By contrast, on the 1914-18 memorial outside the Protestant church at Lagorce a few miles to the North, with its recurrent local patronyms, such information was both known and unnecessary, the Christian name alone adequately differentiating between the dead from the same family (four Silhol, two Tendil, etc.).

The relatively few 1939-45 memorials of the military type are well represented by Rombas (Moselle) and Clermont-Ferrand (Puy-de-Dôme). Redolent of what, "faute de mieux", I am inclined to call the "socialist-realist" style of the 1940s and 1950s, they portray uniformed and partisan combatants with, at Clermont-Ferrand, the figure of the "déporté civil" emerging from the shadow behind. If the idiom is sombre, the aesthetics representational, the intention is inclusive, to unite retrospectively, in the memory if not in the fact, the different constituencies of a movement which remained heterogeneous and, until the end, vide Le Chagrin et la Pitié, filmed in Clermont-Ferrand, far from endorsed by the whole population.

Second World War memorials are inclusive in another sense too, namely that unlike those of the earlier conflict, they eschew separate representation of the dead warrior and the grieving survivors (widow, children) of the type illustrated in the previously-mentioned examples of Grammat and Saint-Malo. This reflects not merely changing aesthetic conventions, but the nature of the conflict itself: the victims of Nazism were indiscriminately soldiers and civilians, women and children, old and young. The inhabitants of a village in the Moselle evacuated to the Haute-Vienne for safety in 1939-40, were among those massacred on 10 June 1944 at Oradour; the six memorial stones at Charly-Oradour list victims from the same families as old as seventy-one and as young as two. At Montigny-les-Metz (also Moselle), a Rodinesque figure which might be a man or a child, framed by dark looming shapes, suggests the ultimate incomprehensibility as well as the enormity of the sacrifice, while at Angoulême and Saint-Georges-de-Didonne in the neighbouring departments of the Charente and Charente-Maritime, it is no longer the statuesque survivor who invites us to remember, at whom we look, it is the whole group which demands our recognition, which looks at us, which accuses: what did you do to prevent this? What are you doing to prevent it ever happening again?

The Second World War was a war of opposing ideologies, a war of propaganda and of words, broadcast on the air-waves ("Les Français parlent aux Français", Lord Haw-Haw's "Germany calling"), and crystallised in slogans ("Radio-Paris ment/Radio Paris est allemand"). The Resistance adopted the binary "Honneur et Patrie", cleverly highlighting the shortcomings in Vichy's triadic "Travail, Famille, Patrie" ("Travail forcé, Famille brisée, Patrie vendue"), while affirming a military and political continuity with the pre-1914 armies of the Republic. "Honneur et Patrie" figure on the two pillars, pillars which are funeral urns and prison bars, of the memorial at Saint-Cast (Côtes-du-Nord) "aux évadés de France qui préférèrent mourir debout que vivre à genoux", a dedication which recalls a Republican slogan of the Spanish Civil War. The municipal cemetery at Levallois-Perret, already distinguished by the grave of the "Communarde" Louise Michel and a 1914-18 memorial which portrays a civilian worker breaking a sword on his knee, contains a stone celebrating "les cochers-chauffeurs de taxi du département de la Seine tombés dans les luttes pour l'émancipation des travailleurs, pour la liberté, pour la démocratie, pour la France et pour la République" (in that order); the "battle honours" recorded include the strikes of 1912, the anti-fascist demonstrations of 1934, and Spain. At Glières, the bodies of "chasseurs alpins", "maquisards" and "foreign" partisans are united under the watchword of the revolutionary Convention of 1792: "vivre libre ou mourir". As in the days of Koblenz and Valmy, alignment with Germany enabled the régime's opponents to claim the patriotic label for themselves. In 1914-18, such a label was unnecessary; from 1940, it was a synonym for the Resistance. Many memorials testify to this assimilation, such as those at Fontainebleau (Seine-et-Marne) to the "mémoire des patriotes français assassinés par les nazis" and Rosporden (Finistère), the latter dedicated "à ceux de la Butte, à quatre patriotes qui le 5 août 1944 tombèrent ici pour que vive la liberté".

Fortunately, there were escapees as well as martyrs, liberators as well as collaborators. At Pont-à-Mousson (Meurthe-et-Moselle), an obelisk commemorates the "passeurs" who risked life and limb to help refugees from the annexed territories into the "zone réservée" (a small progress, but a progress). This theme of liberation which, with the exception of Alsace-Lorraine, had not featured prominently in the iconography of 1914-18, loomed larger in that of 1939-45. Moreover, despite official preference for the non-allegorical and the non-representational, many memorials did attempt to fuse aesthetic values and ideological statements. The monuments at Draguignan (Var) of a muscular, bare-chested civilian breaking the chains of oppression and taking up arms seems deliberately to eschew Aryan gigantism and

238

conventional, statuesque beauty. At Châteaulin (Finistère), two partisans express a heroism on a human scale whose ideological significance is completed by a leading female figure whose "chevelure" and demeanour replicate the "Republican" aesthetic of Rude and Delacroix. The inscription reads: "Gloire à la Résistance Finistérienne, à ses Morts pour que Vive la France, 1940-1944". The re-discovery, not just of the slogans of a previous Republic but of some of its central artistic and iconographical conventions, can also be seen in the imposing memorial to the "Bretons de la France Libre" at Camaret. On the fresco, regular and irregular fighters, soldiers and civilians, men (and a woman), answer De Gaulle's "appel du dix-huit juin 1940". The massive female figure around which they assemble is framed against a Cross of Lorraine, but also symbolises Liberty breaking its chains, Marianne, the Republic which, De Gaulle affirmed in August 1944, had never ceased to exist. At Niort (Deux-Sèvres), the memorial is a great block of crudely jointed irregular stone whose leading edge resembles the prow of a ship, while at the base, a hand brandishing a sword symbolises the emergence of the "soldats sans uniforme" from the anonymous mass. Like the combatants it celebrates, it is a creation in hard, "resistant" material whose naturalness and spontaneity are the antithesis of the unnatural, imposed orthodoxies of Nazism. These values are expressed also in the well-known monument at Le Cerdon to the "maquis de l'Ain", subsequently adopted as a national Resistance memorial. The soaring female figure breaking the chains of oppression seems to emerge bowsprit-like from the cliff face, a surging natural force, the well-springs of renewal. A quotation from Aragon's "Chanson du Franc-tireur" - Aragon who, despite his Communist appartenance might be considered as having succeeded Victor Hugo as poet of "la France éternelle" - underlines the cycle of sacrifice and rebirth: "où je meurs renaît la patrie".[36]

Such continuities are real as well as symbolic: when in defiance of the

---

[36] Aragon, *La Diane Française* (Seghers, 1944), Gallimard, 1965, p.38.

occupiers the "maquisards de l'Ain" paraded in Oyonnax on 11 November 1943, the wreath they placed on the war memorial bore the words "les vainqueurs de demain aux vainqueurs de 1914-1918".[37] Having helped to liberate Belvianes in 1944, Gaston Bonheur returned to his old classroom to salute the portrait of his father who was killed thirty years before.[38]

In the house in Céreste from which he organised the reception of allied parachute drops, René Char ("Capitaine Alexandre"), was equi distant between the local war memorial and the village "Marianne", two spatial and ideological expressions of the place (his native Luberon) and the values for which he fought. His work includes a homage to the young Resistance writer Roger Bernard, shot by the Gestapo at the age of 23 in June 1944 at a roadside between Céreste and the neighbouring village of Viens, within earshot of Char and the rest of the group, armed but powerless to intervene for fear of provoking reprisals on the villagers. The stone, which I came across by coincidence this summer, has a side plaque inscribed "A la mémoire de Roger Bernard, la douleur d'un Allemand". The poem evokes "la foudre au visage d'écolier".[39] But another photograph, taken by a former student at Tourettes (Var), and hence equally coincidental, will perhaps be a more appropriate conclusion to an exposé begun with the stone schoolboy at Argelès-Gazost: it shows his real-life descendant, a young workman, nicely unaware of the camera, paint-brush in hand, renewing the names on the memorial.

---

[37] This well-known episode is recalled by Patrick Vavre in *La Mémoire des Français*, p.337.

[38] Gaston Bonheur, *Qui a cassé la vase de Soissons?*, pp.25-26.

[39] René Char, "Affres, Détonation, Silence", in *Oeuvres complètes*, Paris, Gallimard, Bibliothèque de la Pléiade, 1983, p.257. For Char's account of the circumstances of Bernard's murder, see p.208.

15. THE RENEWAL OF WRITTEN FRENCH

RODNEY BALL

There was a time not so long ago when dictionaries of argot, langue
verte, and colloquial French more widely, used to take the form of
unpretentious and faintly seedy paperbacks compiled in some cases by retired
policemen (Sandry & Carrère's *Argot Moderne*[1] is a distinguished example of
the genre). In the last few years, however, such works of reference have
undergone a veritable metamorphosis. This can be seen if one compares the
original (1977) edition of the Larousse *Dictionnaire du français argotique et
populaire*[2] with its 1988 successor[3] - a glossy, larger format hardback, elegantly
and quite spaciously printed, and costing three times as much. The inclusion
of a couple of hundred additional items in 1988 is counterbalanced by the
deletion of quite a few others, so the number of actual entries in both editions
is around 5,000. However, the original Introduction has been enormously
expanded, so the change is essentially one of format and presentation, not one
of lexical content. A cheap and handy pocket guide seems to have set out on
the road to being a de luxe, coffee-table item. The first and second editions
of Claude Duneton's collection of regional and familiar expressions, *La puce
à l'oreille*[4], show the same kind of development, and a particularly good
example of this intriguing concept of the dictionary of colloquial French as an
art-form is provided by Bernet and Rézeau's *Dictionnaire du français argotique*

---

[1] G. Sandry and M. Carrère, *L'Argot Moderne*, Paris, Editions du Dauphin, 1953.

[2] F. Caradec, *Dictionnaire du français argotique et populaire*, Paris, Larousse, 1977.

[3] F. Caradec, *N'ayons pas peur des mots: dictionnaire du français argotique et populaire*,
Paris, Larousse, 1988.

[4] C. Duneton, *La Puce à l'oreille: anthologie des expressions populaires avec leurs origines*,
1st edition, Paris, Stock, 1978; 2nd edition, Paris, Balland, 1985.

et populaire of 1989.[5]

Far from being ex-employees of the Sûreté, these compilers are CNRS researchers - a measure of the rapidly increasing respectability of the demotic. The physical quality of production of the Bernet and Rézeau volume is at least as good as that of the new Larousse dictionary of popular and familiar French; its price is even higher; and, at an average of just three entries per page, the item-to-page ratio is unprecedentedly generous. As there are only 370 pages, the usual practical consequence is that the word or expression one is after isn't actually included. But this doesn't really matter too much, now that more and more colloquialisms have found their way into the standard Larousse, Robert and other dictionaries. Elegant format apart, the distinctive characteristic of the *Dictionnaire du français parlé* is the fact that the 1,200 words it *does* list are the object of copious exemplification and illustration - the intended readership evidently consists of leisured browsers rather than hurried seekers of lexical information. Reading a dictionary for its own sake seems no longer to be a rather odd perversion, but to have become a socially accepted pastime, and dictionaries are modifying their format accordingly. As the motto of the 1988 Larousse argot dictionary so appropriately puts it: *"Un dico sans baratin est un sac d'os"*.[6]

Now, as K. George has pointed out in a recent review,[7] the ironic thing about the 3,000 or so quotations which are such a feature of the *Dictionnaire du français parlé* is that every single one of them is taken from a written, published source. George takes this as indicating a lack of adventurousness on the part of the compilers, and, more generally, of a lack of innovativeness

---

[5] C. Bernet and P. Rézeau: *Dictionnaire du français parlé: le monde des expressions familières*, Paris, Seuil, 1989.

[6] Caradec, *N'ayons pas peur des mots*, 1988, p.99.

[7] K. George, "Old for New: 'Non-assurance linguistique?'", *French Studies Bulletin*, 39 (Summer 1991), pp.1-3.

242

characteristic of the contemporary French language and its users. It might, however, be possible to take a slightly different perspective, and to view the phenomenon as being symptomatic also of a noteworthy extension in the scope of the written code. This brings us to the main topic of this chapter. I would like to draw attention to some features of contemporary written usage, referring to published material of a formal or relatively formal kind (i.e. disregarding letters to friends, notes, graffiti and the like), and suggesting that considerable changes are afoot in the dominant mode of expression of French culture.

The traditional representation of the division of labour between spoken and written French might be along the lines of the diagram in (a), adapted from a representation proposed by Colette Stourdzé in 1969,[8] and echoed, with variations, in many standard analyses of register.

(a)

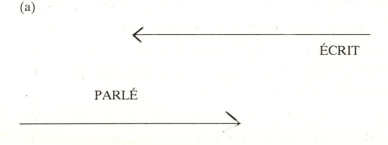

fr populaire --- fr familier --- fr courant --- fr soigné --- fr littéraire

Five levels of formality/informality are postulated here, ranging from the quasi-archaic *français littéraire* through to *français familier* (often defined as "relaxed middle-class speech" and to the working-class vernacular labelled *français populaire*. The written language occupies the formal end of the spectrum, with

---

[8] C. Stourdzé, "Les Niveaux de langue", *Le Français dans le monde*, 65 (June 1969), pp.18-21.

only quite a small degree of overlap between written and spoken language in the zone designated *français courant*. Standard examples would be the variation found in a lexical series such as *un mec, un type, un homme, un monsieur*, or a grammatical series such as *j'ose pas le faire, je n'ose pas le faire, je n'ose le faire*.

Obviously such schemata have attracted criticism because of the way in which they superimpose situational social criteria, because of the resultant implication that working-class users have only one variety at their disposal (namely *français populaire*), whereas the middle and upper classes have at least two, and, in general, because of the excessive rigidity of the classification.

However, as far as the position of the written code is concerned, this kind of representation seems to correspond well enough to the state of affairs that obtained until quite recently, in journalistic, fictional and documentary texts alike. To the extent that one can speak in the French context of an essentially diglossic or quasi-diglossic situation (i.e. co-existence within the same speech-community of two or more functionally differentiated "high" (H) and "low" (L) language varieties), then the standard written code restricted itself to "high" features (extensive use of subject-verb inversion, *ne* never omitted, past historic quite normal, avoidance of argot, presence of numerous vocabulary items felt to be of a "literary" type, and so forth). This is of course in conformity with the mutually reinforcing associations traditionally encountered in literate societies between writing, formality of situation, formality of expression and "correctness" - all these being characteristic of High as opposed to Low varieties.

The strength of these associations is reflected in the relative lack of success of some of the attempts made at various times, and for various reasons, to produce written texts exhibiting Low features. One thinks of the Hébertistes during the French Revolution and their practice of inserting *bougre* and *foutre* at frequent intervals into documents couched in an otherwise impeccable *français littéraire.*[9] Or of the weirdly unnatural juxtapositions of register found in the writings of Céline. Or indeed of the way in which many modern novelists happily allow colloquial dialogue to co-exist with a narrative text (even a first-person narrative) in which imperfect subjunctives, past historics and inversions abound.

It seems possible to identify three principal and interconnected ways in which this state of affairs has evolved since the 1960s (no doubt the timing is sociologically significant). Firstly, the zone of overlap between *français écrit* and *français parlé* has widened. Secondly, there have been changes within *français parlé* itself, affecting the relationship between "familiar" and "popular" French (or, if one prefers, between the "colloquial" and the "very colloquial" levels). Thirdly, innovations have occurred at the formal end of the spectrum, with "literary French" no longer the unchallenged or even the dominant archetype. Let us consider these one by one.

From being a bold departure on the part of a handful of innovative writers, the use of colloquial lexis for purposes other than the reproduction of dialogue has become the unremarkable stock-in-trade of large numbers of contemporary journalists and novelists. In terms of the diagram, the domain of *français écrit* is being extended a long way over to the left-hand side.

One thinks, obviously, of *Le Nouvel Observateur* or *Libération* in this connection. Undoubtedly, there were noteworthy pioneers - and from them it is possible to obtain some idea of the chronology of the changes: a comparison of early 1990s issues of *Le Nouvel Observateur* with issues from no further back than the early 1970s reveals something like a five- or sixfold increase in their respective proportions of colloquialisms. However, many other publications have followed in their path and some have exceeded them in innovativeness (*Actuel*, for instance, or *L'Evénement du jeudi*). Even serious business journals are not averse to using the resources of the colloquial:

---

[9] See F. Brunot, *Histoire de la langue française*, Vol. X, Paris, A. Colin, 1939, pp.173f.

245

(b) A 20 ans, il avait plaqué la fac de droit pour lancer, avec des copains, une société de multiservices aux entreprises. A 33 ans il contrôle un groupe qui pèse plus de 700 m de francs de chiffre d'affaires. Entretemps, Olivier Ginon a découvert un secteur en plein boom et pas encore structuré: celui des expos et salons. Ce sera son créneau. (*L'Expansion*, 02.05.91).

(c) Bouquins-vacances: la sélection des manageurs. (*L'Expansion*, 04.07.91).

And Claude Sarraute's daily column in *Le Monde* is as typical an example as one is likely to find of what might be termed the "jokey colloquial" style. Outside journalism proper, imaginative fiction and autobiography are areas in which this style abounds. The *Dictionnaire du français parlé* lists some 500 titles of works of fiction in its Bibliography. One way and another, it is not always helpful any more to say to foreign learners that such and such an expression is "not used in writing": a written text may well be where they have come across it. And native speakers can be equally uncertain about the distinction, to judge from Jacques Julliard's recent report of the occurrence in essays by Terminale pupils of statements like "Baudelaire n'est pas mon trip".[10]

One or two qualifying points ought to be made at this stage. The term "jokey" was used advisedly just now: unlike the real thing, "written spoken French" is, to a greater or lesser extent, self-conscious and artificial, at times amounting to pastiche, with the language-games taking precedence over the content. Furthermore, the changes just referred to relate more to vocabulary and idiom than to syntax. As will be seen in a moment, there appears to be no limit to the degree of colloquialness of the lexical items commonly encountered in written texts, but writers are less daring as far as grammatical items and constructions are concerned. Omission of *ne* is widespread enough, so is the

---

[10] J. Julliard, "La Dérive populiste", *Le Nouvel Observateur*, 11.8.91.

substitution of *on* for *nous*, and so are sentence dislocations like *je le connais, son père*. However, the same could not be said, for example, of the use of "pronoun-retention" type of relative clause found in *Son père qu'il est sans nouvelles de lui*. This discrepancy can result in texts combining formal syntax and informal lexis, along the following lines:

> (d) Pour trois mille balles, cette escapade fait du bien. Les pensions honnêtes vous attendent dans le quartier près de la gare. Pour manger, évitez les restos clinquants pour ne rentrer que dans les "cervezerias", restos popus aux menus à 1000 pesetas. (*Actuel*, 02.91, p.124).

Many writers in fact, seem to display a remarkable unsureness of touch as far as syntax is concerned, with forms from widely separated registers juxtaposed in the same sentence:

> (e) ... aussi nombreux soient-ils et le fussent-ils plus encore, c'est eux qui ont tort (F. Cavanna).[11]

> (f) Suffisait que la télévision acceptât de jouer le jeu (F. Cavanna).[12]

In some cases, this may create a specifically ironic effect, but often any satirical effect or intention is difficult to discern. Claude Sarraute's inclusion or omission of *ne*, for example, seems totally haphazard. This kind of fluctuation may be best accounted for in terms of the structural gulf between spoken and written syntax. In other words, "downgrading" one's grammar in a consistent manner is as hard as "upgrading" it: Cavanna's deleted impersonal pronoun in (f) is on a par with Le Pen's intrusive imperfect subjunctive in (g):

---

[11] F. Cavanna, *Coups de sang*, Paris, Belfond, 1991, p.176.

[12] Ibid, p.19.

(g) Ça m'étonnerait que ces initiatives débouchassent sur un accord. (J.-M. Le Pen, radio interview, 1987).

Now, if written French makes increasing use of linguistic forms hitherto peculiar to spoken communication, as a result wreaking havoc with diagrams like the one referred to earlier, the picture is further complicated by a process of restructuring occurring within spoken usage itself. This involves the dissolution of the traditional barriers separating *français familier* and *français populaire*, and both of these from *argot*. The validity of these divisions was probably always somewhat questionable, and their recent erosion has been quite widely commented on. Bodo Müller, for instance, referring to the "upward" dissemination of popular and *argotique* items and to the "downward" dissemination of elements associated with *français cultivé* comments: "Il se forme peu à peu un système qualitatif largement indépendant de la stratification sociale, accompagné d'un nivellement des différences de registres vers le bas de l'échelle".[13] In other words, the choice between *foutre le camp* and *ficher le camp*, for instance, is no longer imposed by speakers' socio-economic backgrounds, but by the extra-linguistic situation in which they find themselves on particular occasions. Müller points out how this process is reflected in the wide discrepancies between the standard dictionaries as regards their classification of items under headings like vulgar, popular, familiar, etc.

In view of this, it is not surprising that, once it had got under way, the incursion of *français écrit* into the domain of *français parlé* should have extended right over into the most colloquial registers. Indeed, the absence in the case of written texts of any constraints imposed by concrete "extra-linguistic situations" may well encourage the kinds of innovation illustrated earlier. As long as their editors or publishers allow them to get away with it, writers are free to use linguistic means to create whatever extra-linguistic situations they

---

[13] B. Müller, *Le Français d'aujourd'hui*, Paris, Klincksieck, 1985, p.230.

248

wish, and the more freedom they have, the more daring they become. To the extent, indeed, of using, in written texts addressed to total strangers, vocabulary items which would be unthinkable in situations where there is face-to-face contact. Consider the following titles of articles from the press:

> (h) "Le fric de la culture" (*Globe*). "Dans la tronche de Dutronc" (*Actuel*). "Les bébés sont pas cons", "Les Nuls de l'année", "Les Mecs bien", "La Déconfiture des mecs pas bien", "Pourquoi Tonton nous gongle", "L'Ouverture, oui ou merde?" (*EDJ*), "La Quéquette à Jésus-Christ" (*Politis*).[14]

The eventual consequence is that innovative influences begin to move in the reverse direction - the written colloquial becoming an input to the spoken colloquial, as it were. One would imagine, for example, that Frédéric Dard's linguistically highly sophisticated Commissaire San-Antonio novels have been a major channel for increasing the general public's knowledge of *argot*. (The author himself, it appears, was heavily reliant on dictionaries of slang). The *bande dessinée* album and the rock magazine have, more recently, played a similar role in disseminating *verlan* and other varieties of teenage vernacular. And that curious amalgam of linguistic registers known as *le français branché* (of which *verlan* forms a small but conspicuous part) is clearly indebted to the written medium not only for its propagation, but for quite a few of its constituent items themselves.

This erosion of the written-spoken barrier is particularly noteworthy in the case of French in view of the extremely strong purist tradition which, for over two centuries, was successful in keeping the two codes apart. But it should be remembered that the current incursion of what sociolinguists term "L" (Low) forms into codes and situations traditionally receptive only to "H" (High) forms is not peculiar to French-speaking cultures. There are many

---

[14] Quoted in P. Merle, *Les Blues de l'argot*, Paris, Seuil, 1990, pp.51-2.

analogous phenomena: the extension, throughout continental Europe, of solidarity-related second-person singular ("T") pronouns at the expense of power-related second-person plural ("V") pronouns; the use in Switzerland of Swiss German dialect in semi-formal circumstances where, a generation ago, only High German would have been acceptable; the parallel preference for Gaelic as against English on the part of younger speakers in the Outer Hebrides when addressing such figures of authority as bank managers or policemen.[15] Nearer home, one thinks of the prevalence in contemporary British academic culture of combinations of formal title and familiarly abbreviated first name of the "Professor Bill Jones" type. Evidently all these phenomena reflect the growing prestige of informality in contemporary social life, with the late 1960s as a turning-point. In France itself, an associated phenomenon may be the so-called *parler cru* currently popular with various prominent politicians, and which recently aroused adverse criticism in, surprisingly enough, *Le Nouvel Observateur*. Examples like the following were quoted:

> (j) "Ces banquiers qui nous piquent notre blé" (M. Charasse), "La Bourse, je n'en ai rien à cirer", "Des sous, il va y en avoir" (E. Cresson), "Tout se déglingue" (V. Giscard d'Estaing), "La France est dans la panade" (V. Giscard d'Estaing").[16]

So far attention has been drawn to the way in which written French has opened itself up in the direction of informality, and the way in which informal registers themselves have undergone restructuring. The third aspect I would like to consider involves the levels of language which are traditionally regarded as properly constituting the domain of the written language, and which in the

---

[15] R.D. Grillo, *Dominant Languages*, Cambridge, Cambridge University Press, 1989, p.54.

[16] Julliard, "La Dérive populiste".

diagram are labelled *français courant*, *français soigné* (also known as *français cultivé, langue soutenue,* or *langue recherchée*) and *français littéraire*. Though originating in the speech of the courtiers of the Ancien Régime, the last two, with their inversions, imperfect subjunctives, past anteriors and equivalent lexical repertoire, are now rarely encountered outside written texts (though perhaps not as rarely as is sometimes assumed). Resources of this kind naturally continue to be utilized in a range of contexts and with varying degrees of literary merit.

Example (k) is from a sports report; the mixed and somewhat faded metaphors of (l) are very typical of a style favoured by the more with-it kind of business magazine:

(k) En amont du canal, le murmure d'un déversoir rythme les heures qui s'écoulent, paisibles, dans la campagne du Morbihan. Hennebont, la ville, est là-bas, de l'autre côté du pont. Juste après la boulangerie, une enseigne discrète. Sur fond blanc, un ballon de football dessiné et enveloppé par le nom du club: Union sportive montagnarde ... Ici le riche et douloureux passé de la cité bretonne se confond en douceur avec le quotidien (*Libération*, 10.03.91).

(l) En ce printemps 1991, la politique industrielle connaît une nouvelle jeunesse. Quatre explications à ce regain de verdeur. La première tient aux médiocres performances des entreprises du secteur public. Partout ou presque, les résultats fondent comme neige au soleil. Dans le cas de Thomson on peut même parler d'hémorragie, et l'Etat va encore passer la serpillière (*L'Expansion*, 02.05.91).

However, it does seem that serious non-fictional writing is making increasing use, not just of these time-honoured literary resources, but also of a type of lexis which can best be described as "technocratic/administrative". Technical jargon of one sort or another has of course been around for centuries (one recalls the strenuous efforts of the seventeenth and eighteenth-century academicians to exclude it from successive editions of the Dictionnaire de l'Académie). The point about the language variety I would like to illustrate is that it appears to have become so prevalent as to constitute a component of the accepted "common core" of the written language - in an intriguingly parallel way to familiar, popular and *argotique* varieties of French.

The importance of the technocratic/administrative register dawned on me when coming across the following notice in the public library in the Centre Pompidou:

(m) Toute personne désirant quitter momentanément la bibliothèque est tenue de reprendre intégralement la file d'attente afin de réintégrer les lieux.

It formed, incidentally, an interesting contrast with the invitingly colloquial title of the neighbouring notice:

(n) La Bibliothèque, comment ça marche?

Having reflected on the problems of translating (m) into English into such a way as to convey the register of the original (clearly it won't do to render it as "queue up all over again so as to get back in", though that's what it means), it seemed to me that it might usefully form part of an advanced translation exercise, provided that more examples of the same kind could be found.

What surprised me was how readily available these were: they were to be found in quite concentrated form in tourist literature, in business journals, in promotional handouts issued by regional *syndicats d'initiative*, in articles by geographers and town-planners, in handy guides for the general reader to the current state of French economics and industry.[17] And isolated instances crop

---

[17] See for example: *L'Etat de la France et de ses habitants*, Paris, La Découverte, 1989.

up all over the place - sports writers refer to *l'intégralité du match* in preference to *tout le match*, or *la quasi-totalité des joueurs* rather than *presque tous les joueurs*. "Une équipe de France en train de se recrédibiliser" is another example from sports writing, as is the reference to a Montpellier-Bucarest football match as "notre prestation contre Bucarest". The President of the Poitou-Charentes regional council describes the electrification of the railway line from Niort to La Rochelle as likely to bring about "le désenclavement de notre façade maritime".[18] And so on.

Linguistically the genre has something in common with the "Hexagonal" satirized twenty years ago by Robert Beauvais,[19] though *that* wasn't used by sports commentators. It is characterised by the prevalence of "learned" Graeco-Latin vocabulary items, including, as the foregoing examples show, a large number of abstract nouns, some of which may replace more everyday terms belonging to other parts of speech. There is also an admixture of various characteristic verbs, again of a distinctly abstract nature, like *réintégrer* quoted earlier, or the already consecrated and ubiquitous *provoquer* (in the sense of "cause"), and the scarcely less prevalent *intervenir* (in the sense of "happen"). One finds some rather banal neologisms of the type illustrated by *recrédibiliser* (derived by affixation from a long-established root), but more commonly there is reliance on somewhat fossilized metaphors (*façade maritime* for *côte*), and, perhaps most distinctively, a wealth of terms derived from specialized domains and put to a range of more general uses. For example: *valoriser*, originally used in economics and mathematics; *assumer*, from philosophical uses like *assumer sa condition; pôle*, taken from geography or more probably from physics, and much used in phrases like *pôle d'attraction et d'animation, pôle d'emploi, pôle universitaire, pôle éducatif*. (Incidentally, the ease with which established

---

[18] In *Le Moniteur du bâtiment et des travaux publics (Spécial Régions)*, June 1989, p.102.

[19] R. Beauvais, *L'Hexagonal tel qu'on le parle*, Paris, Hachette, 1970.

253

meanings can be lost sight of is shown in a recent statement in *Le Nouvel Observateur* that "Raymond Barre prendra la tête d'un grand pôle centriste lors de la prochaine legislature").

The denotational (though not of course, the connotational) meaning of some of these items can be quite elusive. While not wishing to suggest that the truth-conditions of the statement in example (p) would remain entirely unaltered if *vecteur* were replaced by *truc*, one is nevertheless sometimes conscious of a certain loosening of the ties between signifier and signified:

(p)   La télévision est le vecteur privilégié par lequel l'enfant perçoit les nouveaux produits [commerciaux] (*L'Evénement du jeudi*, 28.02.91).

This seems particularly characteristic of the very pure example of the "turgid technocratic" style exemplified in (q). This is from a monthly newsletter published by the Conseil Régional de Picardie, written by local councillors and administrators, and intended, it should be emphasized, for the general public, not for any specialized group of readers:

(q)   Abbeville.   Ayant entrepris de conforter ses fonctions urbaines, la ville s'attache parallèlement depuis quelques années à renforcer sa vocation sportive et culturelle.   Dotée d'installations sportives performantes et d'équipements culturels de qualité, elle est à même de renforcer sa polarisation sur l'ensemble de la Picardie Maritime, en visant une démarche de promotion et de communication.[20]

The following excerpts from another entirely banal and unpretentious source - a report in the Socialist Party's weekly magazine - will perhaps give some idea of the overall shape sometimes assumed by the written French of the

_____

[20] Conseil Régional de Picardie: *La Lettre d'information du Conseil Régional*, 36 (November-December 1989), p.11.

1990s, when the various components that have been referred to are combined in a single text, as is more and more frequently the case:

(r) *Angers assume ses déchets. Mieux, il les récupère et les valorise. Elus, professionnels, population, décident de ne pas glisser, en catimini, les détritus sous la carpette.* ...

Récupérer les huiles de vidange: "Un nouveau geste vert qui n'est pas bidon". C'était l'une des adresses lancées aux Angevins en 1987. Dès la fin des années 70, la mairie d'Angers, entraînant le district, concoctait une politique de l'environnement, gestion des déchets incluse.   Quelques mots clefs: récupération, recyclage, valorisation. "Cela paraissait idiot de tout balancer dans un trou", explique Jean-Claude Antonini, maire adjoint, chargé de l'environnement. La gestion des déchets s'est installée sur deux pieds, nommés très doctement recyclages individualisé et centralisé... "Comme on est en avance, on rame", admet Jean-Claude Antonini.   Innovez, innovez, pour que la douceur angevine ne soit jamais polluée! (*Vendredi*, 15.02.91, p.16).

Here one notes the technocratic *assumer* and *valoriser* (collocated rather incongruously with *déchets*), side by side with colloquialisms like *bidon, balancer* and *ramer* - as well as quasi-anglicisms like *glisser sous la carpette*, fashionable catchphrases like *en catimini*, and reassuringly literary references like *la douceur angevine*.   Holding all these together is a backcloth composed of *français courant* syntactic constructions (still largely the norm in written texts, as we have seen), together with various unmarked lexical items.

A much more contrived, self-conscious and indeed self-reflexive instance of this juxtaposing of styles and registers occurs in (s) - note the purely graphic puns.   The reference is to a female rock group: writing on popular music, be it in the national press or in specialized magazines, has for many years been a prolific source of experiment with the renewed written code:

(s) Il fut un temps, pas si forclos que ça, où la new wave était assez exclusivement affaire de gars. Aujourd'hui, tiens, c'est un peu l'inverse. Cette musique que nous aim(i)ons bien est en train de se transformer, jusqu'à l'ovairedose, en gynécée (*Libération*, 21.03.91).

Such are the phenomena that have struck me. Now for a few concluding comments.

Firstly, the straightforward linear mode of representation of levels of language along a parameter of formality/informality no longer seems particularly well adapted to the written code as it has just been characterized. It seems rather to consist of a core of neutral, unmarked material, together with a range of choices of more marked items, the choice being governed not just by a sense of formality/informality and still less by any class-related parameters, but by such speech-act related criteria as the desire to be ironic, flippant, reassuringly "matey", intimidatingly scientific or whatever. Maybe these choices should be represented graphically as encircling the core in the manner of satellites. But perhaps the situation is too fluid at present for there to be much point in diagrammatic representation.

Secondly, these linguistic developments seem rather obviously to run in parallel to changes in society, or at least in social attitudes, that have occurred in recent decades. One thinks of the post-1968 challenge to authoritarian structures and modes of discourse, and the accompanying fashion for informality and democratization - neither of them, as will be suggested in a moment, necessarily any more genuine than *Libé's* phoney popular French. One thinks, too, of the vogue for computerized efficiency and the rise of the enterprise culture - phenomena which it is tempting to associate with the spread of the technocratic style. High-tech efficiency combined with informality and solidarity: watchwords of contemporary French society, perhaps? Even the frequent self-reflexiveness of the new written colloquial and the increasing elusiveness of signifieds in technocratic discourse seem appropriate to the post-modern age.

Thirdly, we seem to have reached a stage where the accepted or mainstream written code not only overlaps the spoken code in all the colloquial registers, but actually offers a wider (not merely a different) lexical and syntactic repertoire. In fact, it *includes* the spoken range, and, as was suggested earlier in connection with *le français branché*, more and more influences its content.

However, it would be wrong, in spite of this, to postulate a complete coalescence of the written and spoken codes. I have already referred to a certain "phoniness" characterizing written texts incorporating colloquial features, be they from the eighteenth or the late twentieth century. They may draw heavily on the repertoire of familiar and popular lexis and syntax, but in terms of discourse organization they remain examples of an "elaborated" code in the sense in which this term has been used by Bernstein and others. That is to say, they lack such characteristic features of authentic spoken texts as unfinished sentences, midstream changes of construction, heavy reliance on extra-linguistic context, or preference for simple as opposed to complex sentences. They are after all planned in advance, and accordingly make extensive and often subtle use of rhetorical devices of various kinds. Compare the genuine article represented by (t) with the fake colloquial of (u), characterized by sophisticated rhetorical questions, rhythmic repetitions, images, neatly balanced contrasts, and so forth:

> (t) Ah bah, une fois, j'en vois un, un matin, c'était ... euh ... y'a combien, trois mois, juste avant mon accident, j'arrive ... j'étais en, au garage là, euh, de vélos, je passe par là, ça coupe, tout d'un coup j'entends broum, broum, je dis qu'est-ce qui se passe, hein, on était à deux, on sort d'un seul coup, qu'est-ce qu'on voit, une voiture qu'avait ... par-dessus le parapet, qu'était plongé dans la Seine, ah, c'était un soldat, il a eu le temps de sauter de sa voiture, hein, alors on voyait les feux rouge encore à l'arrière, qu'est-ce qu'on fait? (From the corpus of conversational

material collected by Denise François).[21]

(u) J'ai une copine au journal, ça va pas, ça va pas du tout.
Tragique! Une crème, cette fille, douce, indulgente, gentille.
Très cool, très relax, très calme. Un lac, une mer étale, jamais
de vagues. Oui et alors? Qu'est-ce qu'elle a? Ben, elle a ça,
bon caractère, et ça ne se pardonne pas. Non, sérieux,
contrairement à ce qu'on croit, c'est pas le stress qui est fatal,
c'est la sérénité. Pour les femmes, attention! Les hommes, eux,
plus ils se contrôlent, mieux ils se portent. D'où je le tire?
D'une étude menée pendant onze ans à l'université du Michigan.
Il en ressort que sa colère faut la piquer, pas la rentrer, si on
veut couper à une mort prématurée. (C. Sarraute, *Le Monde*,
22.11.90).

There are more actual colloquial items in (u) than in (t), but there can
be no doubt as to which of the two texts is the more formal in its discourse
practice. A text like (u) is in fact a curious hybrid: to use the terminology of
sociolinguistics once again, it exhibits High features in respect of one set of
parameters (organizational), but Low features in respect of another
(syntactical/lexical). Like much contemporary social informality, which
misleadingly obscures power relationships while doing little, if anything, to alter
them, (u) is essentially spurious and contrived. This underlying importance of
"elaboration" may explain how the written code has been able to assimilate both
the "jokey colloquial" and the "turgid technocratic" registers with such apparent
ease.

---

[21] D. François, *Français parlé*, Paris, S.E.L.A.F., 1974, p.819.

NOTES ON CONTRIBUTORS

MAGGIE ALLISON is Lecturer in the Department of Modern Languages at the University of Bradford.

RODNEY BALL is Lecturer in French at the University of Southampton.

TONY CHAFER is Senior Lecturer in the School of Languages and Area Studies at Portsmouth Polytechnic.

ROSEMARY CHAPMAN is Lecturer in French and German at the University of Nottingham.

PHILIP DINE is Lecturer in French at University College, Swansea.

JILL FORBES is Professor of French at the University of Strathclyde.

THIERRY GROENSTEEN is the Director of the Centre National de la Bande Dessinée et de l'Image, Angoulême.

RENATE GUNTHER is Lecturer in French at the University of Sheffield.

GEOFFREY HARE is Senior Lecturer in French at the University of Newcastle Upon Tyne.

ALEC HARGREAVES is Senior Lecturer in the Department of European Studies at Loughborough University.

NICHOLAS HEWITT is Professor of French at the University of Nottingham.

WILLIAM KIDD is Lecturer in French at the University of Stirling.

BILL MARSHALL is Lecturer in French at the University of Southampton.

MICHAEL PALMER is Professor in the Département des Sciences et Techniques de l'Expression et de la Communication at the Université de la Sorbonne Nouvelle (Paris III).

BRIAN RIGBY is Lecturer in French Studies at the University of Warwick.

PIERRE SORLIN is Professor in the U.F.R. "Cinéma et Audiovisuel" at the Université de la Sorbonne Nouvelle (Paris III).

BIBLIOGRAPHY

- "Les Bilans 1989 de Radio-France, RFO et RFI", *La Lettre du CSA*, 11, August 1990.

- "Les Bilans 1990 de Radio-France, RFO et RFI", *La Lettre du CSA*, 23, August 1991.

- "La CSA définit sa politique d'attribution des fréquences radiophoniques", *Le Monde*, 1 September 1989.

- "De quelques réseaux FM", *Antennes*, 26, June 1990.

- *Dossier de presse sur l'affaire du foulard islamique*, Paris, ADRI, 1990.

- "La Fin d'une vraie radio locale", *Le Monde*, 14 November 1990.

- "Les Limites de l'ouverture", *Le Monde Radio Télévision*, 24-25 February 1991.

- "Médiamétrie", *Antennes*, 26, June 1990.

- "Médiamétrie abat les cartes de l'audience radio", *Libération*, 7 November 1988.

- *La Mémoire des Français. Quarante ans de commémoration de la seconde guerre mondiale*, Paris, Editions du CNRS, 1986.

- "Le Paysage radiophonique et les nouvelles règles du jeu", *Antennes*, 26, June 1990.

- "Pourquoi Carat provoque Eurocom", *CB News*, 3 June 1991.

- *Pratiques culturelles des Français en 1974*, Paris, La Documentation Française, 1978, 2 volumes.

- *Pratiques culturelles des Français. Description socio-démographique. Evolution 1973-1981*, Paris, Dalloz, 1982.

- *Les Pratiques culturelles des Français 1973-1989*, Paris, La Découverte et La Documentation Français, 1990.

- "Le Président de Skyrock entame une grève de la faim", *Le Monde*, 8 June 1991.

- "Radio-France enregistre de bons résultats", *Le Monde*, 17 July 1991.

- "La Radio, l'entendre ou l'écouter", *Dossier de l'Audiovisuel*, Special Number, 32, July-August 1990.

- "Une Radio islamique conteste les choix du CSA", *Le Monde*, 17 November 1990.

- *La Radio la plus au point. RFM! la radio FM*, Sales Brochure of RFM, December 1989.

- "Les Radios nouvelles dans le monde", *Notes et Etudes Documentaires*, 4770, 1984.

- "Les Réseaux FM", *Le Monde*, 10 February 1989.

- "Tout sur la publicité", *L'Expansion*, July-September 1990.

Alavardo, Manuel; Gutch, Robin; Wollen, Tania, *Learning the Media. An Introduction to Media Teaching*, Basingstoke, Macmillan Education, 1987.

Albert, P., et al., *Histoire générale de la presse française*, Paris, PUF, 1972.

Albert, Pierre and Tudesq, André-Jean, *Histoire de la radio et de la télévision*, Paris, PUF, coll. "Que sais-je?", 1986.

Albert, Pierre, *Les Médias dans le monde 1990-1991*, Paris, Editions Européennes Erasme, coll. "Documents pédagogiques", 1990.

Agulhon, Maurice, *Marianne au pouvoir. L'Imagerie et la symbolique républicaine de 1880 à 1914*, Paris, Flammarion, coll. "Histoires", 1989.

Amengual, Barthelemy, *Le Petit monde de Pif le chien*, Alger, Travail et Culture d'Algérie, 1955.

Aragon, Louis, *La Diane française*, Paris, Seghers, 1944.

Arnoult, P., *Les Courses de chevaux*, Paris, PUF, 1962.

Arvidsson, K.-A., *Henry Poulaille et la littérature prolétarienne française des années 1930*, Paris, Jean Touzot, 1988.

Bacconnier, Gérard; Minet, André; Soler, Louis, "Quarante millions de témoins", in *Mémoire de la Grande Guerre. Témoins et témoignages*, sous la direction de Gérard Canini, Nancy, Presses Universitaires de Nancy, 1989.

Bakhtin, M., *Rabelais and his World*, trans. Helene Iswolsky, Cambridge,Mass., MIT Press, 1968.

Barr, Charles, *Ealing Studios*, London, David and Charles, 1977.

Barthes, Roland, *Mythologies*, Paris, Seuil, 1957.

Baudrillard, J., *La Société de consommation*, Paris, Denoël, 1970.

Beauvais, R., *L'Hexagonal tel qu'on le parle*, Paris, Hachette, 1970.

Becker, Annette, *Les Monuments aux morts. Patrimoine et mémoire de la grande guerre*, Paris, Editions Errance, 1989.

Benetière, Jean and Sancin, Jacques, *Au Coeur des radios libres*, Paris, L'Harmattan, coll. "Logiques sociales", 1989.

Benoit, Jean-Marc; Benoit, Philippe; Lech, Jean-Marc, *La Politique à l'affiche. Affiches électorales et publicité politique*, Paris, Editions du May, 1986.

Bergala, Alain, ed., *Jean-Luc Godard par Jean-Luc Godard*, Paris, Cahiers du Cinéma, 1985.

Berger, John, *Ways of Seeing*, London, BBC and Penguin, 1977.

Bernard, J.P.A., *Le Parti communiste et la question littéraire, 1921-1939*, Grenoble, Presses Universitaires de Grenoble, 1972.

Bernet, C. and Rézeau, P., *Dictionnaire du français parlé: le monde des expressions familières*, Paris, Seuil, 1989.

Betterton, Rosemary, ed., *Looking On: Images of Femininity in the Visual Arts and Media*, London, Pandora Press, 1989.

Bonheur, Gaston, *Qui a cassé la vase de Soissons? (L'Album de famille de tous les Français)*, Paris, Robert Laffont, 1963.

Bouche, D., *L'Enseignement dans les territoires français de l'Afrique Occidentale de 1817 à 1920.* Paris, Librairie H. Champion, 1975.

262

Bouche, D., "L'Ecole rurale en Afrique Occidentale Française", in *Etudes Africaines offertes à Henri Brunschwig*, Paris, Publications de l'EHESS, 1982.

Bougnoux, D., *La Communication par la bande*, Paris, La Découverte, 1991.

Bourdieu, P. and Darbel, A., *L'Amour de l'art: les Musées d'art européens et leur public*, Paris, Minuit, 1966.

Bourdieu, P., *La Distinction, critique sociale du jugement*, Paris, Minuit, 1979.

Boutelier, Denis and Subramanian, Dipil., *Le Grand bluff*, Paris, Denoël, 1990.

Boutet, Jacques., "Inauguration du CTR de Dijon. Le Discours de Jacques Boutet", *La Lettre du CSA*, 4, January 1990.

Boyd-Barret, O. and Palmer, M., *Le Trafic des nouvelles: les agences mondiales d'information*, Paris, Alain Moreau, 1981.

Brémond, Claude, et al., "Les Héros de films dits 'de la nouvelle vague'", *Communications*, I, 1961.

Brévié, J., "L'Enseignement massif et l'école indigène", *Bulletin de l'Enseignement de l'Afrique Occidentale Française*, 74, 1931.

Brosse, G., "La Cinq gagne le tiercé", *Le Monde*, 30 November 1990.

Brunot, F., *Histoire de la langue française*, X, Paris, Armand Colin, 1939.

Burgin, Victoria, "Looking at Photographs", in Victor Burgin, ed., *Thinking Photography*, London, Macmillan, 1982.

Caradec, François, *Christophe Colombe*, Paris, Grasset, 1956.

Caradec, François, *I Primi Eroi*, Milano, Garzanti, 2nd Edition, 1965.

Caradec, François, *Dictionnaire du français argotique et populaire*, Paris, Larousse, 1977.

Caradec, François, *N'ayons pas peur des mots: dictionnaire du français argotique et populaire*, Paris, Larousse, 1988.

Cas, G. and Bout, R., *Lamy droit économique*, Paris, Lamy, 1989.

263

Cathelat, Bernard, *Publicité et société*, Paris, Payot, 1987.

Cavanna, F., *Coups de sang*, Paris, Belfond, 1991.

Cazenave, François, *Les Radios libres*. *Des Radios pirates aux radios locales privées*, Paris, PUF, coll. "Que sais-je?", 1984.

Chafer, T., *The Politics of Adapted Education in French West Africa 1903-1939*, MA Dissertation, School of Oriental and African Studies, University of London, 1986.

Champeaux, Antoine, "Les Guides illustrés des champs de bataille, 1914-1918", in *Mémoire de la Grande Guerre. Témoins et témoignages*, sous la direction de Gérard Canini, Nancy, Presses Universitaires de Nancy, 1989.

Char, René, "Affres. Détonations. Silence", in *Oeuvres complètes*, Paris, Gallimard, coll. "Editions de la Pléiade", 1983.

Chipman, J., *French Power in Africa*, Oxford, Blackwell, 1989.

Clarens, Bernard, "Parcours sans faute de Jean-Paul Baudecroux entrepreneur de radio", *Médias Pouvoirs*, 15, July 1989.

Cojean, Annick and Eskenazi, Franck, *FM, la folle histoire des radios libres*, Paris, Grasset, 1986.

Cojean, Annick, "Les Sages de NRJ", *Le Monde*, 5 December 1989.

Cojean, Annick, "La Stratégie des périphériques", *Le Monde*, 5 December 1989.

Cojean, Annick, "1989 sera l'année de la concentration dans le monde de la FM", *Le Monde*, 10 December 1989.

Cojean, Annick, "Questions à Martin Brisac, Directeur Général d'Europe 2", *Droit et Communication Audiovisuelle*, 7, March-April 1990.

Conseil Régional de Picardie, *La Lettre d'information du Conseil Régional*, 36, November-December 1989.

Debray, R., *Cours de médiologie générale*, Paris, Gallimard, 1991.

Debusscher, Jean-Marie, "A l'ombre des monuments aux morts", in *Entre deux guerres (la création française entre 1919 et 1939)*, sous la direction d'Olivier Barrot et de Pascal Ory, Paris, Editions François Bourin, 1990.

Delannoy, P., "Loteries: progression fulgurante du loto", in Potel, J.Y., *L'Etat de la France et de ses habitants*, Paris, La Découverte, 1985.

Désalmand, P., *Histoire de l'éducation en Côte d'Ivoire*, Abidjan, Editions CEDA, 1983.

Duneton, Claude, *La Puce à l'oreille: anthologie des expressions populaires avec leurs origines*, 1st edition: Paris, Stock, 1978; 2nd Edition: Paris, Balland, 1985.

Dunkley, J., *Gambling: a Social and Moral Problem in France, 1685-1792*, Oxford, Voltaire Foundation, 1985.

Dutourd, Jean, *Les Taxis de la Marne*, Paris, Gallimard, 1956.

Eco, Umberto, "The Frames of Comic Freedom", in Eco, Umberto, et al., *Carnival!*, Berlin, Mouton Publishers, 1984.

Eustache, Jean, *La Maman et la putain*, Paris, Cahiers du Cinéma, 1986.

Evans, Caroline and Thornton, Minna, "Fashion, Representation, Femininity", *Feminist Review*, 38, 1991, pp.48-66.

Ferry, L. and Renaut, A., *La Pensée 68: Essai sur l'anti-humanisme contemporain*, Paris, Gallimard, 1985.

Feyel, G., "Correspondances de presse parisiennes des journaux de province de 1828 à 1856", in *Documents pour l'histoire de la presse nationale aux XIXe et XXe siècles*, Paris, Editions du CNRS, coll. "Documentation", 1977.

Fiske, J., *Television Culture*, London, Methuen, 1987.

Flügel, J.C., *The Psychology of Clothes*, London, Hogarth Press, 1930.

Forsans, D., *Le Tiercé, racket ou divertissement?*, Domène, SOGIREP, 1971.

François, D., *Français parlé*, Paris, SELAF, 1974.

Fresnault-Dervelle, Pierre, *La Bande dessinée, essai d'analyse sémiotique*, Paris,

Hachette, 1972.

Gbagbo, L., *Réflexions sur la Conférence de Brazzaville*, Yaoundé, Editions Clé, 1978.

George, K., "Old for New: 'Non-assurance linguistique?'", *French Studies Bulletin*, 39, Summer 1991.

Girardin, E. de, *L'Impuissance de la presse*, Paris, Plon, 1879.

Giraud, Michel, *Raconte-moi, Marianne, ce qu'a fait la République. Les 36000 jours des 36000 communes*, Paris, Editions Jean-Claude Lattès, 1984.

Goffman, Erving, *Gender Advertisements*, New York, Harper and Row, 1976.

Goguel, François, *Géographie des élections françaises sous la Troisième et la Quatrième Républiques*, Paris, Armand Colin, coll. "Cahiers de la Fondation Nationale des Sciences Politiques", 1970.

Grillo, R.D., *Dominant Language*, Cambridge, Cambridge University Press, 1989.

Guillaumin, Colette, "Question de différence", *Questions féministes*, 6, September 1979.

Gurevitch, Michael, et al., *Society, Culture and the Media*, London, Routledge, 1990.

Habermas, J., *L'Espace public*, Paris, Payot, 1986.

Hamelin, Daniel, "Décentralisation de Radio-France", *Médias Pouvoirs*, 18, April-June 1990.

Hamès, Constant., "La Construction de l'islam en France: du côté de la presse", *Archives en Sciences Sociales des Religions*, 68, i, July-September 1989.

Hardy, G., *Une Conquête morale. L'Enseignement en A.O.F.*, Paris, Armand Colin, 1917.

Harrison, C., *France and Islam in West Africa, 1860-1960*, Cambridge, Cambridge University Press, 1988.

Hayward, P., "Betting 'War' in Europe", *The Independent*, 15 February 1990.

Hayward, Susan, "Television: a *Transparence* on Modern France?", in Cornick, Martyn, ed., *Beliefs and Identity in Modern France*, Loughborough, ERC and ASMCF, 1990.

Hebdige, D., "The Bottom Line on Planet One", in Rice, P., and Waugh, P., eds., *Modern Literary Theory: a Reader*, London, Edward Arnold, 1989.

Hill, C., "French Providing a Profitable Lead", *The Times*, 7 February 1989.

Holt, R., *Sport and Society in Modern France*, London, Macmillan, 1981.

Holt, R., "Ideology and Sociability: a Review of New French Research into the History of Sport under the Early Third Republic (1870-1914)", *International Journal of the History of Sport*, 6, III, December 1989.

Humblot, Catherine, "Les Emissions spécifiques: de 'Mosaïque' à 'Ren contres', *Migrations-Société*, 1, IV, August 1989.

Huss, Marie-Monique, "Virilité et religion dans la France de 1914-1918: le Catéchisme du Poilu", in Cornick, Martyn, ed., *Belief and Identity in Modern France*, Loughborough, ERC and ASMCF 1990.

Jameson, F., "Postmodernism, or the Cultural Logic of Late Capital", *New Left Review*, 146, July-August 1984.

Jeanneney, Jean-Noël, *Echec à Panurge. L'Audiovisuel au service de la différence*, Paris, Seuil, 1986.

Julliard, J., "La Dérive populiste", *Le Nouvel Observateur*, 11 August 1991.

Kane, Cheikh Hamidan, *L'Aventure ambiguë*, Paris, 10/18, 1961.

Kidd, William, "Figures in a Landscape: Literature and the 'lieux de mémoire'", *Contemporary France*, 43, October 1990.

Kopferrer, Jean Noël, *L'Enfant et la publicité*, Paris, Denoël, 1985.

Legman, George, "Psychopathologie des comics", *Les Temps Modernes*, May 1949.

Lesparda, R., *La Maffia du tiercé*, Paris, Editions et Publicitaires Premières, 1970.

Lewis, M.D., "One Hundred Million Frenchmen: the 'Assimilation' Theory in French Colonial Policy", *Comparative Studies in Society and History*, IV, 1962.

Lipovetsky, G., *L'Ere du vide: Essai sur l'individualisme contemporain*, Paris, Gallimard, 1983.

Lob and Gotlib, *Superdupont*, 4: "*Oui nide iou*", Paris, Audie, 1983.

Lorcey, J., *Les Scandales des courses et du tiercé*, Le Havre, P. d'Antoine, 1978.

McKibben, R., *The Ideologies of Class: Social Relations in Britain 1880-1950*, Oxford, Clarendon Press, 1990.

Mattelart, A., *L'Internationale Publicitaire*, Paris, La Découverte, 1989.

Mattelart, A., *La Publicité*, Paris, La Découverte, 1990.

Mauriat, Caroline, *La Presse audiovisuelle 1989-1990*, Paris, Editions du CPFJ, coll: "Connaissance des médias", 1989.

Méjean, Robert, "Stratégies et concurrence de la radio", *Médias Pouvoirs*, 16, November-December 1989.

Merle, P., *Les Blues de l'argot*, Paris, Seuil, 1990.

Mermet, G., *Francoscopie: les Français. Qui sont-ils? Où vont-ils?*, Paris, Larousse, 1985.

Molloy, John T., *The Women's Dress for Success Book*, New York, Warner, 1977.

Morgenthau, R. Schachter, *Political Parties in French-Speaking West Africa*, Oxford, Clarendon Press, 1964.

Morin, Edgar, *Commune en France. La Métamorphose de Plodémet*, Paris, Fayard, 1967.

Morris, T. and Randall, J., *Horse Racing: Records, Facts and Champions*, London, Guiness Books, 1990.

Müller, B., *Le Français d'aujourd'hui*, Paris, Klincksieck, 1985.

Mumford, W.B., *Africans Learn to be French*, London, Evans Brothers, undated.

Neale, S., and Krutnik, F., *Popular Film and Television Comedy*, London, Routledge, 1990.

Nicholson-Lard, David, "Radio-Growth is put in Doubt", *The Independent*, 8 August 1991.

Palmer, M., *Des Petits journaux aux grandes agences*, Paris, Aubier, 1983.

Perec, Georges, *Les Choses*, Paris, Julliard, 1965.

Perotti, Antonio, "Les Relations de la guerre du golfe sur les relations franco-maghrébines", *Migrations-Société*, 3, 15, May-June 1991.

Perotti, Antonio and Thépaut, France, "L'Affaire du foulard islamique: d'un fait divers à un fait de société", *Migrations-Société*, 2, 7, January-February 1990.

Perotti, Antonio and Thépaut, France, "Les Répercussions de la guerre du golfe sur les arabes et les juifs de France", *Migrations-Société*, 3, 14, March-April 1991.

Petitjean, G., "Un Book contre le PMU", *Le Nouvel Observateur*, 18-24 July 1991.

Petitjean, G., "Courses: des milliards sous la botte", *Le Nouvel Observateur*, 18-24 July 1991.

Picant, C., *Dossier T comme tiercé*, Paris, A. Moreau, 1979.

Pilven le Sevellec, Yves, "Les Monuments aux morts de la Loire-Atlantique", II, *Visions Contemporaines*, 4, March 1990.

Portevin, Catherine and Gustave, Anne-Marie, "La Libération des ondes", *Télérama*, 2085, 27, December 1989.

Poulet, M., *Le Tiercé: les règles d'un jeu hippique moderne*, Verviers, Gérard et Cie, 1964.

Preel, B., "1989: an I des nouveaux loisirs?", in Verdié, M. *L'Etat de la France et de ses habitants*, Paris, La Découverte, 1989.

Prost, Antoine, *Les Anciens combattants et la société française 1914-1939*,

III, Paris, Presses de la Fondation Nationale des Sciences Politiques, 1976.

Prost, Antoine, "Les Monuments aux morts. Culte républicain? Culte civique? Culte patriotique?", in *Les Lieux de mémoire, I: La République*, sous la direction de Pierre Nora, Paris, Gallimard, 1984.

Prot, Robert, *Des Radios pour se parler. Les Radios locales en France*, Paris, Documentation Française, 1985.

Raffalovitch, A., "... l'abominable vénalité de la presse...", Paris, Librairie du Travail, 1931.

Ragon, Michel, *L'Espace de la mort. Essai sur l'architecture, la décoration et l'urbanisme funéraires*, Paris, Albin Michel, 1981.

Rebérioux, Madeleine, *La République radicale, 1898-1914*, Paris, Seuil, 1975.

Remonté, Jean-François and Depoux, Simone, *Les Années radio*, Paris, Gallimard, coll. "L'Arpenteur", 1989.

Rieffel, R., *L'Elite des journalistes*, Paris, PUF, 1984.

Rigby, Brian., *Popular Culture in Modern France. A Study of Cultural Discourse*, London, Routledge, 1991.

Rigby, Brian and Hewitt, Nicholas, *France and the Mass Media*, Basingstoke, Macmillan, 1991.

Ritaine, E., *Les Stratèges de la culture*, Paris, Presses de la Fondation Nationale des Sciences Politiques, 1983.

Roucaute, Y., *Splendeurs et misères des journalistes*, Paris, Calmann-Lévy, 1991.

Sabatier, E., *Chevaux, courses et jeu*, Paris, Crépin-Leblond, 1972.

Sabatier, P., *Educating a Colonial Elite: the William Ponty School and its Graduates*, PhD Thesis, University of Chicago, 1977.

Sandry, G. and Carrère, M., *L'Argot moderne*, Paris, Editions du Dauphin, 1953.

Sarraut, A., *La Mise en valeur des colonies françaises*, Paris, Payot, 1923.

270

Schifres, A., "A la tienne Etienne", *Le Nouvel Observateur*, 25 March 1988.

Seguret, Pierre, "Images des immigrés et de l'immigration dans la presse française", Thèse de 3e Cycle, Montpellier, Université Paul Valéry, 1981.

Semidei, M., "De l'Empire à la décolonisation à travers les manuels scolaires français", *Revue Française de Sciences Politiques*, XVI, 1966.

Senarclens, P. de, *Le Mouvement "Esprit" 1932-41*, Lausanne, L'Age de l'homme, 1974.

Spitzbarth, R., *L'Economie du jeu et du sport hippiques*, Thèse de Doctorat, Université de Nancy II, 1981.

Stam, R., *Subversive Pleasures: Bakhtin, Cultural Criticism and Film*, Baltimore, Johns Hopkins University Press, 1989.

Steiner, G., *After Babel*, London, Oxford University Press, 1978.

Steiner, George, *Réelles présences*, Paris, Gallimard, 1989 (translation of *Real Presences*, London, Faber and Faber, 1989).

Stoneham, D., "A Pari-Mutuel Society", *Pacemaker*, February 1977.

Stourdzé, C., "Les Niveaux de langue", *Le Français dans le monde*, 65, June 1969.

Strinati, Pierre, "Bandes dessinées et science fiction. L'Age d'or en France (1934-1940)", *Fiction*, 92, July 1961.

Tanner, Tony, *Adultery in the Novel*, Baltimore, Johns Hopkins University Press, 1979.

Taylor, A.J.P., *From Sarajevo to Potsdam*, London, Thames and Hudson, coll. "Library of European Civilisation", 1966.

Truffaut, François, *Jules et Jim*, London, Lorrimer, 1968.

Tunstall, J. and Palmer, M., *Media Moguls*, London, Routledge, 1992.

Vaillant, J.G., *Black, French and African. A Life of Léopold Sédar Senghor*, Cambridge, Mass., Harvard University Press, 1990.

Vandromme, Pol, *Le Monde de Tintin*, Paris, Gallimard, 1959.

Vincenot, Henri, *La Billebaude*, Paris, Denoël, 1978.

Virieu, F.H. de, *La Médiacratie*, Paris, Flammarion, 1990.

Wangermée, R. and Gournay, B., *La Politique culturelle de la France*, Paris, La Documentation Française, 1988.

Wolton, D., *Eloge du grand public*, Paris, Flammarion, 1990.

Woodrow, Alain, "Ondes oecuméniques", *Le Monde Radio Télévision*, 9-10 June 1991.

Yahiel, Michel, "Le FAS: questions de principe", *Revue Européenne des Migrations Internationales*, 4, 1-2, 1988.

Yonnet, P., *Jeux, modes et masses: la société Française et le moderne 1945-1985*, Paris, Gallimard, 1985.

Zeldin, Theodore, *France 1848-1945*, II: *Intellect, Taste and Anxiety*, Oxford, Clarendon Press, 1977.

Zitrone, Léon, *Mon tiercé*, Monaco, R. Salar, 1966.

INDEX

A.A.C.C., 85, 86

Ache, Caran d', 212

Achille Talon, 214

Actuel, 245, 249

Adhémar, Jean, 211

A.E.A.R., 15

Aegis, 94

Agence Im'Média, 173

Agulhon, Maurice, 224, 231

Albert, P., 91

Alvardo, Manuel, 42

Amengaul, Barthelemy, 210

Amsterdam-Pleyel, 20

Annaud, Jean-Jacques, 126

Antenne 2, 65, 170, 171, 174, 176

Antonini, Jean-Claude, 255

Apostrophes, 13

Arab, Rachid, 174

Aragon, 239

Ariès, Philippe, 227

Arnoult, P., 184

Aron, Raymond, 141

Arvidsson, K.-A., 18

Astérix, 214

(A Suivre), 215

Auchnie, A., 160

Audoux, Marguerite, 23

Auteuil (Racecourse), 197

Aventure FM, 34

Bacconnier, Gérard, 227

Bachelier, Christian, 221

Bakhtin, Mikhail, 131, 132, 133, 134, 135, 137

Balisto, 77, 78-9

Balcon, Michael, 114, 115

Balzac, Honoré de, 20, 95, 100

Baraka, 173

Barbusse, Henri, 15, 19, 20

Barr, Charles, 115

Barre, Raymond, 254

Barrot, Olivier, 221

Barthes, Roland, 83, 89, 201, 205

Baudecroux, Georges, 30, 41

273

274

Forest, Jean-Claude, 210, 211, 214

Forlani, Remo, 210, 214

Forsans, D., 188

Fourastié, Jean, 191

Fournier, Marcel, 88

Franc, Régis, 214

France-Culture, 28, 30, 38

France-Info, 38, 39, 40

France-Inter, 27, 38, 39

France-Musique, 28, 30, 38

France-Soir, 194, 214

Francis, Dick, 191

François, Lucien, 52

Fred, 214

Fréquence Gaie, 40

Fresnault-Dervelle, Pierre, 215

Freud, Sigmund, 139

Froissart, André, 211

Front National, 165, 167, 168

F.R.3., 126, 171, 173, 175

F.U.N., 39, 41

G.A.N., 87

Garetto, Jean, 38, 39

Garrell, Philippe, 119, 120

Gassot, Charles, 126

Gbagbo, L., 142, 144

Gélin, Daniel, 126

George, K., 242

Gide, André, 16

Giff-Wiff, 211, 213

Giono, Jean, 17

Girardin, Emile de, 85, 86, 90, 95-6, 100

Giraud, 214

Giraud, Marcel, 232

Giraudoux, Jean, 221

Giscard d'Estaing, Valéry, 29, 250

Gladiateur, 184

Globe, 249

Godard, Jean-Luc, 116, 117, 118, 119, 122, 123, 218

Godfather, The, 115

Goffman, Erving, 56

Goguel, François, 231

Gorbatchev, Mikhail, 49

Gorky, Maxim, 20, 23

Goscinny, René, 211, 214

Goude, Jean-Paul, 89

Gournay, B., 4

Grand Bluff, *Le*, 88, 89

Grasset, Editions, 16, 17, 210

Grillo, R.D., 250

Gross, Gilbert and Francis, 87-8, 92, 93, 94, 97

Groupe d'Ecrivains Prolétariens de Langue Française, 16, 19

Guillaumin, Colette, 69

Guillaumin, Emile, 23

Guilloux, Louis, 23

Gurevitch, Michael, 42, 45

Gutch, Robin, 42

Habermas Jürgen, 84

H.A.C.A., 31, 32, 34, 35, 37

Hachette, 32, 93

Hamès, Constant, 166, 167

Hamsun, Knut, 23

Hardy, G., 148, 149, 150, 162

Harrison, C., 152, 161

Havas (agency), 28, 83, 85, 86, 88, 89, 91, 92, 93, 94, 95, 97, 104

Havas, Charles-Louis, 85, 95, 96, 100

Haw-Haw, Lord, 237

Hayward, P., 189, 205

Hayward, Susan, 165

Hebdige, D., 138

Hector, 38

Hegel, Friedrich, 99

Heimat, 115

Hergé (Georges Remi), 213

Hill, C., 188

Hit-FM, 37

Holleaux Commission, 31

Holt, R., 181, 182, 184, 194, 205

Hugo, Victor, 232, 239

Humanité, L', 15, 19, 204

Humblot, Catherine, 171

Huppert, Isabelle, 12 2

Huss, Marie-Monique, 229

Hussein, Saddam, 169

I.M.A. Productions, 176

283

285

Subramanian, Dilip, 83, 86, 92, 99

Sud-Radio, 27, 41

Sullerot, Evelyne, 210

Sunday Express, The, 54, 57

Superdupont, 200, 201

Sveltesse, 70-2, 79

Tanner, Tony, 114

Tardi, 214

Tarzan, 212

Taylor, A.J.P., 221

Téchiné, André, 121, 124

Téléma, 126

Temps Modernes, Les, 209

T.F.I., 93, 174, 176

Thatcher, Margaret, 58, 59, 66, 67, 165

Thépaut, France, 168, 169

Thompson, J. Walter, 86

Thornton, Minna, 57

Tiercé, 189, 190, 191, 192, 193, 194, 195, 196, 197, 198, 199, 200, 201, 202, 203, 204, 205, 206

Tolstoy, Leo, 23

Tintin, 210

Torrente, 62

Tour de France, 198, 204, 205

Troyansky, David G., 224

Truffaut, François, 116, 118, 122, 124

Turenne, Henri de, 175

Turnstall, J., 84

Twain, Mark, 140

Unilever, 93

Vaillant, 210

Vaillant, J.G., 158

Vaillant-Courturier, Paul, 15

Vallès, Jules, 184

Valois, Georges, 17, 18

Vandromme, Pol, 210

Vavre, Patrick, 240

Vendredi, 255

Vercingeix, 220

Verdi, G., 102

Verdie, M., 182

Verney, Françoise, 175

Vertigo Productions, 175, 176

Victor, 38